Pūtea Whakairo

Kia ora Ansley

He Kaupapa purakau

He Kaupapa tuhituhi

He Kaupapa whanau ora

He Kaupapa whanau ora

Story & writing. Keeps the family name

alive.

Naku noa na

Brad Haami. 2007.

Pūtea Whakairo

Māori and the Written Word

Bradford Haami

First published in 2004 by Huia Publishers
in association with the Ministry for Culture and Heritage.

Huia Publishers
39 Pipitea Street, PO Box 17-335,
Wellington, Aotearoa New Zealand.
www.huia.co.nz

ISBN 1-86969-082-6

National Library of New Zealand Cataloguing-in-Publication Data

Haami, Bradford, 1966–
Pūtea whakairo : Māori and the written word / Bradford Haami.
Includes bibliographical references.
ISBN 1-86969-082-6
1. Maori (New Zealand people)-History-Sources. 2. Maori
language-Written Maori. 3. Archival materials-Conservation
and restoration. I. Title.
993.00499442-dc 22

He tohu maumaharatanga mō Dr Miria Simpson QSM
i ariari i te maha, kia kakea te taumata mōhiotanga
i te reo, ngā tikanga, toi whakaari me te mātauranga.

Dedicated to the memory of Dr Miria Simpson QSM,
who encouraged many of us to seek the heights
in reo, tikanga, arts and the pursuit of knowledge.

Te rārangi kaupapa
Contents

He mihi
Acknowledgements

He mihi tino whakamiharo ki ngā koreheke, ngā kaumātua, ngā taua, ngā rūruhi, ngā whanaunga katoa, ngā hoa mahi, i awhina, i tuku kōrero mai, i whakawhānui, i tautoko tēnei kaupapa. Nā ō koutou kupu kōrero i awhina te whakatinana i ōku nei whakaaro. Ki a koutou o Ngāti Hikatoa, arā, te whānau Maaka, nā tō koutou whakaaetanga i rui te kakano o tēnei mahi; anei rā, kua pūāwai. Nō reira, ki a koutou ngā hunga ngākaunui e whai nei i te mātauranga o ngā mātua tīpuna, me ōna māramatanga, tēnā koutou katoa.

Many people have assisted me in compiling this work. Jock Phillips, Claudia Orange and the staff of the History Group of the Ministry for Culture and Heritage gave me the chance, as the Fellow in Māori History, to bring this project to fruition; special thanks to David Green for his thoughtful editing; Bronwyn Dalley steered the book through production. A number of people have been invaluable in allowing me to give form to my ideas. I am indebted to my whānau from Whakatāne and Heretaunga, especially Florence Maaka (now deceased), Roger Maaka, Matangihau Maaka, Aritaku Maaka Chadwick, Cynthia Taiaroa, Roseanne Jones, and Maanu and Gwenda Paul. To the many elders, friends and acquaintances, whose verbal comments I have noted over the past ten years and drawn upon here – Ted Butt, Major Mason, Toby Rikihana, Bill Solomon, Barney Ihimaera, Max Mouatt, Koa Murdoch, Tiny Metzger, Wishie Jaram – my greatest appreciation.

I must make special mention also of Miria Simpson, Mere Roberts, Danny Keenan, Pat Parsons, Te Ahukaramū Charles Royal, Jenifer Curnow, and Roger Maaka, whose academic contributions have inspired me. Thanks to the team at Huia Publishers, particularly Māori language editor Brian Morris. There are many others I have not mentioned here to whom I would also like to express my gratitude. Finally, I'd like to thank the Maaka family for sanctioning this project, which I hope will be instrumental in inspiring younger Māori to recognise not only the need for oral tradition but also the written tradition of our people. Mā te Karaiti me ōna kupu koutou e ārahi e manaaki, e tiaki.

Nāku noa,

Nā Bradford Haami,
Tāmaki-makau-rau

TE WHAKATŪWHERATANGA
INTRODUCTION

When Māori children in the 1940s and '50s brought schoolbooks home to study, their grandparents often hid or burnt them because they believed books were a Pākehā tool teaching Pākehā views to help assimilate the next generation. Many of my peers were of a similar mind, seeing reading and writing as Pākehā things that Māori weren't interested in and didn't need. I was stimulated to write this book after wondering what difference it might make if rangatahi (the younger generation) knew how enthusiastically their tipuna (ancestors) had utilised and adapted literacy for their own purposes.

A great mass of manuscript material and many books were kept well guarded in my grandparents' house in Whakatāne. As youngsters, my brothers and I were astounded at the number of books in the home. My memories of our grandfather are of a seemingly stern, physically large and robust man who sat at the head of the kitchen table or at his doctor's consulting desk, reading, writing or – to relieve stress – playing patience. Every day we saw him reading or writing. His vast collection of books ranged through every conceivable subject. I remember thinking that they were tapu (sacred) – even entering his library without asking permission seemed a sin.

Our grandfather's handwritten journals were perhaps the most astonishing of all his books for us, his mokopuna (grandchildren). We would sometimes sneak a look at them, with our eyes and ears on the qui vive. I was always held spellbound by the copious writing, in a beautiful close hand, using black or purple ink, or sometimes pencil, and often in a language we could not comprehend – Māori.

I was not only intrigued by the manuscripts themselves, but also wondered at their contents. We knew that the lists of people's names must have been important for Papa to have written them down, but I had no understanding then of what a whakapapa was, let alone its significance in the Māori world. Years later, my mother told me that her father's books were tapu to her: she was never allowed to read or even touch them. To this day she has not read all his writings.

As a child I never had the patience to sit down and read a book because our lives were lived outdoors. However, whenever my fertile mind was attracted to a subject, my grandfather would buy me a book on my new interest. I loved animals, so he bought me a complete wildlife encyclopedia collection; I loved early Greek and Roman history, so he gave me a book on ancient Mediterranean civilisations; I loved Māori art and legends, so he bought me numerous books on Māori art and fables. In the early days, grandparents often recited and sang songs before dawn, hoping that their sleeping grandchildren would retain the vital tribal information these contained. My grandfather's way of passing information on to me, in my pre-teens, was through books and writing.

After his death when I was twelve, my life changed. His library of books and private journals was locked away, and the adrenalin rush from mischievously creeping into his room to read his journals and diaries ended. I received no more reading material, and reading and writing became just tasks for high school assignments.

Our family moved to Australia and I finished my secondary schooling in Queensland. When I returned to Whakatāne ten years after my grandfather's death, my grandmother gave me the key to a small room in which all Papa's books had been locked away. That room held all the family treasures we considered sacred. Now here I was, allowed access also to a suitcase full of 'whakapapa books' on condition that nothing left the homestead and they did not come too close to food. Reverence for books, and for the information contained therein, was still very much part of the mindset of the old people. This was a turning point in my life, as it opened the pathway for me to learn things Māori. It has taken me roughly fifteen years to get the collection into some sort of order and fully comprehend its worth. I was overwhelmed to discover a historical record of my ancestors' writings spanning more than 120 years. I was astonished to find how literate and meticulous the writers of this material had been.

I found many references for the contents of the manuscripts in the extensive library of published books which had belonged to both my grandfather and my great-grandfather. This contained a great quantity of published material on Māori history, as well as novels, and magazines like *Lilliput* and the pink-covered *Auckland Weekly News*. There were books by English, French and German poets and Shakespeare, and history books about every country in the world, from Thor Heyerdahl's book on Easter Island to a history of the Russian emperors. Piled to the roof were Māori periodicals such as *Te Puke Ki Hikurangi*, *Matuhi*, *Te Wananga*, *Te Kopara*, and the Rātana publication *Te Whetumarama o te Kotahitanga*. This room was something like Sir Āpirana Ngata's Māori room at his residence at Waiōmatatini, or the Grace family library/museum in Tokaanu.

These books had been read and critiqued by my grandfather and my great-grandfather; their comments and corrections were everywhere. In time these treasures led me to write and keep historical records. I write my own daily notebooks of whakapapa and kōrero, in the same manner as my forebears. Reading and writing opened my mind to a new body of knowledge and gave me an appreciation and a thirst not only for Māori knowledge but also for a wide range of other subjects. I could not get enough of the tribal histories, proverbs, whakapapa, and letters. In every spare moment I had my nose in these books. I became frustrated that no one in my immediate family knew anything of what they contained, that it all seemed over their heads. When I told them stories about historical events involving Ngāti Kahungunu, they were quite uninterested.

In 1986 I studied journalism, which led me to a position as a researcher for TVNZ's Māori programmes. The range of Māori subjects I was able to research for documentaries was wide, and the collection of family manuscripts became an invaluable source of ideas and references over the next decade. In those years as a travelling journalist I entered many Māori homes, from Rakiura to Te Reinga, and found much similar material. The writers were lucky that their books were saved. Even in recent times, many books like these were regarded as tapu and buried with their owners.

My grandmother recalled how much she lamented the loss of some of her father's manuscripts and papers. During the cleaning-up process after his death, family members who thought they were helping threw important written material onto a fire behind the house. Efforts to salvage some of the papers from the ashes were in vain. I abhor the loss of such books, whether it occurs because of tapu or through ignorance. This material is priceless, not only for family records, but for tribal claims and historical purposes. These taonga must be kept in safe and responsible hands. To be chosen as the guardian of ancestral knowledge, oral or written, is an honour weighted with heavy responsibility. The guardians of such precious material have an important and difficult role to play as the family's reference books and lawyers.[1]

I am grateful to my Waimārama kin and the Maaka whānau of Ngāti Hikatoa for allowing me to use family manuscript material which was under the custodianship of my grandfather to compile this book. It is my wish to show that reading and writing is not exclusively for Pākehā, but has also been entrenched in Māori society for over a century. The old people saw literacy as 'he mahi rangatira' – a chiefly pursuit. Although it was obviously a western skill, Māori were quick to learn and adapt literacy for the betterment of themselves and their society.

This book is an attempt to analyse some of the writings in this collection, and provide a glimpse of the type of knowledge and information that this particular whānau considered important enough to record in written form. It will explore possible motives for these writings, and examine the effects on Māori society of the introduction of print literacy.

The unpublished material in my grandfather's care, which I have called the Maaka Collection, consists of 40 books containing lists of genealogies, songs, minutes of hui, and traditional stories; a typescript copy of Mohi Te Atahikoia's manuscript, 'Ko tenei korero no Hawaiki ranoa'; an original handwritten book containing the teachings of Moihi Te Matorohanga, dated 1865; 31 letters (including an original letter sent by Tamehana Tarapīpipi to Donald McLean in 1861); eight waiata (on single pages); five maps; nineteen written whakapapa (on loose pages); 100 pages of loose notes; and eight diaries. This is thought to be only a quarter of the family manuscript material that was held in the Maaka homestead at Takapau.[2] When this house was burnt to the ground, a room full of written records was lost. The material which miraculously survived is now in my care.

I have chosen to publish family manuscript material selected from the writings of seven people from four generations of the Maaka whānau over a period of 130 years. Material deemed too personal for publication has not been included. Where practicable, an annotated transcription of the original manuscript is given, together with a translation. The genealogical relationship between the authors is shown opposite.

It seemed appropriate to briefly examine pre-literate forms of Māori communication and the period when literacy was introduced to Māori before undertaking an in-depth study of these family writings. These subjects are covered in chapter 1.

In the subsequent chapters, selected material from the Maaka Collection is examined. Building on the context provided in chapter 1, different aspects of the use of writing are discussed. Each chapter begins with a brief biography of each author, followed by an analysis of the selected material which discusses its contents, purpose and significance. Each chapter concludes with examples of their writings.

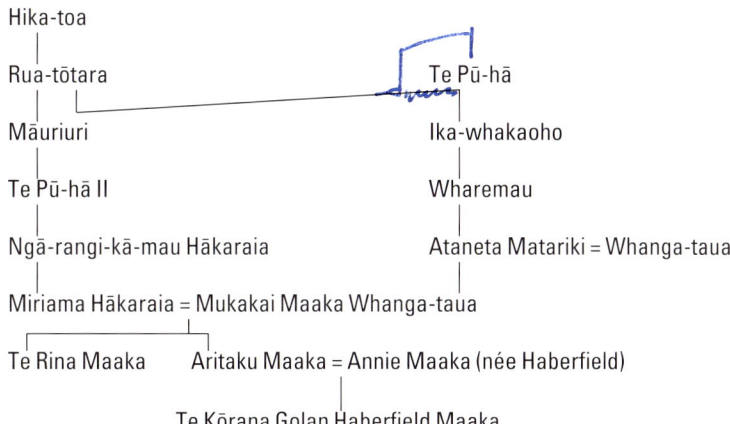

Ngāti Hikatoa of Waimārama

Hika-toa
|
Rua-tōtara — — — — — — — — — Te Pū-hā
| |
Māuriuri   Ika-whakaoho
| |
Te Pū-hā II   Wharemau
| |
Ngā-rangi-kā-mau Hākaraia   Ataneta Matariki = Whanga-taua
| |
Miriama Hākaraia = Mukakai Maaka Whanga-taua
|
Te Rina Maaka   Aritaku Maaka = Annie Maaka (née Haberfield)
|
Te Kōrana Golan Haberfield Maaka

The first essay, in chapter 2, discusses the writings of Ngā-rangi-kā-mau (Hākaraia Maumau), found in a book dated 1884 listing pepeha (aphorisms) and place names in the Waimārama district. Chapter 3 looks at the genealogies written by two women, Miriama Maaka and her daughter Te Rina Maaka. Chapter 4 examines the writings of Mukakai Maaka Whanga-taua, which include a letter, documents and a waiata (song). Chapter 5 discusses the writing of a traditional historical narrative found in Aritaku Maaka's whakapapa book, while chapter 6 deals with the diaries of his wife, Annie Haberfield. In chapter 7 the writings of Dr Golan Haberfield Maaka, the eldest son of Aritaku and Annie Maaka, which include diaries, whakapapa, letters and essays, are investigated.

The conclusion will, I hope, give families holding private written material ideas about the ownership and publication of Māori manuscripts, as well as useful hints on how to preserve the precious works hidden in cupboards or suitcases, or under beds.

I also wish to introduce writers and researchers of Māori-language manuscripts to a convention that Māori may choose to follow when presenting or publishing these treasures. On many occasions when Māori manuscripts, letters, diaries or narratives have been transcribed or translated for publication, the beauty of the original written work has not been reproduced, for a variety of reasons. Having discussed this issue with others, I propose the use of a convention that will highlight the characteristics of the original written work, as well as give the transcription and translation. This can be accomplished using either one or two pages in landscape mode, divided into four columns.

This is not an original idea, but one that came into use centuries ago. Early translators of the Bible utilised a form of this four-column page layout to reproduce the text in several languages. This practice arose out of the adfontem ('return to original sources') movement of the fifteenth century. Polyglot and diglot Bibles were compiled in a columnar format which enabled the simultaneous viewing of the scriptures in Hebrew, Aramaic, Latin, Greek, Arabic and other languages. This form was developed in Europe between 1509 and 1517.[3]

My suggestion is to adapt this format for the publication of Māori manuscripts. The original document is laid out in the first column. This gives a sense of the writer's style and the period in which the text was written, as well as showing the reader the difficulty of deciphering it. The second column is an exact transcription, line by line, of the original document. The third column is a modern version of the transcription, with grammar corrected, macrons added, and phrases ordered properly, while the final column is an English translation.

The portion of a waiata on the next page, in Mukakai Maaka Whanga-taua's handwriting, found in a whakapapa book in the Maaka Collection, illustrates the use of this convention:

Waiata

Kaha te whai tītiri
ka hiko te wira te
tara ki, te iringa. Ka
rere kai raro. Ka tā
ka te tara. Wharama
Haere ra chika ki te
pouri wri, te mate
o te tangata. Ka rū
te wahenua. Karere
tai tau toru, te rua
Mata riki. Ko te
tohu o te mate. E hoa
ma e, He aha tenei
haranga. He mahi
an, e toru, te mūhi
hoa te mamae, te
riri a te Atua. Ka i
Kino, ia hou, te
taku poto tia kia
wawe te tae, ki te
makau i te mate.

Te kape tuhinga	**Te whakatikatika**	**Te whakapākehātia**
(Transcription)	(Modern Māori)	(English translation)
Waiata	He Waiata tangi	A Lament
Papa te wha titiri	Papā te whatitiri,	Thunder clashes,
ka hiko te uira te	Ka hiko te uira.	Lightning strikes.
tara ki te iringa ka	Te tara ki te iringa,	The new moon
rere kai raro. Kata	Ka rere kai raro.	Appears in the north.
ka te tara. otemarama	Ka taka te tara o te marama.	The moon waxes.
Hare ra ehika ki te	Haere rā e hika	Farewell, O sir,
pouri uri, te mate	ki te pō-uriuri,	to the dark dark night,
o te tangata ka ru,	te mate o te tangata.	the death of man.
te whenua. karere	Ka rū te whenua,	The earth rumbles and
tau toru, te rua	Ka rere Tautoru.	Orion appears.
omata riki Ko te	Te rua o Matariki	The Pleiades portend
tohu ote mate. Ehoa	Ko te tohu o te mate.	death.
ma e, he aha tenei	E hoa mā e!	O Friends!
haanga. He mahi	He aha tēnei hānga	Why do I
au e tonu, te mutu	He mahi auē tonu?	Weep so?
noa te mamae. te	Te mutu noa te mamae,	The pain gnaws,
riri ate Atua kai	Te riri a te Atua,	Like the wrath of God
kino. ia hau, te	kai kino i ahau.	It consumes me.
tuku poto tia kia	Te tuku pototia	O that I may
wawe te tae ki te	kia wawe te tae	soon meet
makau i te mate.	ki te makau i te mate.	my beloved in death.

Obviously this format will not be appropriate for some material, because of its length, layout or illegibility, or the cost of reproduction. In this book, I have used this convention only in chapter 4.

I believe it is important to keep these precious writings alive, so that they can be widely read and discussed. Setting conventions for the bilingual publication of Māori material may help ensure that the tradition of Māori-language literacy is retained by those who are interested. Many Māori wonder whether information that is held in manuscript form should be published or kept hidden. While this is a question for the kaitiaki (guardians) of this material, my personal view echoes that expressed by Sir Āpirana Ngata in a letter to a friend in 1943:

> The time has long passed, when the heirlooms and treasures of Maori culture can be hidden in the memories of a fond few or in laboriously compiled manuscripts dedicated to descendants, who may never prize them. They can be forgotten, my friend, and lost. And they should not be lost. So you and I and others should have them kept, as the Pakeha keeps his records and knowledge, in print on bookshelves, that those who care may read and learn.[4]

The first pages of a hexaglot bible, in which the text is reproduced in six different languages. The Hexaglot Bible, Comprising the Holy Scriptures of the Old and New Testament in the Original Tongues, Part 1, Genesis I to XXXIII, *Henry Cohen, 1856,* Neg no. A14667, Auckland Public Library

CHAPTER ONE

Mai te kupu-ā-waha ki te kupu-ā-tuhi
From the spoken word to writing

The introduction of literacy changed forever the world of Māori communication. The written word had huge implications for the validation and mana of oral expression, which had been all-powerful, and for Māori 'ways of knowing'. Writing seemed a miracle to Māori. They were amazed that marks on paper could '"talk" … have … meaning … elicit responses … preserve the Word accurately … last through time and space', and be repeated many times without changing.[5] Literacy opened up both new forms of communication and new trains of thought. The enormous benefits of literacy were seen to include access to the divine word of God as well as to European knowledge.

Māori could not anticipate that traditional society would inevitably change dramatically following the introduction of the written word and everything that accompanied it. No longer would its 'reality' be 'what a person "said" it was'; no longer would its words be those of its leaders '"speaking" the world – [it] fell to those who could read and write to determine the future realities and the ways of the world'.[6] It would become a world far removed from that of oral communication, which had kept people together, with conversation, recitals, story-telling and song acting as catalysts for collective memory.

Ngā kōrero tuku iho
Words handed down

The traditional Māori world was an oral culture. Language and memory (aided by mnemonic devices) were used by pre-literate Māori to preserve and communicate information and knowledge. Such a world reproduces its culture by embodying memories in words and deeds; 'the mind through the memory carries culture from generation to generation'.[7] A society dependent on memory 'employs every device of the demagogue and the poet: rhyme, melody, structure, repetition'.[8] These techniques were utilised by Māori in waiata (songs), of which there were many forms; whakatauki (proverbs); pūrākau (folklore); and other traditional oral forms of communication. Those who succeeded in memorising tribal histories and narratives became leaders of their communities.[9]

Spoken words were both 'symbols of thought',[10] and the means by which reliable information and knowledge was expressed. As Margaret Orbell expresses it, 'language was always experienced as a part of lived reality, and because of this it possessed great weight and finality'.[11] The words and compositions of revered ancestors were sacred, and had great power and validity. They were 'kōrero tuku iho' ('words handed down').

The spoken word has been explained by Māori Marsden and Te Aroha Henare as the fusion of two major elements. They believe that Te Whe (sound, 'the word in embryo') and wānanga (discussion, debate, the imparting of knowledge) were inseparable, 'each indispensable to the formation and existence of the other'. Te Whe was the dress in which the seed word was 'clothed and articulated, then thought may be conceptualised and expressed in word'. Is it possible to think without words? 'For the Maori the answer was in the negative. One cannot exist without the other'.[12] The spoken words of chiefs possessed potency, the power to curse or bless. Words were uttered with great caution, lest they be regarded as an insult or breach of etiquette and provoke punishment. This concept is expressed in the proverb, 'He tao rākau e taea te karo; he tao kī, e kore e taea' ('A wooden spear may be parried, but not the shaft of the tongue').[13]

Whakapapa (genealogy) was essential to the preservation and recitation of oral history. Whakapapa remains the 'skeletal framework' which validates traditional history.[14] Genealogy formed the basis for the order of life and acted as a marker in tabulating the chronology of human history, and that of the universe. As Pei Te Hurinui Jones wrote, 'it was the time-honoured Polynesian method of memorising and tabulating the chronological sequence of events and order of birth.'[15] Genealogy gave Māori a tangible relationship to all things, living and inanimate, connecting everything together in 'a single "family tree" or "taxonomy of the universe"'.[16] The creation of the universe, the formation of the earth and its elements, the emergence of biodiversity, the source of knowledge, the creation of humans, the arrival of people in Aotearoa, and their subsequent travels, were all remembered through genealogies.

Genealogies of biota and environmental phenomena produce a classification system derived from the Polynesian/Māori practice of observing the connections between different entities, taking into consideration location and habit, shape, form, texture, colour, smell, seasonality, change, human usage and adaptation. The southern tribe of Ngāi Tahu developed 'extensive whakapapa that defines and orders … weather patterns and other meteorological phenomena'.[17] Integral to these lists of genealogies were allegorical and analogical oral narratives which often used specialised language. Without an understanding of these accompanying narratives, the genealogies make no sense. Māori use of 'organic analogies' in whakapapa allowed them to link diverse biological phenomena.[18]

Whakapapa and kinship were an essential part of the Māori social fabric. Genealogical relationships were important in forming political alliances, especially in wartime, as well as in the inheritance of status and possessions. It was considered essential that people knew at least their direct lines of descent. Chiefs were also expected to know their links to the most distant branches of their whānau.[19]

Genealogies were examined and argued over by elders on the marae, sometimes even at the point of a weapon, and corrected amid much fury if a mistake was made. To forget a name or place an ancestor in the wrong order slighted the descendants and sometimes provoked retaliation. Great effort was taken to ensure that whakapapa were memorised correctly. The numerous forms of genealogical recitation included kōrero pūtake (whakapapa of origins before the canoe migration), tāhū (single lines of descent), tararere (similar to tāhū but with some names omitted, usually because the ancestor was so tapu that their name could not be uttered), whakamoe (showing wives' names in a male line, or siblings in order of birth), karapitipiti (showing grandparents, siblings, parents, and childen), kōrero whenua (land-based genealogies), whakapapa (all the above), and whaiwhaiā (genealogies used to inflict harm or to search out connections).[20]

Storytelling was a major factor in the survival of historical memory, the formulation of folklore and the retelling of ancestral deeds. A favourite pastime of the elderly and the young, it kept traditional history alive. Stories, especially those about wars, were taonga (treasures). The deliberate construction of myths and legends allowed Māori to conceptualise their perceptions of their physical and mental environment into value systems.[21] While many Māori narratives appear to modern minds to be simplistic fairy tales, the 'myth-messages' woven through them actually provided 'precedents, models and social prescriptions for human behaviour'.[22] At another level, they provided important observations and understandings of the natural world. Many of the ancient narratives have Polynesian origins and were reconstructed and adapted to suit the New Zealand environment.

All forms of information – sacred and profane, prophetic and factual, historical and emotional – were transmitted orally in waiata. Specialised language and archaic expressions were used in various forms of waiata to create a visual image of the subject of the song. Many of the images embodied in waiata portrayed a belief in the unity of or connections between phenomena: stars were carriers of food, while light was associated with life and success, darkness with death and failure, and stormy weather with human strife and emotional turmoil.[23] For Āpirana Ngata, 'a wealth of meaning was clothed within a word or two as delectable as a proverb in its poetical form and in its musical sound.'[24] The classes of waiata identified by Ngata were oriori (songs composed for children containing ancient history, genealogies and accounts of battles), tangi (laments), patere (abusive songs), waiata aroha (love songs), ruri (ditties), mata (prophetic songs), ngeri (chants), haka (posture dances), and karakia (ritualistic chants).[25] Today the ancient texts of waiata are used by many Māori as reference points in traditional accounts of oral histories.

Often the spoken word was expressed not merely verbally, but also through dancing, beating drums, rocking or walking, or playing string games.[26] Whai, the Māori version of cat's cradle, used body movements and often waiata to retell a kōrero pūrākau (traditional narrative). Each pattern exemplified an ancient tradition which was elaborated on by the accompanying songs and puzzles.

Ngā pūrere whakamahara
Mnemonic devices

The mnemonic devices used by Māori included whakairo (carving), mahi tauira (design and weaving), whai, moko (body tattooing), tohu (physical or metaphysical signs), and tuhi (physical markings). These transmitted in a symbolic form information that helped in the retention of oral traditions and history. Carving – perhaps the most visible mnemonic system in Māori society – has become more prominent over the last century. One object often used in remembering genealogies was the rākau whakapapa (genealogy stick). As Jones observed, 'in the course of centuries the Polynesian genealogist had hit upon the device of the carved board and notched stick or rod as a visual aid to the memory.'[27] The carved whare tupuna (ancestral houses) have been likened to 'libraries and learning centres',[28] with the carvings seen as books of knowledge. Highly symbolic forms and elaborate patterns were carved into wood to memorialise ancestors and the traditions associated with them.

The most important aspect of Māori carvings is the messages they hold. Paki Harrison believes that without these messages one would be unable to carve anything. 'Without the korero you have nothing to learn. Without it you have nothing to understand'. Many people think that the basis of Māori carving is the appearance of the finished product, but this is only one consideration. A carving must speak or say something to people.[29] This idea is embodied in ancient stories about how people gained knowledge of carving. One tradition tells how Rua-te-pupuke plunged into the sea to find his son Manuruhi, who had been kidnapped by Tangaroa (the deity of the sea) and transformed into a tekoteko (gable) of his house. Rua-te-pupuke looked into the house and heard the poupou (carved posts) on each side conversing with each other. Eventually he burnt Tangaroa's house and returned to the surface with some of the carvings from its porch. Unfortunately these carvings could not talk.[30] The fact that carvings and decorations on wood convey messages is alluded to in the term pūrākau (traditional narrative). Te Maire Tau describes pūrākau as 'a form of oral tradition [that] … refers to the act of carving a tradition (pu) upon wood (rākau). In this sense, the carving signifies the thought and beliefs of the community just as the word is a signifier of thought.'[31]

Anything within the Māori world-view could be represented by the numerous designs and patterns of Māori artforms. These patterns can be seen in the arts of tukutuku (latticework), raranga (weaving), tāniko (the ornamental bordering of cloaks, or macramé), and kōwhaiwhai (painted designs). The patterns used in these crafts are divided into three categories: skeuomorphs (forms and patterns derived from the structure of houses), physicomorphs (representations of objects or operations of the physical world), and the three kinds of biomorphs – zoomorphs (representations of animals), phyllomorphs (representations of plants), and anthropomorphs (representations of humans).[32]

Meaningful inscribed or written symbols were not unknown to Māori. The word tuhi refers to writing, but it also means to delineate, draw, cause to glow, redden, shine, or adorn with painting. Throughout New Zealand there are numerous examples of tuhi: paintings and drawings on rocks and cliffs, and in caves. Most are found in the South Island, where fairly linear depictions of animals, humans and mythical creatures can be identified. The meanings and historical contexts of these drawings are unclear.

Some traditions of ancient inscriptions have survived. The Wairarapa tohunga Moihi Te Matorohanga told the scribe Te Whatahoro Jury of Te Ana Whakairo (the adorned cave), a cave in the South Island on whose walls Tamatea of the *Takitimu* canoe tradition carved designs he had brought from Hawaiki. The elements of the drawings in Tamatea's cave included a long stroke ⎯⎯ meaning 'Haere mai' ('Come hither'), a straight line curving downward ⎯⎯⎤ meaning 'Kei whea koutou?' ('Where are you?'), this symbol ⎯⎯⎦ meaning 'Hoki atu koutou' ('Go back'), a curved line with a dot under it ⌒•⌐ meaning 'No hea koutou?'('Where are you from?'), and this arrow formation ⬊ referring to insects. A symbol cut on a blade of flax ‿⌒ means 'Kai te whawhai' ('Gather for war').[33] Other paintings and figures represented ngārara (lizards of Hawaikian origin), decorations on the *Takitimu*, and moko patterns on the faces of friends and relatives left behind in Tahiti.[34]

Caves with carvings of canoes and rocks bearing mystical inscriptions can also be found in the North Island (some of the latter are believed to be boundary markers). Among the most famous inscribed stones remembered in Māori tradition are the 'papa tatau', sacred inscribed stone emblems which were part of a tohi ritual performed by the high priests in the Waikato whare-wānanga system.[35] It is not known exactly what 'papa tatau' were or what they meant, as they were lost during warfare in the early nineteenth century.

Te kupu-ā-tuhi

The written word

Once the written word was introduced, eyes (and ears) could access the New Zealand world in different ways. The eye of 'civilised man' depended on books and writing, and this rather than the auditory world became the pathway for information. For the early missionaries, the printed word was an essential tool in bringing Christianity to Māori.

Māori enthusiasm for reading and writing meant that the best way to Christianise them was through literacy and the distribution of printed material containing the gospels, catechisms and tracts in their own language.[36] While literacy was thought to be 'essential to being civilised', the acquisition of British 'social graces' was also vital.[37] The 'improvement' of the 'heathens' by teaching them to read was a necessary part of the Christianising process. Becoming a Christian meant becoming civilised, which meant becoming culturally British.

The first attempts to teach the rudiments of literacy to Māori were made in the early nineteenth century at Parramatta, near Sydney. The students were young men who had joined Pākehā whaling crews. Church Missionary Society missionaries led by the Reverend Samuel Marsden encouraged these Māori to attend the mission school in the hope that they would spread the Christian message to their kin on their return to New Zealand. In 1814 Marsden arrived in the Bay of Islands with three pioneer missionaries and their families. 'Marsden wanted practical men in his team … in order to gain the confidence of Maori by impressing them with British "superior" technological skills', such as carpentry, twine-spinning and blacksmithing.[38] His intention was to introduce 'the "benefits" of a refined society'.[39] Marsden believed that 'trade and … teaching … the decencies and handicrafts of civilized life … was the best path to religious life'.[40]

One of Marsden's pioneer missionaries, Thomas Kendall, was commissioned by the Church Missionary Society to develop an orthography of the Māori language. After settling at Rangihoua pā, Kendall compiled *A Korao no New Zealand* in 1815 as a teaching aid for Māori students.[41] By 1816 Kendall had ten children in his school, and by April 1817, 70. He employed the 'monitorial system', in which children taught others through repetition, to hasten the spread of literacy.[42] In 1820 Kendall accompanied the Ngā Puhi chiefs Hongi Hika and Hōhaia Parata Waikato to Britain. Hongi Hika and Kendall worked with Samuel Lee at Cambridge University compiling a Māori grammar which was published in 1820.[43] Over the next 25 years the Māori alphabet was standardised, and its grammar was described in more detail.[44]

When Henry Williams arrived in 1823 as the new leader of the Church Missionary Society in New Zealand, he abandoned Marsden's strategy of 'artisan education' in favour of 'introducing forms of civilisation which would enable the missionaries to communicate the gospel'. Williams encouraged missionaries to become fluent in Māori and teach Māori to be literate. Schools were the 'key to evangelisation'.[45] The missionaries were to utilise the written language to Christianise the people by using only religious texts. All religious instruction would be in Māori.[46] Limiting reading material to that of a 'sacred nature' would facilitate a 'great moral change',[47] not least by reducing the risk that Māori would learn profanities. However, many Māori had already had contact with Europeans and learnt their language and manners, with some being drawn into the 'purgatory' of shore-whalers' incessant drinking, foul language and other bad habits.

Restricting Māori access to non-religious material was to have more general political and social implications. The rapid increase in the number of European settlers arriving in New Zealand meant that Māori needed greater access to secular literature to improve their understanding of the wider world. This was slow to come because the missionaries saw their primary task as preaching the gospel and converting Māori, rather than fostering their welfare in other ways. Māori were not prepared to cope with the 'acquisitive and materialistic, if nominally Christian, Pākehā society which swept into the country'.[48]

The first Bible in the Māori language was published by the British and Foreign Bible Society in 1868. Before this, other religious material, including books of the Bible, the complete New Testament (1837), hymns and catechisms had appeared. From the late 1840s, grammars and dictionaries, books recording oral traditions, and government publications became available.[49]

By the 1830s, Māori society had been devastated by introduced diseases and musket warfare. European commodities were replacing traditional tools, and Māori sought the power that was promised by European wealth. They assumed this could be found in religious ritual, which had always been influential in Māori society. This belief fostered enthusiasm for baptism as well as for reading and writing.[50] Literacy was the mechanism through which Māori gained access to the Pākehā God. The missionaries, they believed, made contact with the Almighty through the power of the word. Māori were persuaded to believe that literacy was a necessity to reach God – only those able to read and write would be admitted to the ranks of his followers. The Bible was the word, 'the word was God', and therefore the Bible was God. It must have seemed divine to Māori, who already believed that knowledge was derived from ancestral mana.

The missionaries sought to break the power of tapu – the force which bound together the whole fabric of social organisation – over Māori thought, religion and ritual.[51] A person, place or thing became tapu when it was 'set aside or reserved for the sole use of [a] deity'.[52] The desecration of a tapu would incur some form of punishment. Until the 1830s, tapu was 'so great an obstacle' to Christianising Māori that 'nothing could be done'.[53] But the Bible came to be seen as the symbol of a divine power which gave Māori access to a new way of life in which sins could be forgiven rather than leading to death. This idea influenced the conversion of many Māori to Christianity.[54] The sacred words of God were made available to all, not only the elite. However, some aspects of Māori belief had to be rejected before a convert would be accepted as a Christian.

Māori imbued the Bible with 'a sense of tapu'. It became a 'propitious talisman'; its words were recited as a 'powerful incantation'.[55] In its very name – 'Paipera Tapu' – old meanings of tapu were applied in new ways. Its pages were used as earrings to ward off kino (evil), tohu (omens) and mākutu (spells), and as wrappings for bullets. Words from the scriptures were carved on the butts of muskets. Testaments, along with drawings of dreams and tohu, became talismans for warriors. The Bible was also used to point out the inconsistencies of the colonisers, whose religion advocated showing love to all men rather than fighting them.[56]

Although missionaries maintained that Māori attended church and read the Bible and catechisms because of their desire to become Christians,[57] the spread of literacy easily outstripped conversion to Christianity.[58] Reading and writing became commodities utilised by Māori to meet Māori needs. By the mid-1830s, the desire for books and other reading material among Māori had become 'virtually insatiable'.[59]

Te urupaenga
The Māori reaction

Books were received enthusiastically by those who could read them. In the Bay of Islands they were even accepted as wages. 'Maori would work a month for the book to call it their own, while five bushels of potatoes were offered ... for a single copy'. By 1844 Māori were said to be able to learn to read and write using only the alphabet, their determination to become literate being greater than that of Europeans.[60] Raw materials were utilised for teaching in inventive ways: pointed sticks were used to write on wooden slabs that had been oiled and dusted with ashes. Richard Taylor received hundreds of letters written on leaves using nails; most asked him to explain passages from the Bible.[61] Bundles of inscribed leaves sometimes served as prayer books.[62] Some Māori acquired a working knowledge of reading and writing within three months.[63]

Memory skills that had been practised for generations enhanced people's ability to read. Anything that could be read was committed to memory; some Māori could recite whole Epistles. Mission spelling books and missionary teachings were also learned in a traditional manner by being sung around fires at night.[64] Such practices have raised the doubts about whether Māori were really able to read and write; was memorising the printed word simply a 'masquerade for being literate'?[65] Whatever the truth, oral learning continued to be preferred by Māori into twentieth century – college students often returned to their kāinga (home) to be tutored by their elders, who read their school material and then recited the information.[66]

People living in the most isolated parts of New Zealand, far distant from any mission station, soon learned to read.[67] Missionaries 'found Men and Women who could say the Catechism and prayers, read and write, that had never seen a Missionary, but ... had learnt it from one that had been taught'.[68] Travellers in the interior were often asked to give writing lessons using wooden boards; Māori also used slates and korari leaves.[69] Pleas to send written material flooded in from all over the country.[70]

Signposts similar to modern road signs were also common. Carved pou (poles) marking incidents, commemorating peace settlements or warning of rāhui ('no-go' areas), included words notifying people of their purpose.[71] Messages or warnings were also written on trees. In 1845 Reverend Alfred Brown stumbled upon this phenomenon while travelling through the Rangitaiki district:

> The knowledge of writing imparted to the New Zealanders is of great use to them. I have been much amused at the various notices which we have read at different places during our journey ... One of these notices was addressed to a Chief informing him that if he persisted in planting potatoes in that wood which did not belong to him, his head would be cut open by the hatchet of the writer. Another requested us not to eat at a certain spot, it being sacred ... Another was a caution not to kill the pigs in that district, they being the property of the writer, and at the door of the hut where my men are resting for the night, travellers are informed that the mat left there was for a Chief named Ahuriri, and requesting them not to steal it.[72]

Māori of both sexes utilised lettering as bodily adornment. Many had their names and those of kin tattooed on their bodies.[73] Some think that this practice was derived from the missionaries, who marked the baptismal names of Māori children on their arms. It may also have influenced the marking of ancestors' names on the chests of poupou (carved images of ancestors) to identify them.

The power of the printed word and European technologies altered traditional Māori social and political organisation. New criteria for mana (personal prestige) based on the understanding of Pākehā knowledge and habits and the ownership of Pākehā goods developed.[74] Missionary school students – young and old, satisfactory and unsatisfactory pupils – often returned home to their tribal rohe (regions) and taught their relatives whatever they knew of the written word. Sometimes specific people were sent from a village to find instruction in writing and return to the hapū (subtribe). Some believe Māori became largely self-taught in the skills of literacy.[75]

Reading, writing and the acquisition of new knowledge crossed traditional status boundaries. Some former students gained great mana by teaching chiefs to read and write. Even slaves could now hope to acquire status in Māori society. By comprehending and controlling European knowledge, anyone could carve out a role for themselves in a rapidly growing bicultural world. Literacy diminished the significance of older chiefs and priests as the task of memorising traditional lore was removed from their hands. Scribes attained mana through their skill in writing.[76] People would travel for miles to get them to write letters, petitions, histories or whakapapa. New ways to acquire mana would have grave effects on the old system, as new roles challenged the pre-eminence of genealogy. However, the status of chiefly lines was not completely lost.

By the 1830s many Māori wanted to become literate. In 1834, William Yate estimated that about 800 Māori in the Bay of Islands area could read, while Edward Markham claimed that 'not less than ten Thousand people … can read, write and do sums in the Northern end of the island'.[77] In 1837 Marsden noted that there were Māori who could read and write throughout the Hokianga and Bay of Islands. In 1839 another missionary believed that up to a thousand Māori in the Thames district could read religious material. William Brown wrote in 1845 that great numbers of Māori 'had these acquirements, and that too amongst tribes who have no intercourse with the missionaries'.[78] Māori who could read well were found even in the remote south-west corner of the South Island.[79] By 1859 half of all adult Māori could read, and a third could write.[80]

Māori even taunted working-class Pākehā about their illiteracy.[81] They had at first assumed that all Pākehā were literate and therefore connected to God. The realisation that they were not – and that the Bible was not a magical volume – brought disillusionment with the Christian message as Māori re-evaluated their allegiance to the missionaries' words, writings and God.[82] In the early 1840s and again in the early 1850s both literacy and belief in Christianity waned; the novelty had worn off.[83]

Māori disillusionment with literacy was not solely disillusionment with the missionaries; there were other influences upon Māori society, and Māori made their own decisions about which western ideas to accept.[84] Literacy had reached artificially high levels in the 1830s because understandings of what it offered were unrealistic.[85] However, neither Christianity nor literacy disappeared from Māori society. Christianity manifested itself in a new form with the emergence of Māori religious sects, while the function of literacy changed from 'ritual significance' in the 1830s to 'a more practical and utilitarian significance' after the mid-1840s.[86]

With the introduction of British bureaucratic systems – national and local governments, contracts, courts – after the signing of the Treaty of Waitangi in 1840, the written word was to take on an even greater (and more sinister) significance for Māori.

Te ao here tikanga

The binding power of literacy

'In the committing of oaths to writing' in northern Europe from about the thirteenth century, Illich and Sanders believe, 'we can trace the shift of trust from the validly given word to a document exerting legal force'. Documents became legally effective instruments of witness, and eventually a signature was required as a mark of authenticity.[87] The extensive European settlement of New Zealand saw the introduction of bureaucratic systems which brought about vast social change for Māori. Weber's 'ideal type' of bureaucracy involves 'the existence of fixed official areas of jurisdiction, a hierarchy in which lower offices are subordinate to higher ones, management according to general rules and by means of written documents ("the files") and the employment of trained officials'.[88] These systems used the printed word to record and verify proceedings and transactions,[89] including those involving Māori, whose political and social systems were tribally based and rested on notions of whakapapa, mana and tapu.

The forerunners for Māori of bureaucratic systems based on oaths and the binding power of the written word were the 1835 Declaration of Independence and the Treaty of Waitangi. Signatures and symbols representing chiefs' names were written on documents that were to have major consequences for the future of New Zealand. Before signing the Treaty of Waitangi, Māori discussed the Māori text. By 1840 many Māori understood the significance of written words for contractual obligations. After the South Island chief Tūhawaiki signed the Treaty of Waitangi, he gave Major Thomas Bunbury a 'memorandum concerning the register of a ... vessel that was being built for him', and asked Bunbury to endorse 'a guarantee, written in English, that Ruapuke [Island] belonged to ... his tribe'.[90]

Over the subsequent decades dramatic changes took place in New Zealand life: an influx of settlers with a continuing need for land, and the establishment of British social and political structures. Māori acquiescence in these developments was essential. George Grey had argued in 1840 that British law should replace native custom as rapidly as possible.[91] George Clarke, the Chief Protector of Aborigines, made a similar point in a memorandum to Grey in 1846 after the latter had become Governor of New Zealand:

> [They] should be instituted as speedily as possible into the common rights and privileges of British subjects, in all matters appertaining to their own possessions, and ... they should be led, not forced, into the observance of British law.[92]

The rapid changes in New Zealand society were to have both advantageous and detrimental consequences for Māori. The new political and bureaucratic structures undermined Māori rangatiratanga over their lands and customs, if only because most Māori had learned to read and write only religious material.

The institution which was to have the most dramatic effect on Māori was the Native Land Court. Established in 1865, its role was 'to bring the European purchase of Maori-owned land within an orderly system, and so promote the peaceful settlement of the new colony'. Land held under Māori customary ownership was upon application 'brought under a system as near as possible to ownership in British law'. This basically imposed individual ownership of land upon 'a people whose lands had always been held communally'. The court was to identify and name individual Māori as the owners of 'all lands in New Zealand held according to Maori custom'. The land would be converted into titles derived from the Crown, a process that was more or less completed by 1909.[93]

'The crux of the matter', as Vincent O'Malley observes, 'lay in the fact that the Native Land Court was intended not merely to determine native title to Maori lands but to extinguish this and replace it with a transferable title which would expedite the alienation of land to the settlers'.[94] As a Royal Commission of Inquiry pointed out in 1980, 'As soon as the titles were vested in individuals, land purchasing officers and settlers would deal with them for purchases, leases, and mortgages. Large areas were sold, in many cases against the wishes of the greater number of the tribal group and without financial benefit to them. The Court at that time had no authority to control the disposal of Maori land ... Thus many injustices were perpetrated'.[95]

This process stimulated a great volume of Māori writing – transcribed oral testimonies, letters, petitions – containing genealogies and histories that were used to prove rights to land. Some Māori kept their own records of court proceedings.[96] Many letters submitted to court assessors by landowners and claimants set out genealogical lines; these were accompanied by written accounts that supported or contested claims to land.[97] This material has provided crucial evidence in the hearing of Treaty claims in recent decades.

Whakapapa, tribal histories and knowledge of place names and boundaries were cited in the courts to authenticate land ownership. Traditional rights to land were governed by noho-roa (occupation), mahinga kai (labour and food production), and raupatu (occupation by conquest). However, these were of no account without genealogical links to those holding mana over the land.[98]

Sometimes whakapapa were used in questionable ways to claim land rights. Māori who could whakapapa (show their genealogical links) to a piece of land they had never set foot on often staked a claim to it. The validity of whakapapa was often questioned. On many occasions ancestors were deliberately omitted in order to extinguish the rights of descendants who were not present in court. Whakapapa were often changed, manipulated or 'adjusted',[99] to enhance the prestige of an ancestor and his/her descendants, or to challenge the earlier social order. Takaanui Tarakawa called land court genealogies 'whakapapa tango whenua'('land-grabbing genealogies').[100] Such behaviour is one reason why tribal histories have become 'more contentious and less openly discussed' in recent times.[101]

An essential aspect of the information concerning land ownership was knowledge of place names and boundaries, which were 'signposts of... history' and 'immutable, tangible markers of tradition'.[102] These names referred to historical incidents, geographical features, human reactions and emotions. Every part of a tribe's domain was named, and boundaries were defined by these names. Place names were 'word fossils'[103] which could reveal a whole body of history. 'The daily use of such place names meant that the history was always present, always available'.[104] The great significance of place names for Māori was embodied in the proverbial saying, 'Ko taku whenua tēnei, kei te mōhio au i ōna kōrero' ('This is my land, and I know all there is to know about it').

While the court process led to much documentation of Māori history, the resulting loss of land also provoked an 'aversion to print' among Maori, who were disadvantaged because the written word was now more powerful than their more flexible forms of oral consensus.[105] Danny Keenan discusses cases in Taranaki associated with the Compensation Court, an extension of the Native Land Court that was set up to hear and determine claims for compensation from Māori for land confiscated under the New Zealand Settlements Act of 1863. The Compensation Court was reliant on 'the comprehensive status of the binding power of *its* written statements, given that its primary function was to aid the process of title transfer from customary law (oral) to English law (statutory documents)'. Māori claimants' oral evidence was 'mediated' to the court 'through written forms and documents', which compromised their ability to cite customary law.[106] Hapū were asked to record the details of their claims to confiscated lands on a printed form entitled 'He Pukapuka Tono Ki Te Kooti Whakawa Maori, Kia Whakawakia Etahi Take Whenua'. These forms compelled claimants to declare kinship details and other interests in land with a degree of rigour to which Māori were not accustomed. Tribes and hapū relied heavily on elders' knowledge of genealogies and land features, and the information recorded on these forms by different claimants 'invariably overlapped.'[107]

The Compensation Court faced an impossible task in attempting to substantiate the claims submitted to it, because of their size, complexity and number. The eventual land allocations 'took little account of the original basis of claims to mana whenua'.[108] Subsequently, the Crown was continually petitioned about these allocations, and many commissions of enquiry were held.

Māori attempted to influence the new structures that were encroaching on their lives. As the alienation of their land continued, Māori realised the necessity of becoming involved in the legal structures that allowed this to occur. Many tribes formed committees and councils based on the traditional rūnanga system in an effort to control their own destinies. Generally the functions of these councils were to police social and moral controls; promote political goals; and function as alternatives to the Native Land Courts by settling land titles and boundary disputes. Some attempted to enforce tribal vetoes on land sales by punishing those who defied them.[109]

Māori were concerned with much more than eliminating petty crime; their real fear was that they were losing control of their destinies and being subordinated to the political and economic power of the settlers. Tribes throughout the country sought the Crown's recognition of some form of self-government.[110] This impulse saw the establishment of Māori movements such as Te Kīngitanga (the King movement) and its parliament, Te Kauhanganui; Hēnare Matua's Repudiation movement; Te Kotahitanga; and Te Whitu Tekau, in addition to the many official and unofficial tribal councils and committees. Despite – and because of – the adverse and sometimes explosive impact of the introduction of British law in the nineteenth century, a huge volume of Māori writing was generated.[111] The Māori struggle for autonomy is documented in minutes, reports, letters, petitions, transaction slips, voting documents, registration forms and many other items. In the religious sphere, Māori clergy provided annual reports to district synods.[112]

Documents related to the workings of the Native Land Court and the rise of Māori committees and councils are discussed in this book. Chapter 2 analyses tribal information written down by elders to authenticate their rights to ancestral lands, while chapter 4 explores the minutes of an unofficial tribal committee in Hawke's Bay.

Te manako o te kōrero-ā-waha

The oral tradition in focus

Māori wrote down whakapapa and traditional narratives, either at the request of Pākehā or for their own reasons, from the mid-1840s. Some of the well-known recorders of this information were Te Rangikaheke, who wrote more than 2000 manuscript pages,[113] Aperahama Taonui, Paora Tūhaere, Te Wheoro, Hoani Nahe, Matiaha Tiramorehu, Matene Te Whiwhi, Te Kahui Kararehe, Te Whatahoro, Wiremu Mahupuku, Mohi Te Atahikoia, Hamiora Pio, and Mohi Ruatapu.

There was a great interest by Pākehā in collecting Māori religious beliefs and traditions, and genealogical accounts of tribal histories. According to Toon van Meijl, as Māori became politically and economically subordinate to Pākehā, only their ideological colonisation remained to be accomplished. This was achieved in part through the collection of Māori traditions by ethnologists aided by Māori informants. Bilingual and literate Māori were essential to this process; they wrote a huge volume of information. From these oral and written Māori sources, Pākehā ethnologists rewrote and reconstructed the traditional histories with scant consideration for tribal variations, and presented tribal accounts as common to all Māori.[114] This had the effect of detribalising Māori, in Pakēhā eyes at least.

Further interest was prompted by expectations that the race would soon be extinct. In 1856 Dr I. E. Featherston declared that Maori were dying out, and nothing could save them. 'Our plain duty as good compassionate colonists is to smooth down their dying pillow. Then history will have nothing to reproach us with.'[115] In 1881 Dr A. K. Newman observed that, 'the disappearance of the race is scarcely a subject for much regret. They are dying out in a quick easy way and are being supplanted by a superior race.' In 1907 Archdeacon Walsh claimed that: 'The race is sick unto death, and is already potentially dead.'[116]

Nevertheless, Māori recognised that writing and publishing was now a means to preserve oral traditions.[117] Texts facilitated discussion and debate by enhancing communication amongst tribes and people. Circulars, letters, proclamations, minutes of meetings, and some 40 Māori-language newspapers arose out of the need of Māori to inform each other about themselves. The newspapers functioned as consciousness-raising mechanisms, and contained religious material, moral instruction, minutes of tribal meetings, letters, official notices, sale notices, tribal accounts and responses to them, whakapapa, histories and waiata. The readership of these early writings and newspapers amongst Māori was enormous. Māori encouraged other Māori to write and publish their own material. Sir Āpirana Ngata, Sir Peter Buck, and Pei Te Hurinui Jones were among the most prolific Māori writers in the first half of the twentieth century.

Perhaps the most common Māori written material is private family manuscript books. Generally known as whakapapa books, these contain not only genealogies, but waiata, hīmene (hymns), maramataka (calendars), rātaka (daily diary entries), kōrero tipuna (tribal narratives), reta (letters), pepeha, kupu whakaari (prophetic utterances),[118] and all manner of whānau information. Collectively they comprise 'the largest single body of writing in Māori'.[119]

These books are usually regarded as taonga, and jealously guarded by Māori families. Their very existence may be kept secret not only from strangers but from family members considered unsuitable to have access to them.[120] They are hidden in high places, under beds, in suitcases and biscuit tins, even in cupboards in cowsheds. Because of the reverence Māori have for their ancestors, great care is taken not to insult their memory by allowing their written names to be defiled in any way.

Among the many factors behind the compilation of whakapapa books were the interventions of missionaries, politicians, officials and ethnologists, and private needs. From the late ninetenth century, fear of losing traditional knowledge was also a factor.[121] Because whakapapa were essential to the establishment of mana, writing down genealogies may have been regarded as a chiefly pursuit. Many chiefs were proud that their ancestors' lineages were recorded in private books.[122] While many wished to publish their genealogies, some still consider it an act of conceit to openly display your whakapapa to enhance your reputation. 'That is a thing for the common man to do, who never was heard of before'.[123]

Ngā tikanga-ā-waha kei roto i ngā tuhituhi
Traditional oral aspects in literacy

By the early 1840s Māori were constantly sending letters to each other. The Bay of Islands postmaster told William Brown that he had had 'a bundle of native letters a foot square, in his office'.[124] Māori brought their own traditional forms of communication to literacy, as well as applying concepts such as tapu. 'Writers wrote as they spoke ... and wrestled with kaupapa in the same way as they would on a marae.'[125] Many letters followed traditional oral forms of communication, utilising techniques used in whai-kōrero (public speech) such as tauparapara (a verse beginning a speech), whakataukī (proverbs), whakatangata (personification), kōrero whakarite (metaphor), and waiata.

Māori often referred to letters as manu (birds) or waka (canoes), traditional forms of communication. These terms were used when an important statement needed to be sent: 'Haere atu ōku kupu i runga i te manu kawe kōrero' ('Go, my words, upon the bird that carries news'). Writers to Māori newspapers also regarded their letters as messenger birds: 'E manu utaina atu enei kupu ki runga i ou parirau hei whakaatu ki nga iwi Maori' ('O bird, put my words upon your wings, that they may be expressed to all the Maori tribes').[126] Other letters refer to being carried in a canoe: 'Tukua atu tenei hei waka kawe i nga kupu riri' ('Send forth this canoe that carries words of anger'). Letters to friends sometimes began with the statement that the writer was sending their word or their love: 'Haere ra e taku pukapuka' ('Travel yonder, my book'); 'Haere ra e taku tuhi aroha ki'('Go, my loving words'). In accordance with Māori protocols for formal oral communication, other letters began with a waiata, or contained allegories and metaphors relevant to their subject matter.

Under the influence of the missionaries, Māori utilised biblical teachings, parables, and proverbs to communicate, validate and emphasise thoughts. Biblical precepts were often used to appeal to Pākehā to act fairly when dealing with Māori and their land.[127]

In pre-literate Māori society, enemies had been enticed to fight through the use of messengers or trickery. In the 1860s, fighting chiefs sent written messages to their Pākehā enemies with the same purpose.[128] Letter-writing also became a tool to accomplish more sinister traditional goals. Words used to cast whaiwhaiā (spells) were now written in letters with the intention of causing illness or death. Sometimes the whaiwhaiā could not be recognised in the written words, but was implied by their hidden meaning.[129]

While some early Māori writings show little understanding of the rules of grammar, and lack commas and apostrophes, others demonstrate the creation of new forms or use traditional Māori oral formula. Many early whakapapa were written in lists analogous to the genealogies recited on the marae. These tāhū, whakamoe, tararere or kōrero whenua often link the speaker to illustrious contemporary chiefs.[130] Other Māori writers created punctuation more suited to the spoken than the written word. In an early text by Te Rangikaheke, full stops indicate pauses in the karakia (incantation) rather than the ends of sentences; capitals place emphasis on certain words; and paragraph breaks probably also correspond to breaks in recitation.[131] Richard Taylor noted that some Māori used 'figures instead of letters' when communicating in writing.[132]

Another traditional concept applied to written works was that of tapu. In Māori society the institution of tapu, with its gradations and extensions, is still very much alive in relation to the committing of sacred knowledge to paper. To have the kōrero (words) and oral traditions recorded on paper in books, letters and diaries gave these documents a degree of sacredness. A special relationship governed by notions of separation, restriction and prohibition was created between the writer, the person written about, and the guardian of the document. The marks, moko images and signatures of chiefs written on paper were deemed tapu. To damage these documents was to insult the signatories.[133]

Māori believed that mana must be transferred to validate the communication of knowledge. The passing on of knowledge deprived the giver of some of his mauri (life-force) and could even cause his death. This was a sharp contrast with the western view that such an exchange had no detrimental consequences.[134] Because it was also believed that anyone misusing whakapapa books would suffer harm, elders preferred that their written knowledge be buried with them.

Often, Christianity contributed to the loss of many family whakapapa books. On conversion, it was believed, the things of the past should be left behind in favour of the new Christian world view. Many of the whakapapa books belonging to members of Rua Kenana's community at Maungapōhatu were destroyed.[135] According to Hikawera Mahupuku of Wairarapa, two of the elders who lived near a mission station also renounced their traditional knowledge: 'their great fear was that the ministers and mission teachers would banish them to the forested wilderness. The deeds of the ancestors were abominations to the ministers of the Church of England.' He wrote down only a fragment of the genealogies and esoteric understandings of his elders, who were unable to recite the ancient incantations.[136]

Students in many whare-wānanga (houses of learning) around the country began writing down their teacher's knowledge. Some permitted this, while others regarded the innovation with caution. When Te Whatahoro Jury and other students of Moihi Te Matorohanga in the 1860s wrote down his teachings, their actions were seen as 'unnecessary' and they were looked upon 'with a great deal of contempt'. The books were referred to as 'putea whakairo' ('repositories of crabbed markings').[137] Te Whatahoro was told that what they were recording was only a fraction of the ancient knowledge, and that no mana would be gained by students of this knowledge because 'the true teaching has been lost'.[138] On the other hand, Paratene Okawhare, a contemporary of Te Matorohanga and an informant of Sir George Grey,[139] agreed to have his knowledge recorded. However, he cautioned Te Whatahoro not to mingle this knowledge with other tribal information, as it was for him and his descendants only.[140]

At the closure of the whare-wānanga sessions in Wairarapa, Te Matorohanga performed rituals over both the students and the books to lift the tapu from them. In similar cases, other chiefs who agreed to have their knowledge written down refused to have some of it 'repeated in a common dwelling-house'; it 'had to be written in the open air' so that the information could be recited freely and recorded in writing without being desecrated.[141] Even in modern times, a tapu has been lifted from books containing tribal histories to protect general readers from its effects. One such book was Matire Hoeft's history of Te Aupouri, *The Tail of the Fish*, published in 1968.[142]

The relationship between manuscript books containing tribal histories and food was also important. Because food is considered noa and has the power to destroy tapu, it was essential not to bring it into contact with sacred ancestral names and the associated histories. Recording tribal histories – even orally – during seasons of vegetable cultivation was also prohibited. Despite this tradition, the author has seen lists of whakapapa written in books that also contained recipes for strawberry jam tarts and other food products. Many people nowadays hold material without considering themselves bound by any form of tapu – but they do allow access only to the 'hunga mōhio' (knowledgeable ones).

Most holders of whakapapa books and other family manuscripts do adhere to some form of tapu when dealing with what is seen as ancestral knowledge. Most kaitiaki (guardians) of such material consider that their ancestors' books should be kept in a high place; not associated with food; accessible only to the 'right people'; only worked on when in the right frame of mind; and not added to or mingled with other tribal and hapū information, or fragmented. This extension of tapu over written material has been emphasised recently by the notion of protecting Māori knowledge by holding it under tribal copyright or custodianship, so that it is not trivialised, commercialised, or used to increase anyone's personal reputation.[143]

He otinga kōrero
Conclusion

Far from ignoring the new concepts and technologies that were presented to them, Māori seized and adapted foreign tools and philosophies to meet their own needs. Māori learned the skills of literacy as soon as they realised its advantages. From its introduction as a means for teaching the word of God, to its use in letters, petitions, court applications and records, newspapers, diaries, whakapapa books and narratives, writing was acknowledged as an essential feature of the new world. Nevertheless, 'oral processes of knowledge retention and mediation' continued to be crucial for Māori.[144] The introduction of literacy brought unanticipated results and an 'extraordinary flowering' of Maori manuscript material.[145] These taonga have become invaluable sources of traditional oral literature.

This brief historical overview of the relationship between Māori and literacy provides some perspective for the following chapters, which explore the motivation for and meanings of selected manuscripts from the Maaka whānau's collection. The writings discussed here offer an important insight into the use of the written word by everyday Māori people over a period of 130 years. It has been important for me to understand the historical context which brought these family writings into being, lest they remain disorganised documents hidden from all but a few and divorced from a full life.

The porch carvings of Te Tokanga-nui-a-noho house at Te Kuiti. Māori carvings function as vital mnemonic devices for preserving traditions and history. The mermaid/merman carved form of the marakihau shown here, with its long tubular tongue and matted seaweed hair, is a metaphor for a tūpuhi (tempest). The tongue represents the 'raising breath' of the sea. When a storm occurs the marakihau rises to the surface; when the storm passes it returns to the caverns of the sea. Photo by Augustus Hamilton, Making New Zealand Collection, F-2203-1/2-MNZ, Alexander Turnbull Library

Rākau whakapapa (genealogy sticks) were important mnemonic devices for remembering cosmogonical and tribal genealogies.   N. Heke, Photo no. B23648, Museum of New Zealand Te Papa Tongarewa

A Māori dance, 1834. The words of songs and movements in dances were significant media for communicating messages and retaining knowledge. Drawn by Edward Markham, MS-1550-006, Alexander Turnbull Library

A cosmogonical genealogy, written by Wiremu Paratene Oka-whare of Wairarapa in a book sent to Sir George Grey in 1853, 'He Pukapuka no nga Tupuna', Maehe 17, 1853. Neg no. A14666, Auckland Public Library

27

Whai (string games) were usually accompanied by song and dance. Not merely an amusement, they depicted tribal stories and traditions.
F-55374-1/2, Alexander Turnbull Library

Māori rock carvings in a cave at Waverley, south Taranaki. F-2431-1/2, Alexander Turnbull Library

The Māori newspaper Te Kopara *was published between 1913 and 1931.*
Photo by the author

Ko Te Katekihama 111 – The Catechisms, 1830. F-54060-1/2 , Alexander
Turnbull Library

NIGHT SCENE IN NEW ZEALAND.

This sketch in the Christmas 1837 issue of the Church Missionary Paper *illustrates a popular perception of the nature of
missionary work in New Zealand.* PUBL-0031-37, Alexander Turnbull Library

A depiction of a dream in a notebook belonging to Aporo, who was shot by Major Gilbert Mair at Poripori on 3 January 1867. A translation of the text reads: 'Governor Grey, "The Enraged One". It is his intention to adopt a threatening course within New Zealand, so he would be justified in eradicating the Māori people.' F-126522-1/2, Alexander Turnbull Library

Minutes of the Kotahitanga movement relating to government land legislation of 1900.
Maaka Collection

'A native way of writing with figures instead of letters', as recorded by Reverend Richard Taylor c. 1854.
Rev. Richard Taylor MS, MSS 297/30, p. 184. Neg no. A14668, Auckland Public Library

Hoani Turei Whatahoro, also known as
Te Whatahoro Jury (1841–1923), of
Wairarapa.
Photo no. C229, Museum of New Zealand
Te Papa Tongarewa, published with the
permission of the whānau

CHAPTER TWO

Ngā tuhinga-ā-rohe
Land boundary records

Hākaraia Maumau's writings are an example of the kinds of written records compiled to authenticate rights to tribal lands for the Native Land Court process.

Ngā-rangi-kā-mau (also known as Hākaraia Maumau) died 1885

Ngā-rangi-kā-mau was better known as either Hākaraia Maumau or Hākaraia Te Kāmau. An elder from the Waimārama district, he belonged to the hapū of Ngāti Hikatoa and Ngāti Ika-whakaoho. He was the son of Te Pū-hā (an elder twin) and Matiore. Ngā-rangi-kā-mau married Hera Pōhue, a descendant of Ngāti Rongo-māiaia of Waimārama and Ngāti Rākai-paaka of Te Māhia.

Very little is known of his life before 1824, when he and his family were taken captive by a war party of Ngāti Raukawa, Ngāti Pakapaka and Ngāti Mutuahi. The people of Waimārama had warning of the impending arrival of this taua, and most had escaped to their island sanctuary of Motu-o-Kura (Bare Island). However, Ngā-rangi-kā-mau, his wife Hera and their children were taken to Ōtaki by Ngāti Raukawa. He escaped and returned to Waimārama after an arduous three-month journey over the Tararua ranges to Akitio and along the coast.[146]

It is probable that William Colenso, who first visted Waimārama in 1843 and established a mission school in Heretaunga in 1844, baptised Ngā-rangi-kā-mau as Hākaraia (Zecharaiah) and taught him to read and write. However, the local mission school attendance registers have not survived. Hākaraia, together with other elders, told Colenso that his maternal grandfather, Te Ori, had tried to abduct 'Tayeto', the son of the Tahitian navigator Tūpāea who accompanied Captain James Cook on his first voyage to Aotearoa. In this incident, on 15 October 1769, two men – Whakaruhe and Whakaika – were killed, and Te Ori was hit by a bullet under the knee, an injury which caused him to limp for the rest of his life. Hākaraia said that their forefathers had been warned by Tūpāea not to approach the ship in a hostile manner, because 'mai mate koe' ('here thou wilt be killed').[147] After this skirmish the name Cape Kidnappers was given to the Te Matau-a-Māui and Te Pōroa areas.

In Native Land Court hearings in 1868, Hākaraia was listed as a grantee to the Waimārama, Waipuka and Ōkaihau blocks; he was given a certificate of title for the Waimārama block.[148] Walter Campbell, an early Pākehā resident of the district, recorded in 1869 that Hakaraia lived 'in the bush' at Ōkaihau with his son-in-law and their families, and owned a number of horses and bullocks that were used for ploughing.[149] In 1884 he was named as a claimant alongside Mohi Te Atahikoia and others in a subdivision dispute, after which he was granted additional shares in the Waimārama block.[150] Hākaraia was a very old man by the time he died on 15 January 1885, when his daughter Miriama Maaka (from whom the Maaka family are descended) and niece Hiromina Koka succeeded to his lands.[151]

Ngā tuhituhi a Hākaraia
The writings of Hākaraia

Two documents attributed to Hākaraia are known to exist. The first is a letter sent to William Colenso at the Waitangi mission station in Hawke's Bay in 1848.[152] The other is made up of pepeha dealing with Waimārama land boundaries that were written down in connection with Native Land Court proceedings. These pepeha are the subject of this chapter.

It has been difficult to determine whether these documents were written by Hākaraia or by a scribe, as many Māori had their letters, whakapapa books and other manuscripts written for them. Much nineteenth-century Māori writing is astonishingly similar, and Hākaraia's material is virtually identical in style to that of another author in the same book. This may be because a single scribe was responsible – or both men may have learned the same style. Mission schools and a church were established at Waimārama and Manawarākau (known today as Kairākau) by 1847. Local Māori Leonard (Rēnata Mekemeke)[153] and Hadfield (Harawira Tātere)[154] taught there.[155] Colenso mentions these schools often in his journals, and it is likely that Hākaraia studied at one of them. Walter Lorne Campbell, an early lessee of land at Waimārama, recorded around 1870 that Harawira Tātere,[156] Ākenehi, Te Hāpuku, Wī Tūroa, Paratene, Mohi, Te Teira Tiaki-tai, Paora Whatuira, all contemporaries of Hākaraia, kept whakapapa and rent books, and constantly wrote letters to each other.[157] It therefore seems probable that Hākaraia was literate in Māori and that these are his writings.

He tuhinga-ā-rohe
Land boundary records

The writings attributed to Hākaraia which are discussed here were made in a small (34 × 28 cm) purple notebook in which at least four people wrote using three or more different pens and pencils. Hākaraia and his cousin from Ngāti Ura, Tiopira Huangō, are the only named authors. Their writings are dated Hūrae (July) 1884.

The notebook includes pepeha concerning 162 place names, lists of tribal boundaries, maramataka (moon calendars), waiata and whakapapa of Waimārama ancestors. It begins with the title, 'He pukapuka whakatu atu tenei naku na Hakaraia' ('The written records by Hākaraia'). In analysing the contents of this notebook, I will focus mainly on the pepeha concerning place names and boundary markers. The material transcribed and translated here is specifically attributed to Hākaraia.

Each of Hākaraia's pepeha name a place and identify it as a pā (stockaded village), pā tuna (eel weir), taupahī (seasonal camping ground), taumata (resting place or lookout), ngakinga kai (garden), ngakinga karaka (karaka ground), aka tororaro (creeping vine), mahinga harakeke (flax-working ground), aruhe (fernroot), or rua kōiwi (burial place). Beside some of these names there is an indication of how many papa whare (house sites) and rua kūmara (kūmara pits) were located there. Usually the name of an ancestor or hapū who owned or had access to the place is given. Here is an example from Hākaraia's list:

> Ko Waiaute he mahinga kai he mahinga karaka nā Aupaki.
> *Wai-aute is a garden and a karaka preparing place that belonged to Aupaki.*

The writer of this list had an intimate knowledge of the local landscape. The place names identify geographical features or commemorate an historical event. Āpirana Ngata regarded place names as being very important in determining tribal boundaries:

> Down to the most recent times a knowledge of boundaries, of the names of natural features or of features commemorating important incidents in border warfare or in the lives of tribal leaders, was as essential as a knowledge of genealogies. In ancient Maori life the younger generation of the tribe was carefully instructed in knowledge of tribal boundaries, and fathers took their sons with them on their excursions and pointed out the tribal landmarks and impressed them and their significance on the young.[158]

In order to place the contents of this manuscript in an historical context, I will now discuss the nineteenth-century land dealings which concerned Waimārama.

Te Kooti Whenua Māori
The Native Land Court

The Native Land Court, which came into being with the passing of the Native Lands Act of 1865, was designed to remove Māori land from collective ownership by enabling the granting of title to individual hapū members. Māori were 'expected to apply to the court for a hearing to grant them "ownership" in the form of a certificate of title for that which they already owned'.[159]

Māori who appeared before the court had to prove their claim to the land by citing traditional evidence concerning ancestral rights, whakapapa, conquest, land boundaries, urupā, cultivations and habitation sites. Those who received certificates of title were often encouraged by speculators or land agents to sell their shares, or to use the land as security for debts. Under the 'ten-owner rule', the court awarded blocks of land to no more than ten chiefs, regardless of the actual number of owners or the size of the blocks.[160] This caused great dissension over who had the right to have their names on the title. The Rees-Carroll Commission reported that:

> It was believed that these ten were trustees for the whole body … The certificate, however, erroneously alleged that they were the absolute owners of the land according to Native custom, and the Crown grants, which were issued to them by name, vested an absolute estate of freehold in possession, uncumbered by any trusts or conditions whatever. Thus, in Hawke's Bay 569,220 acres of the finest land in New Zealand … which belonged to nearly four thousand Natives … were vested in about two hundred and fifty grantees.[161]

The Native Lands Act 1867 modified the ten-owner rule, but neither this nor the Native Land Act 1873 made much practical difference. 'The basic thrust of the legislation remained ... to treat those listed as individual owners with power to alienate'.[162] Before long, succession and partition led to the fragmentation and eventual loss of land.

The information recorded by Hākaraia was the type of evidence needed in court to verify ancestral rights to blocks of land. Similar information is found in the Native Land Court application forms, 'He Pukapuka Tono ki Te Kooti Whakawa Whenua Maori, kia Whakawakia etahi Take Whenua', on which applicants recorded the boundaries of land to which they believed they were entitled, in the column headed, 'Whakaaturanga o nga rohe'. Descriptions of land, place names, and boundary points were written here.

The District Commissioner, G. S. Cooper, attempted to purchase the Waimārama block for the Crown in the early 1860s, but the price offered was not accepted. Uniquely in Hawke's Bay, Europeans did not acquire freehold land in the block until the twentieth century.[163] By 1865, the graziers ('squatters') J. Morrison, Francis Bee, W. F. Hargreaves, Reynolds and W. J. Birch had obtained unregistered leases to land around Waimārama,[164] without pastoral licences and probably through oral agreements with local chiefs and hapū. After Morrison died and the others left the area, a 21-year lease of approximately 35,000 acres was taken up by a partnership of Frederic Meinertzhagen and Walter Campbell in 1868. After the death of Campbell in 1874, Meinertzhagen took on his brother-in-law Thomas Moore as a partner. The Māori owners had applied for the partitioning of the Waimārama block in 1867, probably because of the 'ready money and trade goods' that were being acquired by their relations and neighbouring tribes.[165] Hearings for the Waimārama lands were held in 1868, and the chiefs Te Teira Tiaki-tai, Te Hāpuku, Wī Rangirangi, Mohi Te Atahikoia, Īhaka Mōtoro and many others, including Hākaraia Maumau, Tiopira Huangō and Mukakai Maaka, were granted titles.[166]

Entering the scene at this time was Airini Tōnore, a granddaughter of Tiaki-tai whose mother Haromi had held title to land. Airini came into possession of large areas of land, and along with her Pākehā husband George Donnelly (Tōnore) persistently thwarted Pākehā efforts to extend or even retain interests in the Waimārama block. This brought her into conflict with Meinertzhagen and his partners, whose 21-year lease would expire in 1889.[167] In a petition to the Legislative Council in 1907, Gertrude Meinertzhagen outlined how her father Frederic had tried to renew the lease from 1883. He had obtained the signatures of a substantial majority of the listed owners – but he needed them all. When Airini Tōnore imposed impossible conditions, he abandoned hope of renewing the lease.[168]

While these negotiations were taking place, an important partition was made by the Native Land Court at Waimārama in 1884 after a hearing was called by Airini and her uncle Te Teira Tiaki-tai to partition. This met with stiff opposition from Mohi Te Atahikoia and many others, including Hākaraia, who disputed Te Teira and Airini's sole right to partition the land. Evidence of ancestral rights to land in the Waimārama, Waipuka and Ōkaihau blocks was given. Mohi was the agent and representative of the majority of elders who sought equal shares in the land.

After a large body of evidence was gathered and read to the court, Mohi and his followers stormed out. While they achieved a partial victory, the judgement gave the mana of the lands to the Tiaki-tai clan. The court ruled:

> We have arrived at the following conclusion: that Te Teira (Tiaki-tai) and those under whom he claims possessed the principal mana over the several blocks and that Mohi and those whom he represents and their ancestors, came from Wairoa as refugees and lived under the mana of Te Teira's ancestors and their right (if any) is derived from long permissive occupation.[169]

The partition was made as follows:

Waimārama block	Te Teira Tiaki-tai, with 41 others named, 14,670 acres.
	Mohi te Atahikoia, with 42 others named, 4,000 acres.
Waipuka block	Te Teira, with 38 others, 6,621 acres.
	Mohi te Atahikoia, with 59 others, 4,379 acres.
Ōkaihau block	Te Teira, with 37 others, 3,757 acres.
	Mohi te Atahikoia, with 46 others, 1,797 acres.

In all, 35,224 acres was partitioned. Airini Tōnore's influence in all the blocks was strengthened, allowing her to oppose Meinertzhagen and Moore effectively.[170] Hākaraia was granted shares in all three blocks thanks to appearing on Mohi Te Atahikoia's lists, and he also gained a grant to the

Waimārama block through his presence on Tiaki-tai's list as a descendant of Hika-toa, who Te Teira agreed was one of the main ancestors of that land.[171]

While the kōrero in Hākaraia's book may have been used to validate the land claims of Mohi and the other objectors, it is interesting to note that Hākaraia's section of this book of pepeha was dated July 1884, after the above hearing. It is possible that this material was compiled because Mohi and his followers wanted to appeal against the court's decision, but there is no other evidence for this speculation.

Further place names, boundaries and associated kōrero similar to those of Hākaraia and Tiopira are recorded towards the end of this book in a different hand which has not been identified. They were written in May 1890, six years after Hākaraia's death but while Tiopira was still alive. Another Native Land Court hearing was held in 1891 to further partition the Waimārama blocks. On this occasion Airini Donnelly was awarded a further 4,026 acres. Mohi Te Atahikoia, who had once again fought to have the land partitioned equally between all the listed owners, reiterated his case to the Rees-Carroll Commission at Waipawa on 6 May 1891.

It is probable that these pepeha and lists of boundary markers were written down because of the need to record in writing evidence of rights to the land in question. Hēnare Matua's evidence in the Pōrangahau case is very similar in form.[172] Many lists of pā, pā tuna, taupahī, mahinga kai and rua kōiwi were assembled for other Māori communities in this period. In pre-European times, the inheritance or gifting of land was recorded by reciting the place names which marked its boundaries. This occurred with several gifts of land at Waimārama, such as those of Poua to Hikatoa,[173] and of Tamariki to Rongo-māiaia.[174]

A map of the plan for the proposed 1884-5 subdivision of the Waipuka, Ōkaihau and Waimārama blocks was held in the Lands and Survey Department's Napier office in 1970. This was unsigned and undated, but the location of some pā, kāinga and burial grounds corresponded closely with the information recorded by Hākaraia.[175] The need to survey and map the land may have been another reason for writing down these place names.

Knowledge about these places has subsequently been lost to local Māori as a result of the sale of land, the dislocation and urbanisation of the people, or the destruction or deterioration of landscape features. Many of these sites have been destroyed or damaged by bulldozing, ploughing, surveying, deforestation and stock grazing, not only in Waimārama but throughout the country.[176] Today most of these places exist only in Native Land Court minutes, maps, and the manuscripts of people such as Hākaraia who once occupied them. In an oral culture, place names serve as memory triggers for the past deeds of both individuals and whole tribes, and reinforce their association with an area of land or sea.[177] Takirirangi Smith believes that Māori were able to 'read' the landscape because 'the landscape and the environment was the text. You didn't need to read a book because all you had to do was read the landscape and the environment.'[178] The loss of place names that were embedded in the landscape has meant the loss of historical memory of events associated with the ancestors of that area.

Ngā hunga papatipu
The people of the land

By studying the evidence given during the 1884 Waimārama hearing and the information in Hākaraia's book, it is possible to develop a sense of how land and resources were shared and managed by the tribal peoples of Waimārama.

The tendency of eighteenth-century hapū to organise themselves in communities often derived from the way they used the land and its resources. The people moved between their different cultivations and resource areas according to the season.[179] 'Nobody lived constantly at one place in those days.'[180] The land not only sustained the people who lived on it, but also held within it the history of the blood that had been spilt to keep it in tribal hands. Māori regarded land as a treasured gift from their ancestors. This whakataukī sums up the rights of people to land:

> Ko te tangata i noho roa te tika, ko te tangata i pikopiko haere, kaore i whai mana. Ko te noho roa te tikanga o te mana, ko te raupatu ko te mahikai hoki.[181]

> The man who lives long on the land has the right to it, not so the man who travels afar. Through long occupation, conquest, and food-gathering upon the land does one have the right to it.

It was on this basis that Te Teira Tiaki-tai claimed greater rights at Waimārama in the 1884 hearings. In giving a whakapapa to the court he asserted that while his ancestors had a right through their occupation of the land, others had lost their rights through non-occupation.[182]

Land ownership rights were gained through inherited mana. Ancestral links provided rights to land that other groups could not claim. As Douglas Sinclair puts it, 'If a Maori could prove land had been continuously occupied by successive and numerous generations of ancestors right down to himself, it was said he had kept his ancestral flame (ahi kaa roa) alive on the land. He had maintained his occupation against all comers and the successful dispersal of other claimants strengthened the ties.'[183]

Te Teira traced the mana of the Waimārama lands back to Ngāti Ira, Rangitāne, Ngāti Awa, Ngāti Apa and Mua-ūpoko. After Te Ao-matarahi from Wairoa defeated these people at several pā in the area,[184] his sons occupied the land and held the mana over the people. However the mana whenua was not obtained until there was intermarriage with the previous owners, when Te Ao-matarahi's youngest son Rongo-mai-pure-ora married Hine-ngāti-ira from Hakikino. Their descendant Hika-rae-roa, his son Tū-māpuhi-ā-rangi and his descendants Hika-toa, Hinu-rewa and Rongo-māiaia became the principal ancestors of this land. It was from Hika-toa that Te Teira claimed his rights, through his father Tiaki-tai. Mohi did not dispute this claim; he traced his descent from Te Ao-matarahi's other sons Te Rongo-mai-raukura and Te Ao-noho-rā, whom Te Teira claimed had no rights there.

Te Teira Tiaki-tai claimed that his father Tiaki-tai and his ancestors held the mana over the land. Ngāti Putanoa, from whom Mohi Te Atahikoia and many of those he represented were descended, had come as refugees from Wairoa after a battle with Tapuwae and had been allowed onto the land by Te Teira's ancestors.[185] Mohi countered that Putanoa had been invited to Waimārama after his defeat by Tapuwae by his brother (some say his son) Tawheto, who was living there under his own mana. Mohi also claimed that Ngāti Putanoa had been given mana over land at Waimārama because of their bravery in aiding another Waimārama chief. The decision of the judge in the 1884 Waimārama partition case upheld Te Teira Tiaki-tai's claim to mana whenua, despite the evidence that will be examined below that Putanoa's descendants had rights to certain places and resources.

Emigrants who were accepted and given rights to use resources 'owned' and exploited those resources jointly.[186] It was usual for the recipient of any gift of land to offer its 'first fruits' to the giver. 'If the cultivator ceases to use it it reverts to the original owner.'[187] While major chiefs controlled large areas, cultivations were often owned by hapū,[188] and sometimes by whānau, while rua kūmara, trees, pā tuna and other specific resources were often owned by individuals.[189] Hākaraia and Tiopira's lists appear to confirm a tradition of giving individuals rights to places and resources. While owners occupied their land, no one else gathered resources there. When they were absent, squatting was tolerated provided the squatters did not attempt to assert rights to the land.[190] The terms denoting squatting included 'whenua pīrere' ('land in temporary occupation'), 'poka noa' (to do things at random, without the sanction of custom), 'manene' (strangers), 'he noho noa iho' ('occupation of no account'), 'he noho tikanga kore' ('occupation without right'), and 'he mahi noa iho' ('work of no account').[191] Conquered tribes lost control over land but were often allowed to remain on it and grow crops provided they acknowledged the mana of the new owners.[192]

The ownership and use of the land and its resources was thus a very complex issue. The names of specific places, including cultivations, houses, trees, burial places, lookouts, eel weirs, traps and tools also identified their owners.

Taupahī (seasonal camping grounds) are mentioned frequently in the writings of Hākaraia and Tiopira. Taupahī were located near resources such as kūmara gardens, karaka groves, aka vines, rat runs, eel weirs, fishing grounds, bird-snaring sites or berry-producing trees. They allowed the people to plant, catch, harvest, and preserve foods close to the cultivation grounds, rather than be based at one pā. It was easier to move to the location of the resource to gather, process and store it than to live year-round in one settlement and travel for short periods. Taupahī usually had one or two papa whare (dwelling sites) that could be re-erected or repaired each season. While different people had rights to specific areas, some were used by an entire hapū and others by individuals from several hapū.

Ngakinga kai, also known as mahinga kai (working places), like taupahī, consisted of a number of houses or dwelling sites which were occupied seasonally by working parties. Usually tools were left there between seasons. Because of the small size of communities, the extent of their territories, and the scattered nature of resources, ngakinga kai were numerous. Waerenga kai (also known as ngakinga kai) were settlements at cultivations, where planting, weeding, and harvesting took place.

Resources such as harakeke (flax), aruhe (fernroot), hua rākau (fruit), and even freshwater pools were named and allocated to individuals or whānau, whose permission was needed for access. According to tradition, karaka trees were brought on voyaging canoes, distributed by people living in coastal areas, and planted on tracks as a food resource, or to identify tapu places, burial grounds or caves.

Pā tuna (eel weirs) were often erected permanently on streams or rivers. These were 'jealously guarded family or individual property',[193] named in commemoration of an historical event to mark their ownership. Pā tuna were often owned by individuals and inherited and used by successive generations. Interference with or use of pā tuna by unauthorised people often led to arguments or fights, sometimes with fatalities.[194] Other types of places mentioned in these documents are pānga tītī (muttonbirding grounds), pā, ngahere (forests), pārae (undulating land), hamuti (latrines), karakia (prayers), tohu (signs), rua kōiwi (burial caves) and taumata (resting places or lookouts).

One of the significant features of these writings is that both Hākaraia and Tiopira Huangō name places that belonged to their ancestors and their wider family groupings. They include the names of numerous places 'owned' both by Hākaraia and by his ancestors; he definitely had ancestral rights to the land as a direct descendant of Hika-toa. While none of the places on these lists were recorded as belonging to Tiopira,[195] his ancestors Ura-ki-te-rangi, Te Rangi-te-auria and Iri-te-kururangi owned or had rights of occupancy at many places around Waimārama. There is no hint of who had mana whenua over the lands and resources these people utilised, but the majority of places named in these documents belonged to the Hika-toa descendants, among whom Tiaki-tai, as the paramount chief, Te Teira and Airini Tōnore were the principal leaders.

While most of these names and places are now lost from memory, many were identified and located in the late 1940s by John Buchanan, who later published them in *The Maori History and Place Names of Hawke's Bay*. An excellent map drawn by Buchanan and published in Sydney Grant's *Waimarama* shows the location of some of these places. Where names in Hākaraia's book have been identified and given a topographical reference point by Buchanan, this information is given in footnotes.

The rest of this chapter presents a selection of pepeha by Hākaraia, and other pepeha which refer to his ancestors. Each pepeha has been transcribed directly from the original text. This is followed by a modern Māori version and an English translation. Insertions for sense by the author appear within square brackets. A genealogical table shows the relationships among the people who are referred to in these pepeha or elsewhere in this chapter. I hope this will help to put in context the relationships between the places, hapū and individuals, as well as reveal something of the history of patterns of land ownership and use around Waimārama.

Waimarama	Waimārama
Hurae 29 – 1884	July 29, 1884
he Pukapuka wha	This is my book
ka atu atu tenei	of records
na aku Na	belonging to
hakaraia	Zechariah
Waipuka Poraka	Waipuka block

1. ko paraerae henga kinga kai Na tu terangi tona tau Pahi kotau mata ohine kona

   Ko Pāraerae he ngakinga kai nā Tū-te-rangi, tōna taupahī ko Taumata-o-Hine-[i]-kona.

   Pāraerae is a garden belonging to Tū-te-rangi, whose camping ground is Taumata-o-Hine-i-kona.

2. he tau mata karakia kai Na teuta moana

   He taumata karakia kai, nā Te Uta-moana.

   This is an altar for prayers associated with cultivations belonging to Te Uta-moana.

3. ko here wahine ote Mauriuri

   Ko Herewahine-o-Te Māuriuri.

   This place is Herewahine o Te Māuriuri.

4. ko Puehu tai he ngahinga kai Na hikatoa

   Ko Puehu-tai he ngahinga kai nā Hika-toa.

   Puehu-tai is a garden belonging to Hika-toa.

5. ko mata huri he ngakinga kai Na hikatoa

   Ko Matahuri he ngakinga kai nā Hika-toa.

   Matahuri is a garden belonging to Hika-toa.

6. ko tau mata a Pakake nona tonu tenei ingoa

   Ko Taumata-a-Pakake nōna tonu tēnei ingoa.

   Pakake's name is still attached to Taumata-a-Pakake.

7. kote Pa ongati apa no hikatoa ko Poianuku

   Ko Te Pā-o-Ngāti Apa nō Hika-toa, ko Poi-ā-nuku.

   Te Pā-o-Ngāti Apa[196] belongs to Hika-toa and is called Poi-ā-nuku.

8. ko waitangi i atu raua kote Manawa akawa

Ko Waitangi i a Tū rāua Ko Te Manawa-kawa.

Waitangi[197] belonged to Tū and Te Manawakawa.

9. ko manga ohewa he hamiti tenei ingoa No hikatoa

Ko Manga-o-hewa, he hamiti tēnei ingoa nō Hika-toa.

Manga-o-hewa was a privy belonging to Hika-toa.

10. ko Rakawhiti he Ngakinga kai Na te Manawa akawa

Ko Rā-kā-whiti he ngakinga kai nā Te Manawa-kawa.

Rākāwhiti is a garden belonging to Te Manawa-kawa.

11. ko te tuhi hepa karaka i ate puha

Ko Te Tuhi he pā karaka i a Te Pū-hā.

Te Tuhi is a clump of karaka trees belonging to Te Pū-hā.

12. koteo Paka ia Hikatoa

Ko Te Ōpaka i a Hika-toa

Te Ōpaka belonged to Hika-toa.

13. ko tuhi ia hika raeroa henga ki nga kai Na Hakaraia

Ko Tuhi-i-a-Hika-rae-roa he ngakinga kai nā Hākaraia.

Te Tuhi-i-a-Hika-rae-roa is a garden belonging to Hākaraia.

14. ko te umu Pohatu he tau Pahi he Rua koiwi kireira kotu terangi kireira e tapukeana Meana Mokopuna

Ko Te Umu-o-Pōhatu he taupahī, he rua kōiwi ki reira, ko Tū-te-rangi kei reira e tapuke ana me āna mokopuna.

Te Umu-o-pōhatu is a camping ground. There is a burial cave here, where Tū-te-rangi and his grandchildren are buried.

15. Ko Waitangi he mahinga hara keke Na Hikatoa

Ko Waitangi, he mahinga harakeke nā Hika-toa.

Waitangi is a flax garden belonging to Hika-toa.

16. kote Rama apakura he Ngakinga Kai Na hikatoa

Ko Te Rama-apakura, he ngakinga kai nā Hika-toa.

Te Rama-apakura is a garden belonging to Hikatoa.

17. kote Pae atu rei a he tau Pahi he Nga kinga kai i a Hikatoa

Ko Te Pae-a-Tūreia he taupahī, he ngakinga kai i a Hika-toa.

Te Pae-o-Tūreia is a camping ground and a garden of Hika-toa.

18. ko manu haro he mahi nga, karaka Nahikatoa

Ko Manu-hāro he mahinga karaka nā Hika-toa.

Manu-hāro is a karaka cultivation of Hika-toa.

19. ko nga ingoa tenei (owaho) Matu noa ia Hikatoa

Ko ngā ingoa tēnei (o waho) ma tū noa i a Hika-toa.

The following names (left out) are still owned by Hika-toa:

20. kote wai o te Moko karere iroto imarae totara Karere i te tahi taha owai matai

Ko Te Wai-o-te-moko, ka rere i roto i Marae-tōtara, ka rere i tētahi taha o Wai-matai,

Te Wai-o-te-moko, carry on within Te Marae-tōtara to the other side of Wai-matai,

21. Kamau ana ko Pohatu turoa

Ka mau ana ko Pōhatu-roa.

until you come to Pōhatu-roa.

22. Kamauana korakawhiti

Ka mau ana ko Rā-kā-whiti

Continue to Rā-kā-whiti,

23. Kamauana kote karaka Amahora

Ka mau ana ko Te Karaka-a-Mahora

to Te Karaka-a-Mahora,

24. kamauana kote rotoiti

Ka mau ana ko Te Roto-iti

to Te Roto-iti,

25. Kamauana kote upokopoito Kamutu Nga wahi ia hikatoa

Ka mau ana ko Te Ūpoko-pōito Ka mutu ngā wāhi i a Hika-toa.

to Te Ūpoko-pōito. Finished are the places belonging to Hika-toa.

26. koko hai Pikonoa i a te mauriuri

Ko Kohai-piko-noa i a Te Māuriuri

Kohai-piko-noa belongs to Te Māuriuri.

27. koko Hai rau mati he mahinga kai i a Apaki

Ko Kōhai-raumati he mahinga kai i a Aupaki

Kōhai-raumati is a garden belonging to Aupaki.

28. Ko tutu kaka he mahinga kai ia Aupaki me te Pohatu ia Aupaki

Ko Tutu-kākā he mahinga kai i a Aupaki, me te pōhatu i a Aupaki.

Tutu-kākā is a garden which, together with the rock, belongs to Aupaki.

The following pepeha associated with Ngāti Hika-toa, Hākaraia and his ancestors were written later in the same book.

kote horenga amanu hengakinga Kai na Ng ahu

Ko Te Horenga-a-manu he ngakinga kai nā Ngahu.

Te Horenga-a-manu is a garden belonging to Ngahu.

ko hora Pokeka i a Ng ahie

Ko Hora-pokeka i a Ngahu.

Hora-pokeka is Ngahu's.

ko nga mangatawai i a Ng ahu

Ko Ngā-manga-tāwai i a Ngahu.

Ngā-manga-tāwai is Ngahu's.

Ko Hawea he mahinga kai he Patuna Kei te awa ko tu ata Koura awai Kote
Maire he Patuna enei ia kumurau i a tahi to i a kao kao i a hakeke i a Mau

Ko Hāwea, he mahinga kai, he pā tuna kei te awa ko Tū-ata-kōura-a-wai, ko
Te Maire, he pā tuna ēnei i a Kumurau i a Tahito, i a Kaokao, i a Hakeke, i a
Mau.[198]

*Hāwea is a garden. At the river are eel weirs named Tū-ata-kōura-a-wai and
Te Maire belonging to Kumurau, Tahito, Kaokao, Hakeke and Mau.*

te putiki He tau pahi Hakaraia tu ahu te whare

Te Putiki he taupahī [nā] Hākaraia, Tūāhu te whare.

Te Putiki[199] is a camping site belonging to Hākaraia. Tūāhu is the house here.

te tarata e wha nga papawhare ia puohia erua ngarua te paratene HareMatenga

Te Tārata e whā ngā papa whare i a Pūōhia, e rua ngā rua [nā] Te Paratene, [nā] Hare Mātenga.[200]

Te Tārata has four house sites belonging to Pūōhia, and two pits belonging to Te Paratene and Hare Mātenga.

He waerenga puru ngaio 13 nga papa whare he tau pahi ia te ika Whaka oho

He waerenga-puru-ngaio, 13 ngā papa whare, he taupahī i a Te Ika whakaoho.

A ngaio grove clearing for thirteen house sites, it is a camping ground belonging to Te Ika-whakaoho.

te umu Hapuku 9 whare He tau pahi ngati Hikatoa … Whakaiti

Te Umu-hāpuku, 9 [ngā] whare, he taupahī [nā] Ngāti Hika-toa [me] Ngāti Whakaiti.

*Te Umu-hāpuku is a place where there are nine houses, and is a camp site belonging to Ngāti Hika-toa
and Ngāti Whakaiti.*

te aka Rarangi He tau pahi no Ngati Hikatoa He tu papa ku tona kai tenei wahi ko rakai tokohā
He kohatu

Te Aka-rārangi, he taupahi nā Ngāti Hika-toa, he tūpapaku tonu kei tēnei wāhi ko Rākai-tokoha,
he kōhatu.

*Te Aka-rārangi is a camping ground of Ngāti Hika-toa. Ancestral remains still occupy this place, namely those
of Rākai-tokohā. A rock marks this point.*

opokopoko ia ngati Hikatoa he mahi nga He tau pahi

Ōpokopoko i a Ngāti Hika-toa, he mahinga, he taupahī.

Ōpokopoko is a Ngāti Hika-toa garden and camping site.

te ahi otai He mahi nga na Hakaraia 4 nga pititi

Te Ahi-o-tai, he mahinga kai nā Hākaraia, [e] 4 ngā pītiti.

Te Ahi-o-tai is a garden belonging to Hākaraia. There are four peach trees here.

Waimārama genealogical table no. 1

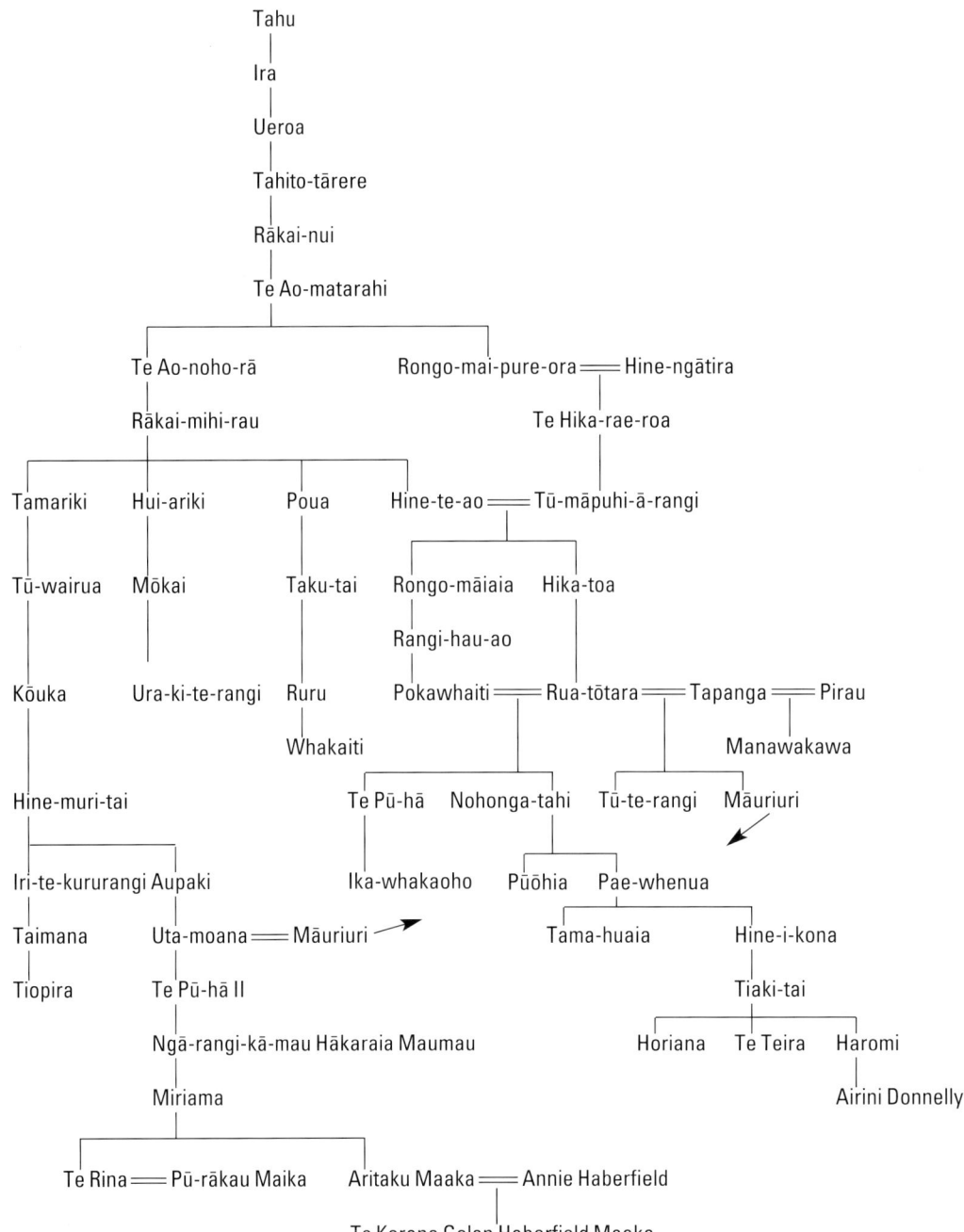

Waimārama genealogical table no. 2

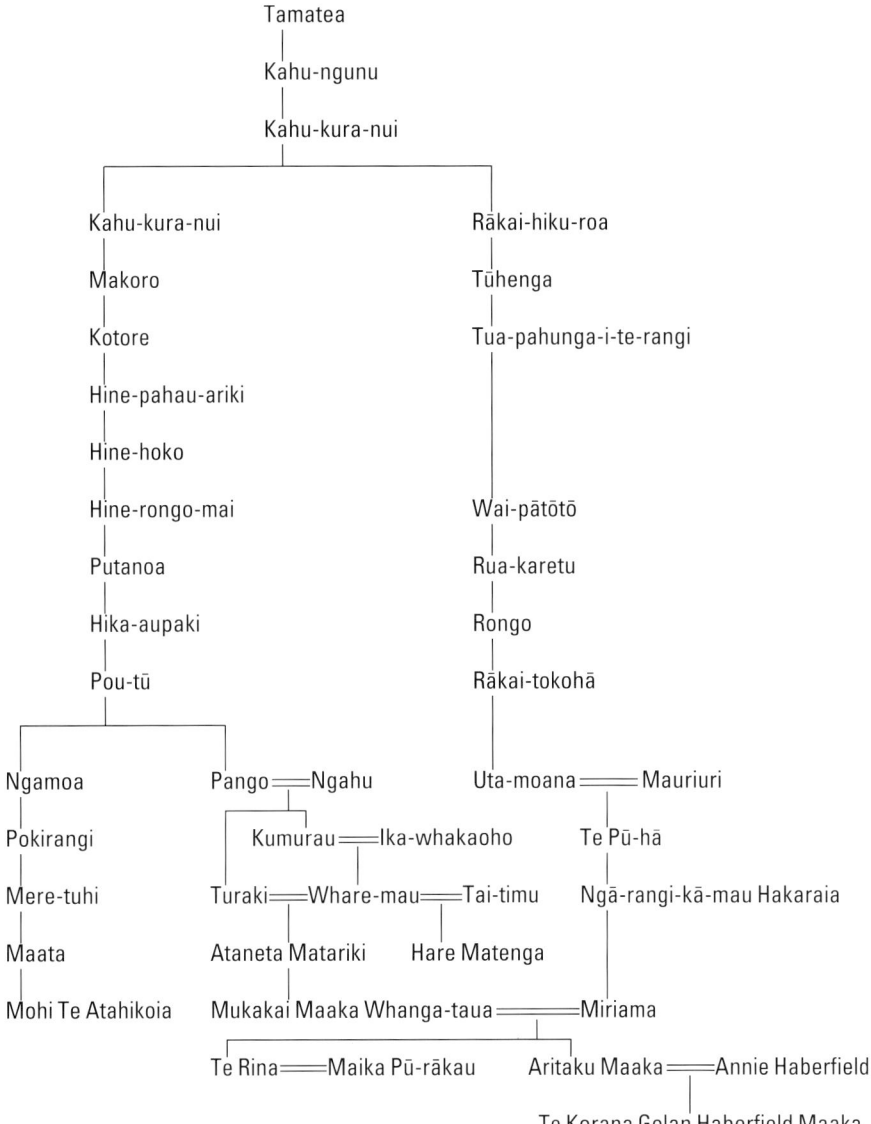

Tiopira Huangō of Ngāti Ura of Waimārama.
Photo courtesy of Pat Parsons

Mohi Te Atahikoia. Photo courtesy of Hawke's Bay Cultural Trust,
Hawke's Bay Museum, Napier, ref no. 7363

The Hakikino pā at Waimārama. Photo by the author

51 Kote iho-ariki he
peito tenei momo
kei konei

Waimarama
Hurae 29, /84
he pukapuka oha
ka atu atu tenei
na aku na.
hakaraia
Waipuka Horaka

1 Ko Pararoa he nga
kinga kai ra tu
terangi tona tau
Wahi kotau mata
Shina kona

2: he tau matua
karakia kai

An example of Hākaraia Ngā-rangi-kā-mau's writing. Maaka Collection

CHAPTER THREE

Ngā whakapapa o ngā wāhine
The genealogies of the women

The whakapapa books of Miriama Maaka and Te Rina Maaka, which are examined in this chapter, illustrate the role of women as the 'natural' custodians of family history. Their writings were penned at a time when recording genealogy was in vogue, especially in connection with the processes of the Native Land Court.

The documents discussed in this chapter were written by two women of the Maaka line, Miriama Hākaraia Maaka and her daughter Te Rina Maaka. Another of the Maaka women who deserves mention, but whose manuscripts will not be discussed here, is Ripeka Tokaanu Īnia (Granny Reko), a first cousin of Te Rina. Each of these women had strong links to Ngāti Hika-toa, Ngāti Kurukuru, Ngāti Rangi-koia-anake and other related hapū of Waimārama, as well as strong ties to Ngāi Tahu of Takapau.

Their only writings which have survived in the Maaka Collection are lists of whakapapa, which was traditionally thought to be a male realm. It is generally believed that women did not attend the whare wānanga which taught tribal history and genealogy.[201] However, women in this family clearly played a major role in the retention of genealogies.

As was discussed in chapter 1, whakapapa has always been the foundation of the Māori worldview and a central part of Māori society. It defines the terms of reference for biological, mythical and historical events, and gives every animate and inanimate object an origin. Whakapapa 'acts as a cognitive template for the ordering and understanding of the visible and invisible worlds, as a paradigm of reality' that is capable of being transmitted orally from one generation of the tribe to the next.[202] In addition, it was a test of memory, which was 'essentially a task of intellectual management'.[203]

Why were whakapapa written down when they were already known? Was the act of recording whakapapa on paper motivated by the need to clarify and assert links to land for the Native Land Court, or simply to keep family records intact in a new medium? Whatever the reason, these whakapapa are today the most venerated writings held by Māori families.

Women may have been entrusted with whakapapa because they were the bearers of the next generation:

> women also must know their ancestral history, and can tell some parts at least with equal authority as the men. But they will tell it in their own contexts. Women are often the first purveyors of history, because they are usually the composers of song … Women may also directly intervene in situations where something has gone wrong – even in the formal speech-making occasions on the marae, normally a male preserve.[204]

The flexible roles of women in traditional Māori society suited them to being the keepers of histories and whakapapa. In the Maaka family, when whakapapa were needed by the men for whatever purpose, they consulted the women.[205] There are a number of family references to women being the writers and holders of genealogies. Aritaku Maaka (a son of Miriama Maaka) noted in his whakapapa book that a whakapapa given to him by his brother-in-law, Pū-rākau Maika of Wairarapa, had been obtained from a high-born woman of the Masterton district.[206] In one of Mohi Te Atahikoia's whakapapa books he names the people who taught him, two of whom were women:

> He whakapapa na nga tipuna i ako mai ki au na Tuahu, na Meretuhi, na Hakaraia, na Matariki, na Tiopiri. Na ratou i korero mai ki ahau i te tau 1864

> Ancestral genealogies were taught to me by Tūāhu, Meretuhi, Hākaraia, Matariki and Tiopiri [sic]. They conveyed this information to me in 1864.[207]

(Meretuhi was Mohi's maternal grandmother, and Ataneta Matariki was Miriama Maaka's mother-in-law). Accordingly, it was both normal and highly appropriate (tika) that these three women of the Maaka family, Miriama Maaka, Te Rina Maaka and Reko, knew and wrote down these genealogies.

In Māori whakapapa, depending on its purpose, women's names were remembered, unlike those of European women in medieval times. Although medieval women were the custodians of lore, it was the histories of husbands and sons that were recalled and mourned, not those of women.[208] Although grandmothers 'survive longer and relay most family annals ... male ancestors are more memorialized and better remembered; women are victims of genealogical amnesia'.[209] Many believe that in Māori society too the lines of men were more important. In some cases this may have been true, but in many of the early whakapapa books I have seen, pains had been taken to record both male and female ancestral lines, showing all the marriages and identifying the gender of those named. It is also noteworthy that women's evidence to the Land Court and their right to own property was recognised.[210]

One noticeable aspect of the whakapapa recorded here is the inclusion of all lines of descent, both illustrious and insignificant. Many of the whakapapa also branch out beyond the immediate family to include notable past and contemporary relations. By demonstrating your links to a well-known, accomplished person, living or dead, you enhanced your own identity. Linking oneself to important characters is common in the whakapapa books I have seen. Miriama and Te Rina have included the genealogies of well-known people of their communities, including Tiaki-tai, Te Teira Tiaki-tai, Te Maari, Airini Tōnore (Donnelly), Mohi Te Atahikoia, Pāora Rerepū, Hōri Niania, Hēnare Matua, Īhaka Mōtoro, Te Hāpuku, Mōrena Hāwea, and Maku Ellison.

As with many Māori families, these writings encouraged subsequent generations of the family to compile their own whakapapa books. The following chapters show how whakapapa became of paramount importance in the writings of Maaka family members, as later generations copied lineages from these books and added to them.

Brief biographies of Miriama and Te Rina are followed by selected genealogical lists from their books.

Miriama Hākaraia Maaka, died 1890

Miriama Hākaraia Maaka, also known as Mereana Puna, was the daughter of Ngā-rangi-kā-mau (Hākaraia Maumau) and Hera Pōhue. Miriama was taken to Ōtaki with her father in the incident described in the previous chapter. She and her husband Maaka Whanga-taua are said to have lived at several places at Waimārama – Pukeake, Ōkaihau and Paparewa – and in a house at Waitangi called Te Ngaehe. It is recorded by the local people that she was the last of her generation to give birth (to her youngest son) in a cave at Pukeake pā, which some say was situated above the Waingongoro waterfall at Waimārama. It is not known whether Miriama attended a mission school, but she was able to read and write Māori. This is apparent from her whakapapa writings and from letters sent to her by her husband.

Miriama recorded whakapapa in a large ledger book that later belonged to her son Aritaku Maaka. This book was seen by the author at the home of Aritaku's son, Īnia Maaka, in 1988. These genealogies are mostly concerned with her immediate family links to Ngāti Hika-toa of Waimārama, and those of her husband. The only other lineages mentioned are those of Hiromina, her cousin, and of Mohi Te Atahikoia, an important relative.

These whakapapa are dated 11 May 1868, at the time the Native Land Court was compiling lists of owners for the various blocks around Waimārama. On 20 August 1868, Miriama's father Hākaraia was named as a grantee on the certificate of title to the Waimārama block. At the same time her husband Maaka Mukakai Whanga-taua was made a grantee for the Ōkaihau block.[211] It is probable that these whakapapa lists were submitted to the court to confirm the rights of Hākaraia and Maaka Whanga-taua as potential title-holders of the lands in question. They may have been compiled and written by Hākaraia and then copied by Miriama into her own book, written by Miriama for her father, or recorded by Mohi Te Atahikoia, who is known to have been a scribe and had collected whakapapa names from Miriama's father in 1864. As they are headed 'Ko enei whakapapa na Miriama' ('These genealogies belong to Miriama'), I have treated them as hers.

Miriama was recorded as succeeding to her father Hākaraia's lands in 1886.[212] Miriama died at Takapau[213] in November 1890,[214] and may have been interred nearby in the old urupā at Ōkahukura, where her husband Maaka Whanga-taua is thought to be buried.

Ko ēnei whakapapa nā Miriama
Miriama's genealogies

May 11 1868
Na Rakainui
Rakaimoehau
Aomutua
Rakaimihiroa
Tamariki
Rehunga
Te Rangitekehua
Rangaranga = Ruapapa
Ruatai
Arahe
Tira
Hera Pohue
Miriama

Kahungunu
Kahukuranui
Rakaihikuroa
Tamanuhiri
Hinepare
Raupare
Ngake
Rangimumutu
Te Aohuakina
Haerengarangi
Wairua = Te Roki
Te Ori
Matiore
Ngarangikamau Hakaraia
Miriama

Na Kahungunu
Kahukuranui
Rakaihikuroa
Kahukuratakapau
Turoimata
Tuwhakawhiurangi
Rangitahia
Taotao
Kiao
Katoa
Na Katoa
    Iritekururangi
    Te Aupaki
    Hikawaipawa
    Tutia
Na Te Aupaki
Utamoana
Te Puha
Hakaraia
Miriama

Na Hikawaipawa
Nohangatahi
Pokirangi
Meretuhi
Maata kotakitaki
Mohi Te Atahikoia

Na Te Ikaraeroa
Tumapuhiarangi
Hikatoa
Ruatotara
Mauriuri
    Te Puha
    Tangorau
Na Te Puha
Ngarangikamau Hakaraia
Miriama = Maaka Whangataua

Na Tangorau
    Patuhoe
    Nīrae
    Te Hei
Na Patuhoe
Hiromona

Na Kahungunu
Tauhei
Tawhiwhi
Rakaimoko
    Kaukirangi
    Rangiwhia
    Haroto
    Hinewhakamauao
Na Hinewhakamauao
Tangataiti i a Kaikoko
    Te Oranga
    Tuohungia
    Ngarokiao
Na Te Oranga ia Hikatoa
Ruatotara
Te Mauriuri
Te Puha
Ngarangikamau
Miriama

He whakapapa ano
Na Kahungunu
    Kahukuranui
    Tamateakota
Na Kahukuranui
Rakaihikuroa
Rakaimoari
Kahukuramango
Humarire
Tataiaho
Tuwairua = Tawhito
Rakaitekura
Tumapuhiarangi
Hikatoa
Ruatotara
Te Mauriuri
Te Puha
Ngarangikamau
Miriama

Te Rina Maaka, c. 1849–1944

Te Rina Maaka was born in 1848 or 1849. The story of how she left Waimārama, where she was raised, is still remembered. The coast between Wairarapa and Waimārama was used as a highway by Māori, and a camping ground named Paparewa was set aside at Waimārama for the Wairarapa people. On one occasion when a group of Wairarapa people were visiting Waimārama, it was suggested that Te Rina, then a young girl, should return with them. Her mother Miriama agreed, and the party departed along the coast on horseback during the night.[215]

When Te Rina's father Maaka Whanga-taua learned that his daughter had gone, he rode after her. Catching up with the party, he angrily ordered Te Rina to return home, but was challenged by a high-ranking woman, who asked him, 'Ko wai koe? Ko wai ia? Ko wai ahau?' ('Who are you? Who is she? Who am I?').[216] The woman was claiming Te Rina as one of their own, whom they had a right to take. Te Rina was related to the Wairarapa people through Maaka Whanga-taua's Ngāi Tahu links, which gave the visitors custodial rights over her. Maaka did not challenge this statement. He turned his horse around and returned to Waimārama.[217]

Te Rina was taken to the Gladstone district and eventually married Pū-rākau Maika, a high-ranking man from Ngāti Hika-rāhui and Ngāti Rākai-rangi of the Masterton area. These tribal names come under the mantle of Ngāi Tahu, the descendants of Te Ao-matarahi. Pū-rākau's ancestors Tū-māpuhi-ā-rangi and the Māhanga brothers had migrated from Waimārama, Te Rina's mother's home, to Wairarapa many generations earlier. Pū-rākau was related to Te Rina on her Ngāti Hika-rāhui side.

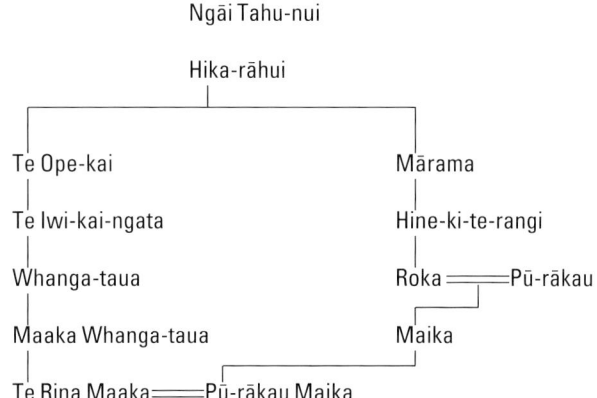

Te Rina and Pū-rākau had no children of their own but raised a number of whāngai (adopted children). Pū-rākau became an important figure in the Kotahitanga movement led by Tamahau Mahupuku, who aspired to make Pāpāwai its base. Pū-rākau led a group of people who were trained as band members and constructed the buildings in which the Kotahitanga parliament met. Tamahau had the idea of a Wairarapa Māori newspaper, *Te Puke ki Hikurangi*, which was first published in December 1897. Pū-rākau was to be its editor for much of its existence. He also became a director of the company which produced another newspaper, *Te Mareikura*. Both ceased publication in 1913.[218]

Pū-rākau and Te Rina were prominent in the politics of their Wairarapa kin, and involved in many tribal hui. For example, both were members of the committee for the opening of the Nuku-tai-memeha house in 1917.[219] Te Rina and Raukura Mahupuku were the head women of the pā, and as kai-karanga called the people onto the marae.[220] Pū-rākau was also a member of the Rongokako Māori Council and the Tāne-nui-a-rangi Committee, which was responsible for the organisation of hui whakapapa. Both Pū-rākau and Te Rina became well known for their knowledge of whakapapa.[221]

Te Rina and Pū-rākau moved to Miramar in Wellington to be close to where the political decisions concerning Māori people were made.[222] After Pū-rākau's death Te Rina sold her Wellington home and shifted back to Takapau, where she spent her final years with her brother Aritaku and his whānau. She paid for an extension to the old homestead which was known as 'Aunty's room'. 'Aunty' Te Rina would sit wrapped in a blanket beside the fireplace, heating up a brick which she wrapped in another blanket and used as a hot-water bottle in her bed.[223] Te Rina died at Gladstone on 14 May 1944 and was buried in the Māori cemetery there.[224] She was the last kuia moko of the Maaka family.

The whakapapa which follow were written by Te Rina in pencil in an address book. All the names are of Ngāti Kahungunu origin, and many of the lines come from Waimārama. Others are those of important contemporaries and relatives, including Te Maari, Maku Ellison, Mohi Te Atahikoia, Piriniha [Pirihira], Henrietta, and the Tiaki-tai family – people Te Rina was related to, or developed relationships with during her travels with Pū-rākau. It was common for writers of genealogies to connect themselves to the aristocracy. The fact that Pū-rākau was known as the scribe of the district may have influenced Te Rina to compile and write down whakapapa.

Ngā whakapapa nā te pukapuka a Te Rina
Genealogies from Te Rina's book

Ko RangimataKoha
Ko RaKaimoari
Ko KahuKuramango
Ko humarie
Ko tataiaho
Ko tuwairau
Ko raKaipa
Ko hikawera
Ko Te Whatiapiti
Ko hikawera
Ko Te roki
Ko Te ori
Ko Matioro
Ko hakaraia
Ko Miriama
Ko Terina

Nā KupaKupa[225]
Ko Tematauote[ra]ngi
Ko Tuteahunga
Ko Tepokawhaiti
Ko Te nohongatahi
Ko Paewhenua
Ko Hine-kona
Ko Tiakitai[226]
Ko Te teira
Ko Tiakitai

Na Te Kipamaro
Ko Tangataiti
Ko Te oranga
Ko Te ruatotara
Ko Te mauriuri
Ko Te puha,– Raua Ko tona Tuahine ko tangorau he whanau tahi enei
Na Tepuha
Ko Hakaraia
Ko Miriama
Ko Te rina

Ko tamatea
Ko Kahungunu
Ko Kahukuranui
Ko RaKaipaKa
Ko Kau ko hea
Ko tutekanoa
Ko tureia
Ko te rauhina
Ko te rangituanui
Ko hine aka
Ko te arahe
Ko tira
Ko hera[227]

he tahu Tipuna
Ko Te Rerenga mai i a whaitiri
na Whaitiri
Ahema
Ko TawhaKi
Ko arawhita
Ko Tura
Ko Tirarangi
Ko Iranuikoiraroa
Ko Iratupata
Ko IratupaeaKau
Ko PoKauwai
Ko Miru
Ko Rere
Ko KuratuKia
Ko Mairurangi
Ko tato
Ko RongoKaKo
Ko tamatea
Ko Kahungunu
Ko KahuKuranui
Ko RaKaihiKuroa
Ko hineteraraKu
Ko tutaetara
Ko Marutauhea
Ko Te ao mataura
Ko Patu tu
Ko amo ake i te rangi
Ko te Kura
Ko te rangi
Ko Teriponga
Ko Kiriwai
Ko hikarahui
Ko Teopekai
Ko Tiro
Ko whangataua
    Ko Maka[228]
    Ko Inia

he tahu tipuna
Ko Potipu
Ko Porea
Ko Te pomarutuna
Ko Te pomaruehi
Ko Raro puare
Ko Raro puano
Ko Te uruehu
Ko tonga
Ko whā
Ko Ira
Ko Maikiroa
Ko Mahuika
Ko Te Kaununui
Ko Te Kauroroa
Ko Te KauwheKi
Ko Te Rupetu
Ko Maui
Ko WhariuKura
Ko uwhenga
Ko Poutama
Ko Whatirangimamao
Ko Kupe
Ko hine
Ko tahuoirangi
Ko tautumu
Ko tutawhiorangi
Ko Rikimaitai
Ko whiti arangi
Ko Karimoe
Ko takoto
Ko Papauma
Ko KahuKurataKapau
Ko hinemoa
Ko tukowhiti
Ko Patu tu
Ko Amoake
Ko Te Kura
Ko Te rangi
Ko Te Riponga
Ko Kiriwai
Ko hikarahui
Ko Te opekai
Ko Ko Tiro
Ko whangataua
    Ko Maka
    Ko inia

Waimārama in 1900. Photo courtesy of Pat Parsons

From left: Te Rina Maika (née Maaka), an unidentified woman, Ripeka Tokaanu Īnia (Reko), and Porangi at Waimārama, 1936.
Maaka Collection

He Tahu Tipuna tenei

Ko   Ueroa
Ko   Tahitotarere
Ko   Rakaimii
Ko   Rakaimohau
Ko   Te aomutua
Ko   Rakaimuhirau
Ko   Tamaakiki
Ko   Te rehanga
Ko   Te rangi e ekehua
Ko   Rangaranga = Ruapapa
Ko   Ruatai
Ko   Te arahe
Ko   Turia
Ko   hera
Ko   Miriama
Ko   Terina

16

Te Rina's whakapapa. Maaka Collection

The remains of the whare called Te Ngaehe at Waimārama, 1997. Photo by the author

Te Rina Maika (née Maaka).
Maaka Collection

CHAPTER FOUR

Ngā waiata, ngā reta me te kātipa
Songs, letters and formal documents

By the 1870s, the written word was being used frequently for many different purposes in Māori society. This chapter studies three very different examples of Maaka Whanga-taua's writings from this period: a letter, a traditional waiata, and the minutes of a tribal 'court'.

Mukakai Maaka Whanga-taua, died 1882

Mukakai Maaka Whanga-taua was the youngest son of the warrior Whanga-taua of Takapau and Ataneta Matariki of Waimārama. Through his father he was affiliated to Ngāi Tahu, Ngāi Tangi-moana and Ngāti Te Ope-kai, all hapū from Takapau, and through his mother he was Ngāti Putanoa and Ngāti Ikawhakaoho of Waimārama.

The birthplace of Maaka Whanga-taua is not known. He married Miriama of Waimārama, where he lived for some time while remaining involved in tribal affairs in the Takapau region. The two are said to have lived at a number of different places at Waimārama: in the bush on the Ōkaihau block,[229] at Pukeake pā, at Waitangi, and at Paparewa.

Maaka was by oral family tradition the first of his line to become a Christian, when the name Maaka (Mark) was bestowed upon him. He was a follower of the Ringa-tū faith formed by Te Kooti, but it is evident from his letters and writings, which include hymns, that he was also active in the Mihinare (Anglican) movement.

From references in his whakapapa writings and also in the diaries of a local Pākehā, Walter Lorne Campbell, it appears that Maaka and other local Māori used Pākehā agricultural and farming techniques in the 1860s and '70s. They owned bullocks, ploughs and horses, raised pigs, grazed sheep, and grew melons and peaches around Waimārama.[230]

While little is known of Maaka's personal life, his name is associated with Māori councils and komiti which administered Pākehā-style law in Heretaunga villages in the 1870s.

Following the Native Land Court's practice of listing individual owners of Māori-owned blocks, Maaka was named as a registered claimant, shareholder and owner of land in the Waimārama district, and also in Tamaki-nui-a-rua and Takapau.

Maaka's use of letter-writing, his role with tribal councils, and his subscriptions to Māori news-papers such as *Huia Tangata Kotahi* and *Te Wananga*, in which he often placed advertisements,[231] suggests that he had a good understanding of the written word. Only a few of his writings have survived, and some of these are presented here.

According to succession applications, Maaka Mukakai Whanga-taua died in September 1882.[232] The family believe he was buried at the old urupā near Takapau known as Ōkahukura.

Ngā rau whārangi a Maaka
Fragmented pages

The writings of Maaka Whanga-taua which are analysed below were not found in manuscript books; they are separate handwritten documents. While this material is not extensive, it gives a glimpse into an interesting period of Māori life in Heretaunga. Although the preservation of whakapapa remained paramount, letter-writing was becoming much more common, and the recording of waiata and traditional information by both ordinary people and the elite was now almost customary.

The three examples of Maaka's writings discussed here are a letter, a waiata, and the minutes of a tribal 'court'.

He reta nā Maaka

A letter by Maaka

This is one of a number of letters Maaka Whanga-taua wrote to his wife Miriama at Waimārama in 1878. It was written at Ōkahukura, a small kāinga (now a cemetery) near the present township of Takapau that belonged to the local Ngāi Tahu hapū. Sending personal news in letters had become a fairly standard form of communication for many Māori by the 1870s, as mail could be sent quite quickly over long distances once railway networks were developed.

In this letter Maaka tells his wife about the problems caused by 'Kiingi', who has been burning (angering) the house (people) of Ngāi Tahu at Takapau by allowing his dogs to kill their sheep. Since 1849, when the first sheep station in the district began operating at Pourerere, Heretaunga lands had been utilised by Pākehā for farming.[233] In the 1870s the chiefs Te Hāpuku and Rēnata Kawepō had flocks of up to 5000 sheep.[234]

Ngāi Tahu owned a number of sheep, and neighbouring hapū such as those of Rākau-tātahi and Ōtāwhao were also grazing sheep and cattle on their lands. There were often boundary disputes when stock fences were erected.[235] Trouble also arose over land sales and surveys, and when Pākehā-owned sheep grazed on Māori lands. If Māori asked for payment for this grazing, 'the Europeans would not give sixpence; but took the Maori horses that were there, and placed them in the pound'.[236] Māori acquired farming skills through experience on settler runs, and some chiefs employed European shepherds. Too often, however, it was left to the energy and ingenuity of individuals to develop pastures. By the early 1900s Māori sheep farming had declined because of continuing land sales.[237]

In his letter, Maaka mentions the purchase of Te Kōpua from the government by 'Pakeha', and that the railway line had reached there. The line from Napier to Takapau (a distance of 59 miles) had opened on 12 March 1877. It had then been extended five or six miles to Te Kōpua, rather than to Norsewood, as many people in the latter town had hoped. The Te Kōpua extension was opened on 25 January 1878,[238] the day after Maaka wrote this letter. More than a thousand people travelled from Hastings in 24 carriages for the occasion.[239] There were disputes over the railway. In May 1879, Maaka's cousin Īhaka Tūhua blocked the line with posts, vowing that the train would not run over his land any longer because he had been thrown off it.[240]

The final comment in Maaka's letter concerns their daughter Te Rina, who was married to Pū-rākau Maika and living at Gladstone in Wairarapa. 'Horomona' had told Maaka that he had seen Pū-rākau, but not Te Rina. On the other side of this letter are fragments of another:

> Kia Kawana Kerei, kia …
> Kia Mainatakena, e hoa me homai e koe he moni kia au, kia mano pauna
> kia haere au ki Ingarangi kia kite au …
> ia Te Kuini Wikitoria weera …

This letter to Kāwana Kerei (Governor Grey) and 'Mainatakena'[241] asks them for £1000 to enable the writer to go to England to meet Queen Victoria. The idea of travelling to England to seek an audience with the Queen to request relief from colonial intrusion onto land and raise other Treaty issues was very common at this time. The subject was discussed by Ngāti Kahungunu in 1876 at a hui at Ōmāhu, for example.[242] Maaka Whanga-taua appears to have been seeking funding for such a trip.

Okahukura
24 - Hanuere - 1878

Kia Miriama e kui te mara koe heoi te mihi
te kupu kia rongo mai koe ka nui te raruraru
kua wera te whare o Ngaitahu i Putaeore i te
ahi na kiingi i tahu ki te ahi, ko te tahi ko
Nga Hipi a Ngaitahu kua mate i a kiingi te Patu
Patu te Whakangau kia ana kuri ko Nga Hipi i
Mate i a kiingi e Whatekau kui atu ranei iti mai
ranei kua tae Ngaitahu ki te tono i nga kuri a
a kiingi kia tukua mai kaore i tukua mai
e rangi kua whaka atu tia ki nga kai-
whaka haere, ko te tahi he Hoko rakau na
kiingi kua panaia nga Pakeha a kiingi e
Ngaitahu heoi kui atu te kino o tana
tangata kino rawaatu kua takoto nui te
kino i roto i tenei tangata
Ko te tahi kupu ko te kopua kai te hokona
e Nga Pakeha i te Rawahataya kua tae
hoki te rerewe ki te kopua
Ko te tahi kupu kua kite au i a Horomona
kaore ia i kite i a terina ko Purakau
anake taana i kite te kupu a Purakau
kia ia kai te tatari tonu Ngaitahu kia
mapaka tenei pea te haere nei
Heoi nga kupu
Na Maka Whangataua

A letter written by Maaka Whanga-taua. Maaka Collection

Te kape tuhinga	**Te whakatikatika**	**Whakapākehātia**
(Transcription)	(Modern Māori)	(English translation)

Okahukura	Ōkahukura	Ōkahukura
24 Hanuere 1878	24 Hānuere 1878	24 January, 1878
Ki a miriama e kui tenara koe heoi te mihi	Ki a Miriama, e kui tēnā rā koe, heoi te mihi.	To Miriama, greetings my dear.
te kupu kia rongomai koe ka nui te raruraru	Te kupu kia rongo mai koe, ka nui te raruraru –	I would like to let you know of the catastrophe –
kua wera te whareoNgaitahu i Putaeore i te	kua wera te whare o Ngāi Tahu i Putaeore i te	the house of Ngāi Tahu at Putaeore has been
ahi na kiingi i tahu ki te ahi, ko tetahi ko	ahi. Nā Kiingi i tahu ki te ahi. Ko tētahi ko	fired by Kiingi. In addition
nga Hipi a ngaitahu kua mate i a kiingi te Patu-	ngā hipi a Ngāi Tahu kua mate i a Kiingi, te patu	Ngāi Tahu sheep have been savaged by Kiingi's
Patu te whakangau kia ana kuri ko nga Hipi i	patu, te whakangau ki āna kurī. Ko ngā hipi i	dogs,
Mate i a kiingi e Whatekau nuiatu ranei i ti mai	mate i a Kiingi e whā tekau nui atu rānei, iti mai	about 40 sheep more or less.
ranei kua tae ngaitahu ki te tono i nga kuri a	rānei. Kua tae Ngāi Tahu ki te tono i ngā kurī a	Ngāi Tahu arrived to demand that
a kiingi kia tukua mai kaore i tukua mai	Kiingi kia tukua mai, kāore i tukua mai.	Kiingi's dogs be handed over, but they weren't.
e rangi kua whaka atutia ki nga kai-	Erangi kua whakaatutia ki ngā	However the managers have been notified.
whaka haere, ko te tahi He Hoko rakau na	kaiwhakahaere. Ko tētahi he hoko rākau nā	Another problem is the sale of trees by
kiingi kua panui nga Pakeha a kiingi e	Kiingi, kua pānui ngā Pākehā a Kiingi e	Kiingi, and the Pākehā have been warned by
ngaitahu heoi nui atu te kino o taua	Ngāi Tahu, heoi, nui atu te kino o taua	Ngāi Tahu. He is a bad man,
tangata kino rawaatu kua takoto nui te	tangata, kino rawa atu kua takoto nui te kino i	really very bad,
kino i roto i tenei tangata	roto i tēnei tangata.	wicked in fact.
ko te tahi kupu ko te kopua kai te hokona	Ko tētahi kupu, ko Te Kōpua kai te hokona	Another thing: Te Kōpua is to be
e nga Pakeha i te kawanatanga kua tae	e ngā Pākehā i te Kāwanatanga, kua tae	purchased by the Pākehā from the government,
hoki te rerewe ki te kopua	hoki te rerewē ki Te Kōpua	for the railway has now reached Te Kōpua.
ko te tahi kupu kua kite au i a Horomona	Ko tētahi kupu, kua kite au i a Horomona,	Also, I have seen Horomona
kaore ia i kite ia Terina ko Purakau	anake tāna i kite. Te kupu a Pū-rākau	but he has not seen Te Rina, only
anake taana i kite te kupu a Purakau	ki a ia, kai te tatari tonu a Ngāi Tahu ki a	Pū-rākau, who told
kia ia kai te tatari tonu ngaitahu kia	Maaka. Tēnei pea te haere nei!	him that Ngāi Tahu is still waiting for
maaka tenei Pea te haere nei		Maaka. He is on his way now!
Heoi nga kupu	Heoi ngā kupu	That is all.
Na Maka Whangataua	Nā Maaka Whanga-taua	From Maaka Whanga-taua

He waiata i tuhia e Maaka
A song recorded by Maaka

In addition to the letters of Maaka Whanga-taua there are a number of waiata and lists of whakapapa. Of four waiata found in his handwriting, the following is the most legible and easily explained. The song was written on both sides of two pages that were pinned together, with his signature at the end.

The song, which appears to be from Wairarapa, discusses two important chapters in the history of the Ngāi Tahu people of Takapau and Wairarapa. It refers to the history of Maaka's own family, and mentions his great-grandmother, Te Ope-kai. This may be one reason he recorded this song. Maaka headed it, 'He oriori nā Te Oka-whare' ('A lullaby belonging to Te Oka-whare'), while in Jock McEwen's *Rangitāne*, where a portion of this song is published, it is entitled, 'A song by Parātene Te Okawhare about Te Whakamana's gift to Pouri'.

Te Oka-whare was a tohunga from Wairarapa who was descended from Te Whakamana. As a contemporary of Te Matorohanga, he too was interviewed by Te Whatahoro in the 1860s or 1870s.[243] It appears from the last line of this song that it was composed as a lullaby for one of the six children of Raharuhi Tūhokairangi of Taua-nui and his wife Hīria Maika.[244]

The first verse recounts the history of the Heretaunga ancestor Te Rehunga, who was visited one day at (Te) Kōpua by Tama-i-waho. When Tama-i-waho commented on how small Te Rehunga's whare was, he replied, 'Ahakoa he iti taku whare, i ahu mai au i te kōpua kānapanapa' ('Although my house is small, I emanate from a deep pool'). In response to this challenge to his mana as a chief, Te Rehunga gathered food from his lands for Tama-i-waho, who was unable to return the compliment and instead made a gift of land to Te Rehunga. After Te Rehunga occupied this land there were several incidents, including the erection by the Rangi-tāne people of a pourāhui (boundary pole), which Te Rehunga felled, leading to several skirmishes. When Te Rehunga eventually retreated to Heretaunga, he sent a number of high-born women to live on the land given by Tama-i-waho at Takapau. These women – Tāwhiri-toroa, Te Ope-kai (Maaka Whanga-taua's great-grandmother), Tau-kahakaha and Mā-runga-o-te-rangi – were accompanied by the men Te Haemata-o-te-atua, Te Wāwāhanga and Ngā-oko-i-te-rangi. The song states that this group of people are those with the name of Ngāi Tahu. A full account of this story, written by Tānguru Tūhua, a descendant of Te Rehunga, Ngā-oko-i-te-rangi, and Te Ope-kai, was published in the *Journal of the Polynesian Society* in 1906.[245]

Below is a genealogy showing the relationships among the people involved in this episode.

He whakapapa mō Ngāi Tahu
A Ngāi Tahu genealogy

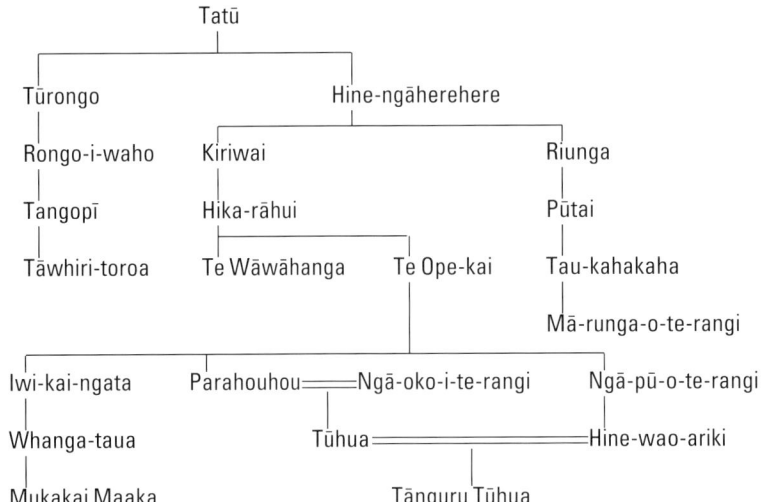

The second verse elaborates on the history of the composer's time, mentioning Pū–rākau, Tarehā and Karauria, who were influential Ngāti Kahungunu men in the nineteenth century. This verse seems to encapsulate a period of migration south from Heretaunga, perhaps during the period of invasions by powerful combined taua (war parties) from outside the district.

The third verse recalls another important historical event, the migration of a second branch of Ngāi Tahu people from Heretaunga to Wairarapa. It refers to the great heke of Te Rangi-tāwhanga and Pōuri, both descendants of Te Ao-matarahi, one of the major ancestors of Ngāi Tahu on the east coast of the North Island. After a squabble between Hine-te-rangi and her brother Rākai-werohia over a kūmara patch, Rākai-werohia was killed. His brothers, cousins and son Te Rangi-tāwhanga decided to leave the Te Mata district for Wairarapa, where the Rangi-tāne chief Te Rerewa, the brother of Rākai-werohia's wife Hine-tauira, lived. A large hikoi (migrant group) including Rangi-tāwhanga's uncles and cousins travelled in canoes, the names of which included *Whakaengarangi*, *Makawhiu*, *Whai-tō-muri* and *Pōkai-kaha*.

When they arrived Te Rerewa was preparing to leave for the South Island, and in an exchange of gifts the migrants from the north were given land. Te Whakamana, another Rangi-tāne chief, refused to leave for the South Island with Te Rerewa and retained control of his own land, but agreed to honour Te Rerewa's gift. Rangi-tāwhanga followed Te Whakamana to his pā, Pōtaka-kura-tawhiti, which was situated on the right bank of the Ruamahanga River a few kilometres upstream from Lake Wairarapa. Pōuri and Rākai-rangi followed also, and Te Whakamana decided to give them land as well. He took them to Puke-wharariki to show them this land.[246] The whakapapa below shows the relationship between those who migrated from Heretaunga to Wairarapa:

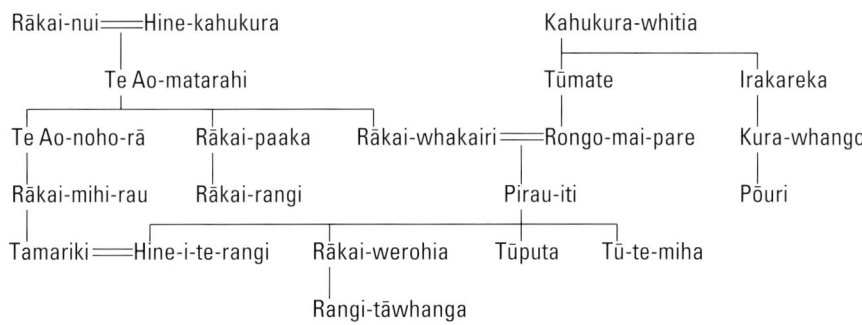

He oriori na te okawohare
te Mate Parae e Moe nei nai
katira ate moe eara kize
ngara, e huri te tarinya
ki te kupu korero e han
maira ra rungai nga hi
wi nai, te raia he kiinga
atu no te waha, te raia
he korero ta nga atu kiai
motana ka whaka hokia
nei ki Heretanga nai, he
morehu ano totana i,
mahue atu i te kainya
ko ta whiritoroa ko te ope
kare tau ka ha ka hae te
marunga o terangi Huema
ta o te atua na, ko te wa
wahanga i hoki atu i

kohei koia te ingoa o
tipuna o Ngaitahu e
maramanga mairana
haere rawa atu to ma
tua te Purakau kize
to Manaia koia taha
e noho maira na, i hara
mai ano to tipuna a ka
rauria i reira, kaore
he Parara i mahue atu
i roto o Kakara he
Hauitia na kera, kaore
he okonga i mahue atu
i runga o Matapane i
roto a huriri na ko ta
reha na ke e a huare
ka maira kaore he pou
ri i mahue atu i

The song ends with a recitation of the whakapapa linking Te Whakamana to the person it was composed for. Explanatory notes follow the song.

Te kape tuhinga	**Te whakatikatika**	**Te whakapākehātia**
(Transcription)	(Modern Māori)	(English translation)

He oriori na te okawhare	He oriori nā Te Oka-whare	A Lullaby by Te Oka-whare
te mate Parae e moe nei nai,	Te Mate-pārae e moe nei,	Te Mate-pārae, asleep here,
katira ate moe e ara ki ru	Kāti rā te moe e ara ki runga rā.	Wake up and arise.
ngara, e huri te taringa	E huri te taringa	Turn your ear
ki te kupu korero e hau	ki te kupu kōrero e hau mai rā,	To the spoken word wafting
maira ra runga nga hi	5 Rā runga i ngā hiwi na-i.	Over the hills.
wi nai, teraia he kiinga	Tērā ia he kīnga	Perhaps it is
atu no te waha, teraia	atu nō te waha,	A direct call.
he korerotangaatu kiaia	Tērā ia he kōrerotanga atu ki a ia	Perhaps it is a message
motaua ka whakahokia	mō taua, ka whakahokia	About us being sent back
nei ki Heretaunga nai, he	10 nei ki Heretaunga nā-i	To Heretaunga.
morehuano totaua i	He mōrehu anō tō tāua i	Our kin
mahue atu i te kainga	māhue atu i te kāinga;	Who survived were
kotawhiritoroa ko te ope	Ko Tawhiri-toroa, ko Te Ope-kai e,	Tāwhiri-toroa, Te Ope-kai
kaie taukahakahae te	Tau-kahakaha e,	Tau-kahakaha e,
marungaoterangi Haema	15 Te Mā-runga-o-te-rangi,	Mā-runga-o-te-rangi,
taoteatuana, ko te wa	Haemata-o-te-atua nā,	Haemata-o-te-atua,
wahanga i hoki atu i	Ko Te Wāwahanga i hoki atu i konei.	Te Wāwāhanga returned from this place.
Konei koia te ingoa o	Koia te ingoa ō tipuna o	Hence your ancestral name
tipuna o ngaitahu e	Ngāi Tahu e.	Ngāi Tahu!
maramanga mai ra na	20 Maramanga mai rā nā,	Arise from your sleep,
haere rawa atu to ma	Haere rawa atu tō matua	Your kinsman
tua te Purakau kiro	Pū-rākau ki roto Manaia	Pū-rākau went as far as Manaia.
to manaia koi a tana	Koia tāna	Indeed that is why
e noho maira na, ihara	e noho mai rā nā	He remans there.
maiano to tipuna a ka	25 I hara mai anō tō tipuna	Your ancestor
rauria i reira, kaore	a Karauria i reira.	Karauria came from there.
he Parera i mahue atu	Kāore he parera i mahue atu	Hardly anyone was left
i roto o kakara he	i roto o Kākara,	At Kākara,

3

roto tukituki i roto Nga
ru rorona ko te kurapara
anake e noho mai ra ko
Nga tihoriahake e no
homaira, e Ngari e tama
ho mua taua i taua i
ki te nei whenua koia
tapuhikura e tu mai i
Polakura la Whitira nai
koia Puke Whararikie
tu maira na taua iho
, atu kia Pouri tipuna
o karauria nei nai, na
to tipuna na te Wha
kamanae nahana a te
Whara o te ranitawhana
nahana torokana o te atu
nana utapu na na

4

tokouru, ka noho ia te
kaiwahie ko ta whakira
ngi, nana a te whakaau
angina nana a te ware,
nana maui nana a te
koromatawerawera ki
roto whakataki; naha
na te Poharu ki te manga
a te Whitau nai, nana
tuhokairangi nana a
Aharu nana Raharuhi
nana hoki Koe naai,

Whangatana

Hauitiana kera, Kaore,	He hauiti anake rā.	Only a very few.
he ohonga i mahue atu	30 Kāore he ohonga i mahue atu	No one was left
i runga o matapane i	i runga o Matapane i	On Matapane
roto Ahuririna ko ta	roto Ahuriri nā,	Within Ahuriri,
rehanake e a huare	Ko Tarehā anake	Only Tarehā,
ka maira kaore he pou	E āhuareka mai rā,	Who is pleased to stay.
ri i mahue atu i	35 Kāore he pōuri i mahue atu	No sorrow is left yonder
roto tukituki i roto nga	I roto Tukituki i roto Ngaruroro na,	At the Tukituki and Ngaruroro rivers,
ru rorona ko te kurapare	Ko Te Kurapare anake	Only Te Kurapare
anake e noho mai ra ko	E noho mai rā,	Is left there,
nga tihorianake e no	Ko Ngāti Hōri anake	And so too is Ngāti Hōri
homaira, e ngari e tama	40 E noho mai rā.	Left there.
no mua taua i taua i	Engari e tama! nō mua tāua,	But O son! long before this,
ki tenei whenua koia	I tau ai ki tēnei whenua.	Did we settle on this land.
tapuhikura e tumai i	Koia Tāpuhikura e tū mai	There is Tāpuhikura, standing
Potakura tawhitira nai	I Pōtaka-kura-tawhiti rā nā-i.	At Pōtaka-kura-tawhiti.
Koia Puke wharariki e	45 Koia Puke-wharariki e tū mai rā,	Puke-wharariki stands there,
tu maira na taua iho	Nā tāua i hoatu,	Given by us
atu kia Pouri tipuna	kia Pōuri tipuna	To Pōuri, an ancestor
o karauria neinai, na	o Karauria nei nā-i.	Of Karauria.
to tipuna na te wha	Nā tō tipuna nā Te Whakamana	From your ancestor Te Whakamana
kamanae nahana a te	50 Nāhana a Te Whara o	Comes to Te Whara o
whara o te rangitawhanga	Te Rangi-tāwhanga	Te Rangi-tāwhanga
nahana torohanga o te atua	Nāhana Torohanga-o-te-atua.	Who begat Torohanga-o-te-atua.
nana utapu na na	Nāna Utapū, nāna Tokouru	Who begat Utapū, who begat Tokouru,
tokouru, ka noho ia te	Ka noho ia Te Kaiwahie.	Who lived with Te Kaiwahie.
kaiwahie ko tawhakira	55 Ko Tawhaki-rangi	Tawhaki-rangi
ngi, nana a te whakaau	Nāna a Te Whakaauangina	Begat Te Whakaauangina,
angina nana a te ware,	Nāna a Te Ware,	Who begat Te Ware,
nana Maui nana a te	Nāna Māui, nāna a Te	Who begat Māui, who begat Te
koromatawerawera ki	Koromata-werawera	Koromata-werawera
roto whakataki, naha	60 Ki roto whakataki,	Who married Whakataki,
na te poharu ki te manga	Nāhana Te Pōharu	And begat Te Pōharu
a te whitaunai, nana	Ki Te Manga-a-te-whitau na-i.	Who married Te Manga-a-te-whitau.
tuhokairangi nana a	Nāna Tū-hokairangi,	Tū-hokai-rangi
Anaru nana Raharuhi	Nāna a Anaru, nāna Raharuhi	Begat Anaru, who begat Raharuhi,
nana hoki koenaai,	65 Nāna hoki koe na-a-i.	Who also begat you.
Whangataua	Whanga-taua	Whanga-taua

Ngā Whakamārama

Explanations

Line 1: Te Mate-pārae: The person to whom this song is addressed, or possibly a feature of the landscape.

Lines 13-15: Tāwhiri-toroa, Te Ope-kai, Tau-kahakaha, and her daughter Te Mā-runga-o-te-rangi, all prominent women of Ngāi Tahu, were sent back to Takapau by Te Rehunga to live on the land given to the people. Another person often named in this group was Ngā-māhiwa-o-te-rangi, which some say was another name for Te Ope-kai.[247]

Lines 16-17: Haemata-o-te-atua was the son of Manawa-kawa, an uncle of Ngaoko-i-te-rangi, and the husband of Mā-runga-o-te-rangi. Te Wāwāhanga was Te Ope-kai's brother.[248]

Line 19: The Ngāi Tahu people of Takapau.

Line 22: Te Pū-rākau lived at Manaia in 1840. He married Roka, a descendant of Hika-rāhui, and had Maika, who had Hiria Maika and Pū-rākau Maika. Hiria married Raharuhi Ānaru Tū-hokai-rangi, who is mentioned in line 64, while Pū-rākau Maika married Te Rina Maaka, a daughter of Maaka Whanga-taua.[249]

Line 26: Karauria: Either Karauria Pūpū of Waimārama or Karauria Ngawhara of Wairarapa.

Line 27: Parera: Grey ducks. A metaphor for a large number of people.

Line 31: Matapane: A large pā at Ahuriri.[250] Goldsmith Terrace near Napier Hospital runs through it.

Line 32: Ahuriri: The area where Napier city was built.

Line 33: Tarehā: Chief of the Waiohiki district.

Line 35: Pōuri: May refer to the Ngāti Kahungunu ancestor Pōuri, who migrated with Rangi-tāwhanga to Wairarapa. Pōuri was in charge of the *Makawhiu* waka and was given land by Te Whakamana.[251]

Line 36: Tukituki and Ngaruroro are large rivers in Hawke's Bay.

Line 37: Te Kurapare: Ngāti Kurapare of the Hastings district. Te Kurapare was the wife of Tama-te-rā, the son of Ngarengare. She was the mother of Rangi-te-kanapa, Kau-te-whata, Hine-te-moa (Whatu-i-āpiti's mother), Te Au-ka-miti and Tahito-ara-moana.[252]

Line 39: Ngāti Hōri: Generally regarded as the descendants of Tahatū-o-te-rangi, the younger brother of Te Rangi-koia-anake I. This hapū lives at Waipatu.

Line 43: Tāpuhikura: May refer to Tapukikuea, an area of land between Gladstone, Martinborough and the coast.

Line 44: Pōtaka-kura-tawhiti was Te Whakamana's pā.

Line 45: Puke-wharariki: The hill from which Te Whakamana pointed out the boundaries of the land given to Pōuri and Rākai-rangi.[253]

Line 49: Te Whakamana was a Rangi-tāne ancestor.

Line 63: Tū-hokai-rangi was a descendant of Rerewa.

Line 64: Raharuhi Tū-hokai-rangi Ānaru was a son of Ānaru Tū-hokai-rangi, whose father was Tū-hokai-rangi.

He tuhi kātipa
Formal documents

The third example of Maaka Whanga-taua's writings to be discussed is handwritten minutes of village committee investigations into matters of public order and morality. These documents are examples of the use of functional literacy in a village society for administrative purposes based on the British legal system. They record five 'court' hearings at Pātangata (a village near Ōtāne) and Tawakeroa in July and August 1878.[254] The men whose names appear at the bottom of each document – Maaka Whanga-taua, Mohi Te Atahikoia and Urupeni Pūhara – were the kai-whakawā (investigators). The latter two were influential Hawke's Bay chiefs.

The origin of these documents is unclear, but they may be a fragment of the records of a local official or unofficial tribal committee or council. For almost 30 years prior to these hearings Māori had tried to form rūnanga, councils and komiti to administer the type of civil law recorded in these minutes, and ultimately to control the destiny of their lands. The origins of these organisations lay in the schemes for self-government that were set up in many areas in the 1850s by emissaries of the King movement or local iwi or hapū, and later by the colonial administration.[255]

From 1840, when the Treaty of Waitangi was signed, it was inevitable that the country would be colonised and Māori assimilated 'into the restraints and principles of British law'.[256] As settlers flooded in, bringing with them European technology as well as a desire to acquire land, it became obvious that Māori must 'come to grips with the now apparently unshakable Pākehā world … to succeed in it'. Hapū asked that 'settlers, gaols, doctors, schools, communications and magistrates … come among them and teach law'; positions for Māori as assessors and policemen were also prized.[257] In 1865 the 'principal chiefs' of Hawke's Bay were reported to be 'anxious to have European laws carried out in every way' in their area.[258] This was a process of 'conscious adaptation' rather than an 'acceptance of total assimilation'.[259]

The new Pākehā colony used Māori in a variety of policing roles. Chiefs and others became informal policemen, usually for some sort of payment. Some Māori enrolled in the Armed Police Forces that were established from 1846. The Resident Magistrates Ordinance of 1846 was intended to facilitate the introduction of European notions of law and order to Māori-dominated areas, but this did not happen to any significant extent until the late 1850s.[260]

In 1861 Governor George Grey advised William Fox's ministry of a 'Plan on Native Government' in which the Native Districts Regulation Act 1858 would validate the delegation of policing and governance to regional rūnanga. The 'Native portions' of the North Island would be split into about twenty districts, each administered by a Civil Commissioner, who would 'preside over the District Runanga and coordinate the activities of the Resident Magistrates'. Districts would be subdivided into half a dozen 'Hundreds' (an old English administrative category), from each of which two 'Assessors or Native Magistrates' would be selected. Each Hundred would have five police constables to enforce the District Runanga bylaws which had been approved by the Governor. These rūnanga would have authority over moral issues such as drunkenness and 'the suppression of common nuisances'.[261] Significantly, they would also define tribal, hapū or individual interests in land, and could authorise its sale to Europeans.[262]

Māori sought to participate in the administration of their own affairs rather than be dictated to by the Crown. Many tribal meetings were called in the post-war period to discuss how to respond to Pākehā domination. One aim of these hui was the abolition of the Native Land Court.[263] By 1872, many Māori communities around the country agreed with Paora Tuhaere and Wiremu Te Wheoro that Māori rūnanga or committees should determine titles, assisted by Resident Magistrates and perhaps using the Native Land Court to hear appeals against or ratify rūnanga decisions.[264] As George Waterhouse told the General Assembly in his first speech as Premier:

> A matter that has excited great interest in the Native mind is what is by themselves called 'Local Committees'. There is among the Natives a general desire that matters simply affecting … the ownership of land, and various kindred matters, shall be settled by means of Committees, to be elected by the Natives in the various districts. I am told by those who are thoroughly competent to give an opinion upon this matter, that so firm a hold on the Native mind has this question obtained, that it has now risen to the prominence the king movement did some years ago.[265]

Later that year, the Native Minister, Donald McLean, introduced a Native Councils Bill, which provided for local councils to be elected by Māori communities. Any district in which the majority of the population was Māori could be declared to be subject to its provisions by the Governor, whereupon a Native Council would elect between six and twelve members, a president and a Resident Magistrate. These bodies would 'pass by-laws on matters of local concern'. Applications to the Native Land Court would have to be made to the Native Council, whose decision would be binding – provided the parties agreed. Councils would also be able to recommend regulations relating to the 'use occupation and receipt of the profits of lands and hereditaments'. Hostile reaction to the bill forced McLean to withdraw it until the following year. Opposition remained strong after its revision in 1873, and McLean withdrew it again. Parliament would not give Māori even limited powers to decide land titles or administer their own local affairs.[266]

Nevertheless, Māori continued to create and modify unofficial committees in an effort to maintain some local control.[267] These committees may have influenced the organisation responsible for the documents considered here. The proceedings of a committee which met at Papawai in Wairarapa in June 1877 were published in *Te Wananga*. It had defined districts and their boundaries, and chosen 'Magistrates for these districts, which were appointed by the meeting to conduct matters of dispute, wherever any such may occur amongst the Maori people.'[268] The magistrates would issue summonses and hear disputes over amounts of less than £20. Three 'chief heads' would decide cases involving between £20 and £50, and both the magistrates and their superiors would adjudicate on larger claims. Cases would be heard only after costs had been paid. The minutes discussed here seem to follow this model, a structure which was clearly 'adapted from that of the Pakeha'.[269]

Hēnare Matua, a Pōrangahau chief, emerged at this time as a powerful influence in the formation of similar committees in Hawke's Bay. Related to both Maaka Whanga-taua and Mohi Te Atahikoia, Matua was very active in both a Ngāti Kahungunu committee and the formation of the Repudiation movement. He strongly advocated both local self-government and a Māori national movement. John Ormond, the Superintendent of Hawke's Bay, wrote that Matua showed 'considerable ability' in these roles.[270] The importance of Matua's 'Committee of Kahungunu', which apparently originated in a meeting of some 500 Māori at Pākōwhai in July 1872, was its effectiveness in rallying opposition to the Native Land Court and stimulating other iwi to elect their own committees and submit petitions to Parliament.[271]

Mohi Te Atahikoia, whose name appears on the following minutes along with that of Maaka Whanga-taua, was very close to the Wairarapa people, having lived amongst them for many years and been active alongside Hēnare Matua. These relationships probably stimulated Mohi's involvement in issues of Māori self-government and local administration.[272]

Maaka's minutes may also have been related to the workings of the Native Circuit Court. Kai-whakawā (assessors) were selected and paid by the government to assist magistrates in Māori cases before the Native Circuit Courts. Many kai-whakawā set themselves up as 'independent founts of justice' and vigorously administered law among their own people. Kai-whakawā or their pirihimana (policemen) often enforced their own laws, which combined Māori customary and European legal norms.[273] The creation of this position enabled chiefs to increase their mana. Some defined as offences 'anything that is offensive to the tribe generally', and dealt out punishments that were based on the Old or New Testament, or corruptions of a Pākehā rule. The colonial state found this ad hoc system to be 'a useful first step in social control'.[274]

Māori were interested in much more than controlling petty crime. Their greatest concern was that they were losing control over their futures to the Pākehā, whose political and economical power was increasing.[275] Tribal committees, official and unofficial, were designed not simply in imitation of Pākehā structures, but as adaptations that would aid iwi in their struggle for autonomy. Voluminous minutes, petitions and other writings of the Māori councils and committees which sprang up from the mid-nineteenth century have survived. They stand as a record of the Māori struggle for a say on issues that concerned them at the national and local level.

A single piece of paper found in the Maaka Collection reveals the existence of a Pākehā-style legal structure amongst the Ngāi Tahu of Takapau in this period. This document records the nomination and election of Maaka Whanga-taua as a kai-whakawā, along with two others as pirihimana and karaipi (scribe), on 9 August 1878 by members of the Ngāi Tahu hapū:

Takapau
9- - Akuhata - - 1878
ko te pooti te nei o Ngaitahu mo Maka Whangataua hei kai whakawa,
Mo Rapana Whiuwhiu hei Pirihi Mana Mo Anaru tu roa hei karaipi koia tenei nga ingoa
o nga tangata[276]
Ko taana Wananga
Ko Horomona tukati
Ko Wi Whiuwhiu
Ko Hiramate opetaua
Ko Taituha kotokoto
Ko Nahi Kauangatahi
Ko Kereopa te he
Ko Patu tuhua
Ko Tamihana tukonohi
Ko Pirihana Whiu
Ko Hemi kepa
Ko Inia Whangataua
Ko tanguru tuhua
Ko Hemi Paikea
Ko Arapata te owai
Ko Anaru turoa
Ko Rapana Whiuwhiu
Ko Henare tititi
Ko Pahata tititi
Ko Tanguru tititi
Ko Inia Maka
Ko Nikora Hori
Ko te Pepene teha
Ko Hori te Aroatua
Ko teretimana Hohaia
Ko Hohepa torohu
Ko Maka Whangataua
Huihui katoa e (28)

Ko Waikohu, (28)

While the specific committee which generated the documents discussed here has not been identified, it clearly was one of the many through which Māori communities sought to control their own affairs in this period. These minutes show that summonses were sent out, a 'court' hearing was held, witnesses were questioned and a judgement was made. The 'crimes' investigated included failure to pay money owed, inheritance disputes, defamation and divorce. Among the notable people mentioned are Mōrena Hāwea of Ngāti Hika-toa at Pourerere; Rēnata Pukututu of Ngāti Whatu-i-āpiti at Pukehou; Hōri Te Aroatua of Ngāti Kikiri-o-te-rangi at Takapau; Te One Neana, a Pākehā settler who lived at Pourerere; and Maika Iwi-kātea of Ngāti Whatu-i-āpiti at Pātangata. The minutes of three cases are shown overleaf.

Patangata Hurae 25 - 1878
Ko te whakawa a Raiha Nikora
mo Hori te Aroatua te take mo
nga Hoiho i riro i a Hori Rana
Hoiho me ana rawa katoa no Arapera
te Ngira i hoatu kia Hori Rana ko
te whatu Hori mahia iho tana tama
na Rika iho e te whakawa kua tika te tamana a Raiha kahinga a Hori
Hori rania e te whakawa nga whana
unga o Arapera i ora i te uo kilea
iho ko Henare Pukngarehu heoi whaka
tana iho e te whakawa me riro i a
Raiha Rana Ko Henare nga rawa katoa
o arapera whakapuare tia ana e te
whakawa kia oho nga marama e kimi ana a Hori he tika mona kiunga
ki tunga ki anarawa kite kilea e Hori
i roto i enei marama e oho he tika
mona ki tunga ki ana rawa ka hoho
a Hori ki ana rawa ki te rore e kilea
e Hori he tika mona ki ana rawa
ka tuturu ana rawa katoa kia Raiha rana
Ko Henare

Heoi ko nga moni e £2......
e rua Pauna hei whaka puta ma Hori
mo tana Hara kua Puta tana moni
i a Hori ki te whakawa

Mohi te Atahikoia
Maka Whangatana
Wiremu Puhara

Te kape tuhinga
(Transcription)

Patangata Hurae 25 – 1878
ko te whakawa a Raiha Nikora
mo Hori te Aroatua. Te take mo
nga Hoiho i riro i a Hori. Koaua
Hoiho me ana rawa katoa no Arapera
te ngira i hoatu kia Hori Raua ko
te whatu. Heoi mahia iho taua tama
na kitea iho e te whakawa kua tika te tamana a Raiha kahinga a Hori
Heoi kauia e te whakawa nga whana
-unga o Arapera i ora i te ao kitea
iho ko Henare Pungarehu heoi whaka
taua iho e te whakawa me riro ia
Raiha raua ko Henare nga rawa katoa
o arapera whakapuaretia ana e te
whakawa kia ono nga marama e ki
mi ana a Hori he tika mona
ki runga ki auarawa ki te kitea e Hori
i roto i enei marama e ono he tika
mona, ki runga ki aua rawa ka noho
a Hori ki aua rawa ki te kore e kitea
e Hori he tika mona ki aua rawa
ka tuturu aua rawa katoa kia Raiha rāua
Ko Henare
Heoi ko nga moni e 2—0—
e rua pauna hei whakaputa ma Hori
mo taua hara kua puta tana moni
i a Hori ki te whakawa.
Mohi te Atahikoia
Maka Whangataua
Urupeni Puhara

Te whakatikatika
(Modern Māori)

Pā-tangata, Hūrae 25, 1878
Ko te whakawā a Raiha Nīkora
mō Hōri Te Aroatua. Te take mō
ngā hoiho i riro i a Hōri. Ko aua
hoiho me āna rawa katoa nā Arapera
Te Ngira i hoatu ki a Hōri rāua ko
Te Whatu. Heoi, mahia iho taua tāmana.
Kitea iho e te whakawā kua tika
te tamana a Raiha, ka hinga a Hōri.
Heoi, ka uia e te whakawā ngā whanaunga
o Arapera i ora ai i te ao kitea
iho ko Hēnare Pungarehu. Heoi,
whakattaua iho e te whakawā me riro i a
Raiha rāua ko Henare ngā rawa katoa
o Arapera. Whakapuaretia ana e te
whakawā, kia ono ngā marama e
kimi ana a Hori, he tika mōna
ki runga ki aua rawa. Ki te kite e Hori
i roto i ēnei marama e ono he tika
mōna ki runga ki aua rawa, ka noho
a Hori ki aua rawa ki te kore e kitea
e Hori he tika mōna ki aua rawa,
ka tūturu aua rawa katoa ki a Raiaha rāua
ko Hēnare.
Heoi, ko ngā moni e 2—0—0
e rua pāuna, hei whakaputa mā Hōri
mō taua hara. Kua puta tana moni
i a Hori ki te whakawā.
Mohi Te Atahikoia
Maaka Whanga-taua
Urupeni Pūhara

Te whakapākehātia
(English translation)

Pātangata, July 25, 1878.
The case of Raiha Nīkora
against Hōri Te Aroatua. The case is for
the horses taken by Hōri. These
horses and everything that belonged to Arapera
Te Ngira were given to Hori and
Te Whatu. And so a summons was served
and the court found in favour
of Raiha and Hōri lost.
Then the court asked if any relatives
of Arapera were still alive and they found
Hēnare Pungarehu.
The court ordered the return
to Raiha and Hēnare of the entire estate
of Arapera, and granted Hōri
six months in which to find
evidence of his
right to part of the estate. If Hōri is able
within the six months to submit a
case for a share in this estate, he will receive
it. If it is found that Hōri has no rights
to the property,
the whole estate will revert to Raiha
and Hēnare.
Meanwhile, £2
is to be paid by Hōri
for the offence. The money was paid
to the court.
Mohi Te Atahikoia
Maaka Whanga-taua
Urupeni Pūhara.

No 2

Patangata - Hurae - 25 - 1878
Ko te Whakawa a te One Neana mo
Renata Pukututu te take mo nga
Nama a te One i a Renata ko ana
Nama no te tau ono tekau mawha te
kau mawha o Ngara o Mei) ko ana nama
e Waru Pauna me te (hikipene, ko nga
kupu tenei o te Whakawa ko Morena te
kai Whaka puaki ara te Matgai o te One
te kupu a Renata e Whaka ae ana au
ki Nga Pauna e Waru, ko Nga Pauna e rima
kaore au e Whakae e pai ana au ki a
ki a korero mana ko te One mo te ritenga
o ana nama, Kapatai tia, e he ana e
nei nama, Ka ki mai a Renata e he ana,
Ka Patai tia, kaore ranei he kupu tono
a te One mo ana nama ia koe, ka kimai a Renata kaore heoi kapa mui tia
te Pukapuka a Renata ki a Morena ko
tana Pukapuka no Whitu te kau ma
ono no te taima i katia ai e te One nga
Hoiho a Matoha mo ana nama koia tenei
Nga kupu o te reta a Renata me tuku
mai Nga Hoiho a Matoha na ana tonu
ana Hoiho e hoa Morena ki atu ki to-
hoa Pakeha e tika ana Waiho kia kite
au i te Moni ka utu atu ai e au heoi
no te Putanga o tana kupu i te reta
a Renata ka whakae a Renata ki ana
nama ara ki te Waru pauna me te hiki
pene mo te Hawene - 10 - Herengi ma te
Whakawa - 7 - hereni Huihui katoa e
£8 - 17 - 6 Kua Whakae a Renata maana
e utu enei moni Ma te Wiremu e utu
ki a te One Neana

Mohi
Maka

Neana

Te kape tuhinga
(Transcription)

Patangata – Hurae 25 – 1878
ko te whakawa a te one Neana mo
Renata Pukututu te take mo nga
nama a te one i a Renata ko aua
nama no te tau ono tekau mawha te
kau ma wha o ngara o (mei) ko aua
e waru Pauna me te hikipene, ko nga
kupu tenei o te whakawa ko morena te
kai whakapuaki ara te mangaio te one
te kupu a Renata e whakae ana au
ki nga Pauna e waru ko nga Pauna e rima
kaore au e whakae e pai ana au ki a
kia korero maua ko te one mo te ritenga
o aua nama, kapataitia, eheana e
nei nama, ka kimai a Renata eheana
Ka, Pataitia, kaore ranei he kupu tono
a te one mo ana nama ia koe, ka ki
mai a Renata kaore heoi kapanuitia
te pukapuka a Renata ki a morena ko
taua pukapuka no whitu no te kauma
ono no te taima i katia ai e te one nga
Hoiho a matoha mo ana nama koia tenei
Nga kupu o te reta a Renata Me tuku
mai nga Hoiho a matoha naana tonu
ana Hoiho e hoa morena ki atu ki to-
hoa Pakeha e tikaana waiho kia kite
au i te moni ka utu atu ai e au heoi
no te putanga o taua kupu i te reta
a Renata ka whakae a Renata ki aua
Nama ara ki te Waru pauna me te hikipene mo te Hamene – 10-Herengi ma te
whakawa – 7 – hereni Huihui katoa e
£18-7-6 kua Whakae a Renata Maana
e utu enei moni mate Wiremu e utu
ki a te one neana
Mohi
Maka
Neana

Te whakatikatika
(Modern Māori)

Pā-tangata Hūrae 25 – 1878
Ko te whakawā a Te One Neana mō
Renata Pukututu. Te take mō ngā
nama a Te One i a Rēnata. Ko aua
nama nō te tau ono tekau mā whā te
kau mā whā o ngā rā o (Mei) ko aua nama
e waru pāuna me te hikipene, ko ngā
kupu tēnei o te whakawā. Ko Mōrena te
kai whakapuaki, arā, te māngai o Te One
Te kupu o Rēnata, 'E whakāe ana au
ki ngā pāuna e waru-6. Ko ngā pauna e rima
kāore au e whakāe. E pai ana au ki a
kia kōrero māua ko Te One mō te ritenga
o aua nama.' Ka pataitia; 'E hē ana ē
nei nama?' Ka kī mai a Rēnata, 'E hē ana."
Ka pataitia; 'Kāore rānei he kupu tono
a Te One mō āna nama i a koe?' Ka kī
mai a Rēnata, 'Kāore.' Heoi, ka pānuitia
te pukapuka a Rēnata ki a Mōrena, ko
taua pukapuka nō whitu tekau mā
ono nō te tāima i katia ai e Te One ngā
hōiho a Matoha mō āna nama. Koia tēnei
ngā kupu o te reta a Rēnata, 'Me tuku
mai ngā hōiho a Matoha nāna tonu
āna Hoiho. E hoa Mōrena kī atu ki tō
hoa Pākehā e tika ana. Waiho kia kite
au i te moni ka utu atu ai e au.' Heoi
nō te putanga o taua kupu i te reta
a Rēnata, ka whakāe a Rēnata ki aua
nama, ara, ki te waru pauna me te hiki
pene. Mō te Hāmene 10 Herengi, mā te
whakawā 7 hereni, huihui katoa e
£18-7-6. Kua whakāe a Rēnata māna
e utu ēnei moni, mā te Wiremu e utu
kia Te One Neana.
Mohi
Maaka
Neana

Te whakapākehātia
(English translation)

Pātangata, July 25, 1878.
The case of Te One Neana [John Nairn] against
Rēnata Pukututu. The charge is for
money owed by Rēnata to Te One. The amount
due since
14 May 1864 is
£8 6d, as outlined by
the court. Mōrena is the
representative of Te One.
Rēnata said, 'I agree
to the amount due of £8 6d. But with the £5
I disagree. I wish to
discuss that amount with Te One.'
Question: 'Do you disagree with
these amounts?' Rēnata stated, 'I disagree.'
Question: 'Do you not have an invoice
from Te One for the amount to be paid by you?'
Rēnata replied, 'No.' Then, the contents of
a letter from Rēnata to Mōrena was read
dated 1876,
from the time that Te One impounded
Matoha's horses in lieu of this debt. These are
the contents of Rēnata's letter, 'Please return
Matoha's horses, they are
his own horses. My friend Mōrena, tell your
Pākehā friend that is the truth. Let me find
the money and then I shall pay you.' And so
with the reading of
Rēnata's letter, he agreed that he owed this
amount of £8 6d.
For the summons 10s, for
court costs 7s, a total of
£8 17s 6d. Rēnata agreed
to pay this amount to Wiremu, who would then pay
Te One Neana John Nairn.
Mohi Te Atahikoia
Maaka Whanga-taua
Nairn

No 15

Tawakeroa Akuhata – 7 – 1878

Ko te Whakawa a te koroneho Hakikino mo tana wahine mo Pirihira
te take mo te whakarere a tana
wahine i a ia

Kapataitia a te koroneho he aha te
take i tamana ai koe i to wahine he
tamana naku kia hoki mai taku wahine ki a au Patai, kai te mohio koe he
wahine nahau tera, ka utua e te
koroneho ae Patai, kowai te tangata
nana i hoatu tenei wahine ki a koe
ka utua e te koroneho ko Matiu na
wai korua i marena, na te Wiremu
Patai he aha te take i whakarere ai
to wahine i a koe ka utua e te koro
neho he moe naku heoi ka korero a te
koroneho i te ritenga o tana moe
ka mutu ki a te koroneho

ka ahu ki a Pirihira te Patai e mohio
ana koe kua tamana tia koe e te koro
neho ka utua e Pirihira e mohio ana
au Patai e tika ana to whakarere i a
te koroneho ka utua e Pirihira, he ma
tenga noku katahi he kai Parapara
karua he Hupe ka toru Patai Pehea
to whakaaro ki a te koroneho i tenei ra
ka utua e Pirihira e kore au e hoki
ki a ia tuturu te kupu a te wahine
e kore ia e hoki ki toha tane heoi
ko te whaka tau a te whakawa ma
Pirihira e utu te tamana $1-0-0 me te
whakawa $1-0-0 Heoi ko tona ture i Potae
tia ki runga ki a Pirihira ahakoa haereia
i te ao Heoi tena Mohi Moka

etika ana

Te kape tuhinga

(Transcription)

Tawakeroa Akuhata – 7 – 1878
Ko te whakawa a te koroneho Hakikino mo tana wahine mo Pirihira
te take mo te whakarere a tana
wahine i a ia
Kapataitia a te koroneho he aha te
take i tamana ai koe i to wahine he
tamana naku kia hoki mai taku wa
hine kia au, patai, kai te mohio koe he
wahine nahau tera, ka utua e te
Koroneho ae ,Patai, ko wai te tangata
nana i hoatu tenei wahine kia koe
ka utua e te koroneho ko Matiu, na
wai korua i marena, na te Wiremu
Patai he aha te take i whakarere ai
to wahine i a koe ka utua e te koro
neho he moe naku heoi ka korero a te
Koroneho i te ritenga o tana moe
ka mutu ki a te Koroneho
ka ahu kia Pirihira te patai e mohio
ana koe kua tamanatia koe e te koro
neho ka utua e Pirihira e mohio ana
au Patai e tika ana to whakarere ia
te Koroneho ka utua e Pirihira e tika ana he ma
tenga noku katahi he kai Parapara
karua he hupe ka toru Patai Pehea
to whakaaro ki a te Koroneho i teneira
ka utua e Pirihira e kore au e hoki
ki a ia tuturu te kupu a te wahine
e kore ia e hoki ki tona tane heoi
ko te whakatau a te whakawa ma
Pirihira e utu te tamana 1-0-0 me te
whakawa £1-0-0 Heoi ko to raua ture i Potae
tia ki runga kia Pirihira ahakoa haereia
i te ao
Heoi tena
Mohi Maka

Te whakatikatika

(Modern Māori)

Tawake-roa Ākuhata 7 – 1878
Ko te whakawā a Te Koroneho Hākikino mō tana wahine mō Pirihira.
Te take mō te whakarere a tana
wahine i a ia.
Ka pātaitia a Te Koroneho, 'He aha te
take i tāmana ai koe i tō wahine?' 'He
tāmana nāku kia hoki mai taku wahine ki a au.' Pātai: 'Kai te mōhio koe he
wahine nāhau tērā?' Ka utua e Te
Koroneho, 'Ae!' Pātai: 'Ko wai te tangata
nāna i hoatu tēnei wahine ki a koe?'
Ka utua e Te Koroneho, 'Ko Matiu.' Nā
wai kōrua i mārena?' 'Nā Te Wiremu.'
Pātai: 'He aha te take i whakarere ai
tō wahine i a koe?' Ka utua a Te Koroneho, 'He moe nāku.' Heoi, ka kōrero a Te
Koreneho i te ritenga o tana moe
Ka mutu ki a Te Koroneho,
ka ahu ki a Pirihira. Te pātai: 'E mōhio
ana koe kua tāmanatia koe e Te Koroneho?' Ka utua e Pirihira, 'E mōhio ana
au.' Pātai: 'E tika ana tō whakarere i a
Te Koroneho?' Ka utua e Pirihira, 'E tika ana, he
matenga nōku ka tahi, he kai parapara
ka rua, he hūpē ka toru.' Pātai: 'Pehea
tō whakaaro ki a Te Koroneho i tēnei rā?
Ka utua e Pirihira, 'E kore au e hoki
ki a ia.' Tūturu te kupu a te wahine,
e kore ia e hoki ki tona tāne. Heoi,
ko te whakatau o te whakawā, mā
Pirihira e utu te tāmana £1 me te
whakawā £1. Heoi, ko tō rāua ture i potae-
tia ki runga ki a Pirihira, ahakoa haere ia
i te ao.
Heoi tēnā.
Mohi Maaka

Te whakapākehātia

(English translation)

Tawakeroa, August 7, 1878.
The case of Te Koroneho
Hākikino against his wife Pirihira.
The charge is of desertion by his
wife.
Koroneho was asked, 'Why
have you served a summons on your wife?'
'My summons was to have my wife return
to me.' Question: 'Are you sure she
is your wife?' Te Koroneho
answered, 'Yes!' Question: 'Who was it that
gave this woman in marriage to you?'
Te Koroneho replied, 'Matiu.' 'Who
married the two of you?' 'Te Wiremu.'
Question: 'Why did your wife
leave you?' Koroneho answered,
'Because of a dream I had.' And so he
proceeded to relate his dream.
When Koroneho's testimony was ended,
Pirihira was asked, 'Do you
know you were summoned by Te
Koroneho?' Pirihira answered, 'I understand.'
Question: 'Do you have a good reason to leave
him?' She answered, 'Yes, firstly I was
abused, secondly I haemorrhaged,
and thirdly mucus ran from my nose.'
'How do you feel towards Koroneho today?'
Pirihira answered, 'I shall not return
to him.' Her mind was firmly made up that
she would never return to her husband.
And so the decision of the court was for
Pirihira to pay £1 for the summons
and a court fee of £1. Furthermore, the court
granted Pirihira the freedom
to go anywhere in the world.
That is all.
Mohi and Maaka

The railway line at Te Kōpua, south of Takapau.
Photo by the author

Mukakai Maaka Whanga-taua. Maaka Collection

Urupeni Pūhara. Photo courtesy of Pat Parsons

Rēnata Pukututu. Photo courtesy of Pat Parsons

TE WANANGA.

Panuitanga.

HE panui tena naku mo taku hoiho i ngaro ki te Hauke No te 4 o nga ra o Akuhata i ngaro ai, e rua nga parani kai te taha maui, nga parani, koia tenei | A H | | A H |, kai te kaokao i te ritenga mai ki te Pakihiwi i te nohoanga o te Tera, tetahi o nga parani kai te kaki tetahi o nga parani, ko te ingoa o tena parani ko Ahu Ahu, He ingoa Tipuna taua parani, ko te ahua o te hoiho he ma, he ma, ma katoa te hoihoi, he rahopoka, he mea hutihuti naku te waero, kai runga ake i nga turi te mutunga o te waero, ko te peke maui o mua i ma iti a waenganui o te putu. He hoiho pai te ahua, ko te Paha te ingoa o taua hoiho.

Ki te kitea taua hoiho me kawe atu ki te Hauke kia Hekangarangi, ka utua te tangata nana i kite ki te £2.

32   NA MAAKA WHANGATAUA.

Panuitangata ki nga Pakeha.

E HAERE mai ana ki te Pereti pa Karongata me mutu ta ratou haere mai ki te pupuhi manu, aha ranei, aha ranei, i muri mai o te putanga o tenei panui, ki te tohe ratou ki te haere mai, ka whakawakia ki te ritenga o te Ture.
                                 IHAKO KAAPO.

HE Panui
kaati te
moana, i Pouk
Pukeko, i te W
te ngahere i P
tangata, ka w

Te Hauke, F

I HEREBY
TRESPAS
tricts, nor to s
caution them
on the Lakes
my land or la

Poukawa, J

An advertisement placed in Te Wananga, *25 August 1877, by Maaka Whanga-taua after the loss of his horse Te Paha, offering a reward of £2 for its return.* Courtesy of Auckland Public Library

CHAPTER FIVE

HE KŌRERO TIPUNA NŌ NGĀI TAHU-NUI
A TRADITIONAL STORY FROM NGĀI TAHU-NUI

From the late 1840s, Māori recorded traditional narratives for a number of reasons: out of personal interest, for use on social occasions, for fear of losing traditions, or in response to requests from Pākehā ethnologists. This chapter surveys a traditional Ngāi Tahu-nui narrative, found in Aritaku Maaka's whakapapa book, which recounts the hapū's origins.

Aritaku Maaka, c. 1866–1936

Aritaku Maaka was the youngest child of Miriama and Maaka Whanga-taua to survive to adulthood, and the only one to have children. Family history records that Aritaku was the last baby to be born in a cave at the Pukeake pā above the Waingongoro waterfall.[277] While Aritaku lived at Waimārama for much of his early life, the family also had strong associations with the chiefs Te Moana-nui of Matahiwi and Hēnare Tōmoana of Waipatu.[278] Because of these links, and those of his paternal grandfather Whanga-taua to central Hawke's Bay, Aritaku spent most of his married life in the Takapau area.

According to family tradition, Aritaku was employed as a harpooner for a whaling station at either Pututaranui or Rangaika, and as a ploughman, farmer, and leather worker. He also worked for the racehorse owner Spencer Gollan. Aritaku was associated with Gollan's most successful horse, the brown colt Moifaa, which won the Grand National steeplechase at Liverpool in 1904 before being sold to Lord Marcus Beresford on behalf of King Edward VII. Moifaa became the king's favourite hack and was ridden by him on state occasions.[279] To commemorate the victory, Aritaku named his first child after Spencer Gollan. Aritaku and Golan often told their families the story of Moifaa, and how it took pride of place in King Edward's funeral procession in 1910.

When he was a youngster at Waimārama, Aritaku and his people were followers of Te Kooti's Ringa-tū movement. According to the Maaka family, the whare named Taupunga after one of the anchor stones of the *Tākitimu* canoe was built as a Ringa-tū house of prayer. Aritaku is said to have travelled with a number of Waimārama people to Te Kuiti to attend the reopening of the wharenui Te Tokanga-nui-a-Noho, which was moved and rebuilt by Te Kooti and his people in 1882.[280] Aritaku became an Anglican lay minister at Takapau in 1917,[281] and in his later years he also attended hui at Rātana Pā.

In 1903 Aritaku married Annie Haberfield of southern Ngāi Tahu, who had been raised at Greenhills, near Bluff. The couple lived in a communal wharepuni at Waimārama for a while before shifting back to Takapau, where Aritaku eventually built their home next to the old whare named Tawari. He later preached often in St Mark's Māori church, which was built nearby. In 1919 Aritaku, Annie and their family moved to Ōhinemutu for three years so he could gain relief from his arthritis by soaking in the hot pools.

Like many Māori of his generation, Aritaku was active in tribal affairs and the fight for compensation for land that had been wrongly sold. He was probably influenced by his father's participation in formal tribal affairs. In 1894 Aritaku was a member of Te Komiti o Te Kotahitanga for the hapū of Ngāti Te Kikiri, Ngāi Tahu, Ngāi Toroiwaho and Ngāti Huringa-o-te-rangi.[282] Later he chaired the Takapau marae committee and was a member of the Takapau Māori Council, and on his return to Takapau from Rotorua in 1922 he became a member of Te Komiti o te Hahi o Te Takapau (the Takapau Church committee).[283]

Aritaku's understanding of the English language was limited, and his younger children often read the daily newspapers to him. He was hard-working and honest, but stern and rather formal in manner. Aritaku Maaka died at Waipukurau hospital on 12 July 1936 from pneumonia, and was taken back to Waimārama to be buried.[284]

Ngā tuhituhi a Aritaku
The writings of Aritaku

To his family, Aritaku was a man of the land, a worker and an administrator. The Maaka Collection includes a number of Aritaku's maps, whakapapa, narratives and waiata; the minutes of local committees he was involved with; and letters he received. All are in Māori.

Most of the manuscript and whakapapa books, and minutes, stored in a back room of the Maaka homestead at Takapau, were lost in a fire.[285] In 1988, while attending the opening of the Rākau-tātahi marae at Takapau, I visited the sites of the old Maaka homestead, Tawari pā and St Mark's church. Where the homestead and Tawari had stood, there were empty paddocks, but the church where Aritaku had often preached was still in use. Inside were a number of his Bibles containing references to sermons and hymns written in his own hand. We left these for parishioners to use, and sadly the church was burnt to the ground some years later.

Like his elders, Aritaku recorded many whakapapa. From the large number of letters he received, it seems that he was an avid letter writer, but unfortunately none of those he wrote are held in this collection. Whakapapa and lists of names are central to the letters addressed to Aritaku, which may often have been related to tribal meetings discussing land or the election of committee members. One 1934 letter in the Maaka Collection is Hori Tupaea's reply to a request from Aritaku to confirm whakapapa connections.

The piece of writing by Aritaku chosen to feature in this chapter is a traditional narrative written in one of his whakapapa books. It has been transcribed (with punctuation, including macrons, added) and translated by Roger Maaka, a grandson of Aritaku.[286] It recounts the well-known traditional kōrero of the Māori view of creation, retracing the deeds of the ancestors from Io to Paikea to Tahu-nui, the progenitor of the Ngāi Tahu people of Takapau. We have entitled the piece by its first line, 'Ko te whakamāramatanga o ngā pūtake o te atuatanga' ('An explanation of the origin of the deity').

This narrative was written in a ledger book that also contains lists of Aritaku's whakapapa. When Aritaku's son Golan Maaka copied portions of it into his own whakapapa book, he attributed it to his father and dated it 1930.[287]

'Ko te whakamāramatanga o ngā pūtake o te atuatanga' is a commentary on the cosmogonical origin and human history of Ngāi Tahu of Takapau. It begins with Io-rangi, the supreme atua, then describes the feats of the primal parents, Rangi-nui and Papa-tū-ā-nuku, and their children, including Tāne-nui-a-rangi. Tāne's works, the creation of humans, the flight of Hine-tītama to Te Pō, and Tāne's ascent to the heavens to obtain the baskets of knowledge are recounted. The narrative then follows the path of that sacred knowledge, through the human lineage from Tāne to Māui and on to the migration of the *Tākitimu* and *Horouta* peoples to Aotearoa. The human lineage given in this narrative is associated with the genealogy of Paikea and Tamatea. The lineage of Tahu-nui (sometimes known as Tahu-makakā-nui or Tahu-matua), the eponymous ancestor of Ngāi Tahu of Takapau, is set out and confirmed.

The other prominent waka mentioned in this manuscript is *Nuku-tai-memeha*, the canoe of Māui-pōtiki. A brief history of *Nuku-tai-memeha* reveals those to whom this canoe was passed down through successive generations. It eventually became the property of Uenuku, the father of Paikea and Ruatapu. *Nuku-tai-memeha* became embroiled in Wai-kōkopu, the famous battle in Hawaiki between Whena and Uenuku, and also in the rivalry between Ruatapu and Kahutia-te-rangi (also known as Paikea). When Ruatapu tried to drown his brothers, who were on board *Nuku-tai-memeha*, Paikea and Tama-rereti survived, and Tama-rereti eventually brought the canoe to Ao-tea-roa.

According to Tanguru Tūhua, Inia Maaka and others, Ngāi Tahu was a hapū of Ngāti Kahungunu based at Horehore pā which occupied the land around Whenuahou and Aorangi:[288]

> Ko nga Hapu nona te pa nei a Horehore ko ngai Tahu i noho tuturu i runga i te whenua nei Ara ngauri o Ngamahiwa te ope-kai a Tawhiritoroa me te taha Toroiwaho hapu me ngati te kikiri hapu To ratou ingoa iwi ko Ngati Kahungunu.[289]

> The sub-tribes who belonged to Horehore pā are Ngāi Tahu; they are entitled to this land and are the descendants of Ngā Mahiwa/Te Ope-kai, Tāwhiri-toroa; Ngāti Toro-i-waho; Ngāti Kikiri. Their tribal name was Ngāti Kahungunu.

The lineage of the Tahu people of Takapau is obscure, as they name Tahu-nui (also known as Tahu-matua), not Tahu-pōtiki, as their eponymous ancestor. Tahu-nui was a sibling of Porou-rangi and Tahu-pōtiki, according to Golan Maaka's whakapapa book:

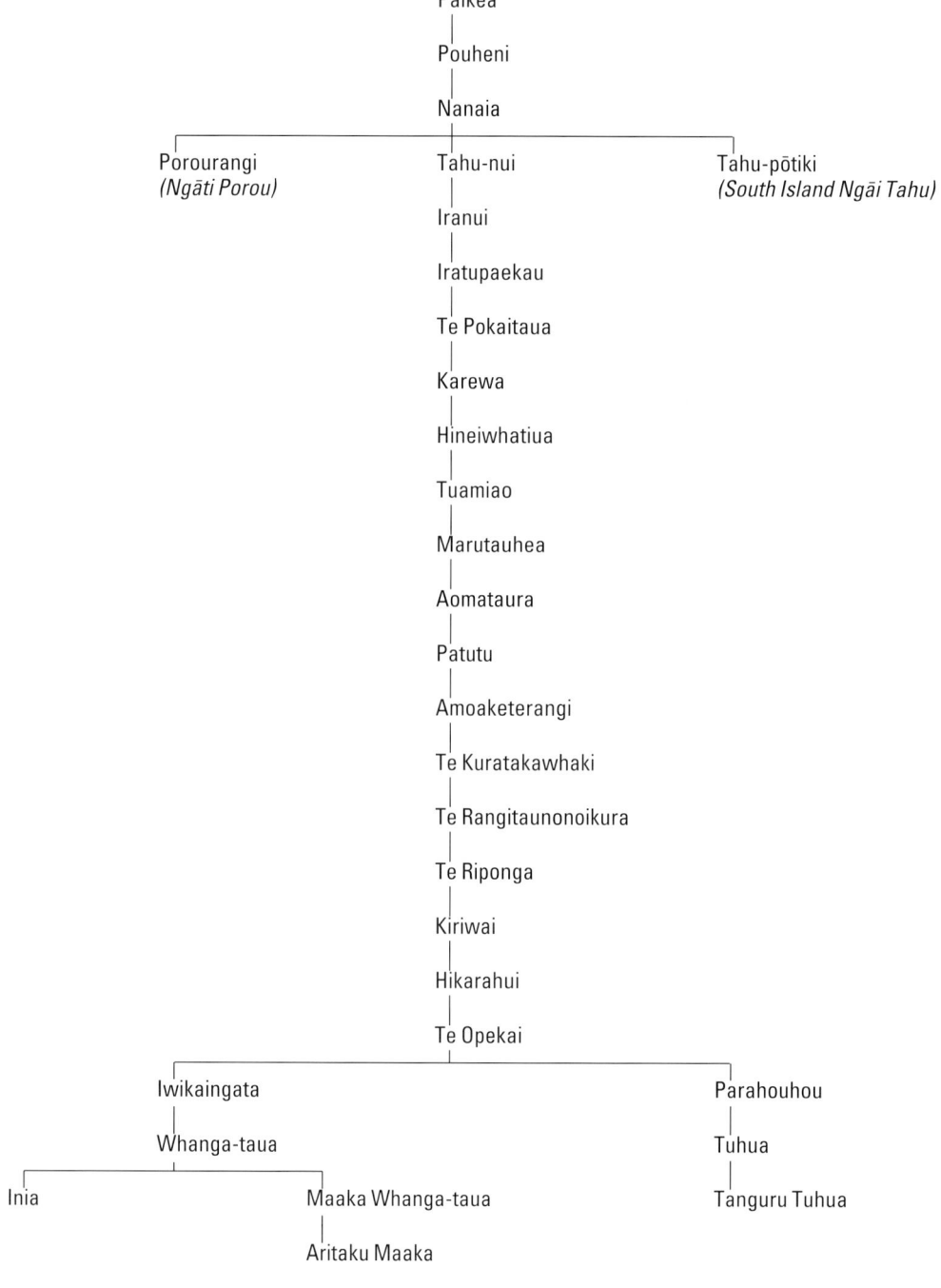

The narrative in Māori is followed by an English translation.

He kōrero pūrākau nō te pukapuka a Aritaku Maaka
Nā Roger Maaka i kape tuhi, ka whakapākehā

Ko te whakamāramatanga o ngā pūtake o te atuatanga: i tohia nei tōna ingoa e ō tātou tīpuna ko Io-rangi-matua-kore. Kāore e mōhiotia e ngā whakatipuranga mai i ō tātou tīpuna te papa me te whaea o Io-matua-rangi-kore. Heoti anō tā rātou whakamārama ki roto ki tō rātou whare wānanga, i a rātou e noho huihui ana i roto ki tō rātou pā, i Te Rauroha o Tikitiki-o-rangi. Koia tēnei.

Ko Io-rangi, nāna i hanga a Papa-tūā-whenua; ka oti, ka hangaia hoki a Rangi ki runga ki te kōpū o Papa; ka oti, ka hangaia ko te moana ki raro iho i a Papa; ka oti, ka hangaia i raro atu i te moana ko Te Waha-o-Te Parata; ka oti katoa i a Io-rangi-matua-kore āna mahi katoa. No te wā ka whakatinia e Io-rangi ki roto ki te moana, hokowhitu tōpū (wāhia ake 140 takitahi): he atua katoa tō rātou āhuatanga. Nā taua wā ka hangaia e Io-rangi a Tāne-nui-a-rangi hei ūpoko mo rātou. Ka hoatu hoki e Io-matua-rangi-kore ngā mātauranga nunui o āna mahi ki a Tāne-nui-a-rangi, ā, nō taua wā tonu, ka mahia e Tāne-nui-a-rangi.

Heoi, i a Tāne-nui-a-rangi rātou ko tōna hokowhitu tōpū e noho huihui ana i runga i a Rangi e tū iho nei, ka hangaia e rātou tō rātou pā, a Te Rauroha. Ka tū, ka mahia te whare; ka oti, ka tūātia e Tāne-nui-a-rangi te ingoa ko Rangi-ātea.

I taua wā tonu, ka whakamaharatia e Io-rangi-matua-kore ki a Tāne kia mahia he uha kia rite ki a rātou te āhua. Mahia ana e rātou ki te one ki Kurawaka; ka oti, ko Hine-hau-one. Nō tēnā wā ke eketia e Tāne a Hine-hau-one; heoi, kīhai i tika tā Tāne tāna mahi. Ko āna tamariki tuatahi, he mea mahi rāwaho noa nā Tāne.

Koia tēnei ō rātou ingoa, ko Te Taniwha, ko Te Pūtoto, ko Te Para-whenua, ko Te Pokiki, ko Te Hore-roa. Tokorima ngā tamariki a Tāne i mahia rāwahotia e Tāne. Nō taua wā anō, ka karanga iho ōna tuākana i runga i te rangi tuarua, mahinga a Ro-iho, a Ro-eke, 'Tāne e!' Ka karanga ake a Tāne, 'E?'

Ka karanga iho rāua, 'Kei te hē koe i te ara ki te uha; kei raro kē te waha.'

Kātahi a Tiki ka whakaaro, ē, kei te hē. Kātahi ka hikaia te ahi a Tiki: aha ki runga, e Tiki-matua, aha ki waho, e Tiki-matua, aha ki te pokopoko. Kātahi anō te tahito o Tāne ka hāngai ki raro ki te waha o te hika o Hine-hau-one, pukepuke maunga.

Ka hapū a Hine-hau-one, ka whānau tā rāua tamaiti, ka tapaina e Tāne te ingoa o tāna tamaiti ko Hine-tītama, he wahine. I muri iho, ka moea a Tāne tana tamāhine, a Hine-tītama, hei wahine māna. Nā, e whakatōhua ana a Hine-tītama i tana tamaiti, ka haere a Tāne, ka piki ki te rangi ngahuru-mā-rua whakaoti ai. Nō te taenga atu ki te rangi whakamutunga, whakaoti ai, ka hoki iho a Paia ki roto ki tō rātou pā, ki Te Rauroha. A, i muri iho ka ui atu a Hine-tītama ki a Paia, 'Kei te kimi noa au, ko wai rā ō koutou tōku pāpā nāna au?'

Ka kī a Paia, 'Me titiro koe ki te tāhū o te whare e mau iho nei, ka tatau e koe i ngā heke, i ngā kāhō, me te pou o te tuarongo, me te pou-toko-manawa, me te pou whatitoka, me te poupou o te pae pae kei waho, me nga poupou o ngā pakitara.'

Ka ui atu a Hine-tītama ki a Paia, 'Koia nei tonu tōku pāpā, ko te tangata nāna i hanga te whare e tū nei?'

Ka kī a Paia, 'Ae, ko te tāne e moe na kōrua, hōhō, tō pāpā.'

Heoi anō, ka whakamā a Hine-tītama i konei, ka kahakina ia e tōna whakamā, ka rere ia i te rangi, tau rawa atu ko te pārae i Whitianaunau. Ka kite ngā tāngata o Te Hono-i-wairua i a Hine-tītama, ka ui atu, 'Nō whea koe?'

Ka kī atu ia, i haere iho ia i te rangi, i a Tikitiki-o-rangi e tū iho nei.

Ka pātai atu anō ngā tāngata, 'Ko wai tō ingoa?'

Ka kī atu te wahine nei, 'Ko Hine-nui-te-pō tōku ingoa.'

Heoi, ka rongo [a] Māui-pōtiki, te tangata nāna i hī a Papa-tūā-nuku, ka whaia kia patua e ia a Hine-nui-te-pō, Heoi, kakari ana rāua, ko Māui-pōtiki i mate. Ko te mate rā tēnei, ko te katinga o te ūpoko o Māui ki roto ki te hika o Hine-nui-te-pō. Heoi, tūtūā tonu iho a Māui, waiho tonu iho hei kupu kī mōkai ma ngā uri o Hine-nui-te-pō ki a Māui-pōtiki.

Heoi, muri iho i a Tāne-nui-a-rangi e whakaotioti ana i a Tikitiki-o-rangi, ko te whakamutunga iho tērā o ngā rangi ngahuru-mā-rua, i mahia ai e Tāne-nui-a-rangi rātou ko tona hokowhitu. Ka hoki iho a Tāne ki Matangi-nui-o-rangi, ki tō rātau pā ki Te Rauroha. Ka ui a Tāne ki ngā tāngata tiaki o tō rātou pā, 'Kei whea taku wahine?'

Ka kī atu ngā tāngata tiaki o te pā, 'Kāore mātou e mōhio. I mahara mātou kua tae atu ki a koe ki runga nā.'

Heoi, ka pōuri a Tāne ki te ngarotanga o tana wahine; heoi, ka haere ia ki te tūāhu ki a Kauahoaho-te-ata, ka kumekumea e Tāne ngā hau o ngā rangi i hangaia ra e ia. Ka kitea e Tāne te huarahi i haere ai a Hine-tītama: i haere ia mā roto i te hau āwhiowhio.

Heoi, ka haere iho a Tāne i roto i Te Koroirangi, whare atua, ka tae ia ki Motu-tapu, ki Hawaiki-nui-a-Ruamatua.

Ka kite a Tāne i a Hine-tītama, ka mihi atu ki tana wahine. Heoi, kāore a Hine-tītama i mōhio ki a Tāne, he āhua kē hoki tōna āhua i tōna taenga atu. Heoi, nō te pō ka whakakitea e Tāne āna tohu ki tāna wahine, ka tae hoki te mōhiotanga ki te wahine rā ko Tāne tonu ia tēnei, e moe tahi rā rāua.

Ka kī atu a Hine-tītama ki a Tāne, 'He iwi kino te iwi e noho nei, he iwi kai tāngata; pono mai au e kai tonu ana i a rātou.'

Ka kī a Tāne, 'E kore rātou e kai atu anō i te tāngata i a tāua e noho nei.'

Ka kī atu a Hine-tītama ki a Tāne, 'I taku taenga mai ki raro nei, i ui mai te iwi nei ki taku ingoa, ka kī atu ana au ko Hine-nui-te-pō taku ingoa. Ka ui mai anō ki a au, "I haere mai koe i whea?" Ka kī atu au ki te iwi nei, "I haere mai au i runga, i Tikitiki-o-rangi e tū iho nei." Heoi, ka wehi te iwi nei i a au. Heoi, ko tā rātou ingoa e karanga ana mōku ko Hine-ariki-rangi.'

Ka kī atu a Tāne ki a Hine-tītama, 'Me kī atu koe ki tō iwi kia whakamutua te karanga i tā rātou ingoa i tapaia nā mōu: me karanga rātou i tō ingoa ko tāu anō i kī atu ai ki a rātou, ko Hine-nui-te-pō tō ingoa.'

Heoi, ka tūturu te ingoa o te wahine, i rere nei te angi ko Hine-nui-te-pō. Nō taua wā tonu ka whānau tā rāua tamaiti; ka tūātia te ingoa; 1. Hine-rauwharangi; 2. Hine-ahurangi; 3. Hine-puarangi; 4. Tangihia-ariki.

I muri iho ka whānau ko etahi o [ā] rāua tamariki i muri iho i a Hine-rauwharangi, te tamaiti tuatahi a Tāne rāua ko Hine-nui-te-pō. Nō taua wā tonu ka whakakitea e Tāne āna tohu nunui ki Hawaiki-nui, te motutanga o Te Hono-ki-wairua. Nō taua wā tonu ka tae te mōhiotanga ki ngā iwi e noho rā i Te Hono-ki-wairua, ko Tāne tonu tērā e moe rā ia Hine-nui-te-pō, ka tau te wehi ki ngā iwi e noho ana rā rātou i Te Hono-ki-wairua.

Heoi, ka huri katoa rātou hei iwi kotahi ki raro i a Tāne-nui-a-rangi, ā, ka atawhaitia rātou e Tāne.

A, i muri iho ka piki atu a Tāne i roto i Koroirangi. Ka tae ia ki runga ki Tikitiki-o-rangi e tū iho nei, ka mauria mai e Tāne te wānanga me te tūāhu, me Kauahoaho, me ngā whatu kura e rua. Koia i kīa ai ko ngā whatu takataka o Io-matua-te-kore, me te kākahu tākai ōna, o aua whatu, me Whare-kura.

Nō te hokinga iho o Tāne ki Motu-tapu, Te Hono-ki-wairua ki Hawaiki-nui-a-Ruamatua, ka hāpainga e Tāne a Whare-kura hei whare mō te wānanga. Ka tīkina e Tāne ngā rākau ki a Rangi-ata-maku: nau mai ai hei whakairo katoa ngā pou, ngā heke me ngā kaho o tēnei whare. He tūāhu, he wāhi tapu nō tēnei whare, arā nō Io-matua. Kei Hawaiki-nui-a-Rua-matua tēnei whare e tū ana; ko ōna taonga i hoatu e Io-matua ki roto ki Whare-kura tiaki ai.

Ko Kauahoaho-te-ata (he tūāhu tērā), ko ngā whatu kura takataka o Io-matua, ko te wānanga. Ka whāia ko te wānanga; i haere iho tōna whakahekenga ki runga ki te kāwai tāngata, arā ki a Tāne-nui-a-rangi, te pūtake mai o tātou. Koia tēnei.

Ko Tāne-nui-a-rangi	moea i a	Hine-nui-te-pō
Ko Hine-rau-wharangi	moea i a	Kawe-kai-rangi
Ko Te Kuku	moea i a	Hine-i-te-ana-nui
Ko Tū-whakaheke-nuku	moea i a	Puau
Ko Rua-taratara	moea i a	Tū-te-amoamo
Ko Ruamano	moea i a	Whareikura
Ko Uenuku	moea i a	Rongo-mai-taka-nui
Ko Paikea	moea i a	Hutu-mahana
Ko Whatu-i-ata-marae	moea i a	Te Au-ripo
Ko Ue-te-koroheke	moea i a	Nanaia
1. Ko Porourangi	2. Ko Tahu-nui	3. Ko Tahu-pōtiki

Ka whakamāramatia te pūtake mai o te taina o Tū-whakaheke-nuku, koia tēnei tōna tātai:

Ko Tū-whakaheke-rangi	moea i a	Punga-toroa
Ko Pito	moea i a	Ngā-tai-āio
Ko Rere	moea i a	Tua-ngahuru
Ko Karotai	moea i a	Tato
Ko Rongo-kako	moea i a	Huri-whenua
1. Ko Kahukura-kōtore		
2. Ko Rongo-rongo		
3. Ko Tamatea		
4. Ko Ūhenga-ariki		

Ko Porou-rangi, Ko Tahu-makakā-nui, Ko Tahu-pōtiki, Ko Taewa-rangi, Ko Ruawhare.

Nō te whakatupuranga i ō tātou tīpuna, e mau iho nei ō rātou ingoa i runga ake nei i heke mai ai rātou i Tawhiti-nui, i Tawhiti-roa, i Tawhiti-pāmamao, i Motu-tapu, i Whare-kura, i Hawaiki-nui, i Te Hono-ki-wairua. Ko tō rātou waka i haere mai ai rātou ki Ao-tea-roa nei, ko Tākitimu.

Mau ana ki te ihi o te whare o tōna tīpuna, o Tonganui, ko Te Matau-a-Māui, Ko Te Kauwae-o-Muri-ranga-whenua. I muri iho i te tokonga a Tāne me tōna hokowhitu i a Rangi ki runga, i a rātou e noho huihui ana i tō rātou pā, i Te Rauroha o Tikitiki-o-rangi, nō taua wā tonu ka heke a Papa-tūā-whenua ki raro. Nā ngā pou i mahia rā e Tāne hei toko i a Rangi ki runga, nāna a Papa i wāwāhi. Ka pākarukaru ana a Papa-tūā-whenua, heke ana ki rire [sic] o te moana, ki Te Waha-o-Te Parata. I muri iho, ka whakamaharatia e Io-matua a Māui-pōtiki i Tikitiki-o-rangi rāua ko tōna teina, ka kohia e rāua a Papa ki ā rāua matau kia autaha te pō, kia autaha te ao.

Ko tō rāua waka i hī ai a Papa ko Nuku-tai-memeha. Ka whiua e rāua ā rāua matau a Māui-pōtiki kia autaha te ao, arā, ki te kauwae o Muri-whenua. Ka waenganui a Māui-pōtiki e huti ana i tana aho, ka ripo te moana, ka hiko te uira, ka tangi te whatitiri a Papa-tūā-whenua i roto i te moana. Ka kitea iho e Māui-pōtiki a Papa-tūā-whenua e pākarukaru haere ake ana, e whakaporotititia ana tō rāua waka e te au kōmingomingo o te moana. Ka mataku ana a Māui-tikitiki-o-rangi, ka karanga atu ki tōna teina, ki a Māui-pōtiki, 'Tapahia atu te aho. Ehara i te ika i kai ake nā ki tō matau. Me hoki tāua ki uta, ka mate tāua!'

Ka kī atu a Māui-pōtiki ki tōna tuakana, 'Kāore! Kia eke rawa ake te ūpoko o te ika i kai ake nei ki taku matau, kia kite tāua i te āhua, ka hoki ai tāua ki uta.'

Nō te ekenga ake o te ūpoko o te ika a Māui-pōtiki, he ūpoko whenua ia: Ko Papa-tūā-whenua e mau ana i te ihu o te waka [ihi o te whare] o tō rāua tīpuna, o Tonga-nui. Heoi, ka hoki rāua me tō rāua waka ki te tuawhenua, ki Te Hono-ki-wairua.

I taua wā tonu, i tae atu rā rāua ki Motu-tapu o Te Hono-ki-wairua, ka kutia e Io-matua te māramatanga ki roto i te kapua hinapōuri. E whā ngā pō e pōuri ana a Rangi e tū iho nei, ka tākiritia e Io-rangi te kapua pōuri, ka puta iho te māramatanga nui i runga i Tikitiki-o-rangi e tū iho nei.

I taua wā tonu, ka piki atu a Tāne-nui-a-rangi ki runga ki te puke i Hikurangi, ka kite atu ia i āta tokotoko te wehewehenga o Papa-tūā-whenua i tēnā takiwā, i tēnā takiwā o te moana, huri noa i te ao. Ka hoki iho a Tāne ki Hawaiki-nui-o-Ruamatua, ki Motu-tapu, ki tōna whare tapu ki Wharekura, tae noa ki te whakatipuranga i a Tū-whakaheke-nuku rāua ko tōna taina ko Tū-whakaheke-rangi.

Nō te takiwā i tō rāua whakatipuranga mai, ka whakahekea iho e tō rāua tipuna, e Tāne-nui-a-rangi, te waka a Nuku-tai-memeha ki a rāua. Koianei te waka i hī ai e Māui a Papa-tūā-whenua. Na Tū-whakaheke-nuku i whakaheke te waka ki tāna mokopuna, ki a Ruamano; ā nā Ruamano i whakaheke te waka ki tāna tamaiti, ki a Uenuku. Ka tūturu te waka nei ki a Uenuku.

Ā, i muri iho i a rātou ko ōna uri e noho huihui ana, ka tāhaetia e Ruatapu te heru o tōna papa, o Uenuku. Heoi, ka pātaia e Uenuku ki tāna tama mātāmua, ki a Kahutia-te-rangi. 'Kei te tāhae pōriro, tirau moko, na Moenga-hau na. Kei a Ruatapu tō heru e huna ana.'

Heoi, ka riri a Uenuku ki a Ruatapu. Ka kīia e Uenuku he tama meamea nāna – nā tana wahine taurekareka, nā Pai-māhu-taka. Heoi, ka mate a Ruatapu i te whakamā, ka tono ki te waka o tōna pāpā hei waka hokinga mōna ki te kāinga i riro taurekareka mai i a tōna hākui, i tō rātou matenga i Te Rā-kumia, i Wai-kōkopu, i Te Whiri-pūreia. Ā, hoatu ana e Uenuku tōna waka, a Nuku-tai-memeha, ki a Ruatapu.

I muri iho ka tono a Ruatapu ki tōna tuakana, ki a Kahutia-te-rangi (arā, ko Paikea) kia haere ki te whakahoki i a ia ki te kāinga i riro herehere mai ai tōna hākui, i a Pai-māhu-taka ... a, moea ana e Uenuku hei wahine māna. Ā, muri iho ka whakaae a Paikea kia haere ia ki te whakahoki i a Ruatapu ki tōna kāinga, ki te Raukumia. I taua wā tonu ka hoe a Paikea rāua ko Ruatapu i te Moana-nui-a-Kiwa. Ā, ka ngaro te wā tuawhenua, ka haere te waka nei i te wā moana anake i te pō. Ka unuhia e Ruatapu te kāremu o tō rātou waka, arā te puru o te waka. Heoi, ka heke te waka nei ki te kōpū o te moana; heoi, ka patua e Ruatapu te hokowhitu o Mahina, arā, te iwi o Paikea, mate katoa.

Ko Tama-rereti anake rāua ko Paikea i puta; heoi, ka warea a Ruatapu ki te whai i a Paikea. Kāore hoki i mau i a ia. Ā, kupa noa mai te ata, ka karanga atu a Ruatapu ki tōna tuakana, ki a Paikea, 'E, nau mai rā, haere. E ū koe ki uta, horahia te tau ki tō taua hākui, ki a Wehi-nui-a-mamao. Popo roroa o te makariri, tēnā au te haere na ki uta, kai Hikurangi te pūpūtanga o te tangata.'

Heoi i a Ruatapu; ka warea ki te whai i a Paikea, kia patua e ia.

Ka kāhakina te waka e Tama-rereti, tau noa mai te waka, a Nuku-tai-memeha, ko te taha rāwhiti ... Ko te putanga mai o te rā. Ā, tūturu atu te tāngata nōna te waka, ko Tama-rereti.

Ko Ruatapu, oti atu koe ki te ... o te Moana-nui-a-Kiwa; kāore hoki ia e hoki mai ki te tuawhenua nei, he whakamā nō Ruatapu i tāna kohurutanga i te hokowhitu o Tū-mahina (arā, te iwi o tōna tuakana, o Kahutia-te-rangi arā o, Paikea). Engari, nō te hoenga i te waka nei i te kōpū o te moana, ka whakawhitia te ingoa o te waka nei e Ruatapu, ko Tū-te-pewa-a-rangi. I mahara hoki a Ruatapu, ka tūturu tonu te waka nei, a Nuku-tai-memeha, ki a ia; heoi, riro atu ana te waka i a Tama-rereti. Kōna [tona] hoa nāna i kāhaki te waka Nuku-tai-memeha, ko te Ngahuru-mā- ru[a] o Matariki. Oti atu te waka nei ki runga ki a Rangi-nui-a-tamaku e tū iho nei.

A traditional story written in the book of Aritaku Maaka
Transcribed and translated by Roger Maaka

This is an explanation of the origin of the deity: he was given the name by our ancestors of Io-rangi-matua-kore. The parents of Io-rangi-matua-kore were not known by the generations who were descended from our ancestors. This is all they would explain in their school of learning, when they gathered in their pā at Te Rauroha-o-Tikitiki-o-rangi. See, here it is:

It was Io-rangi who created Papa-tūā-whenua. When that was done, he also created Rangi, through the womb of Papa; when that was done, he created the sea beneath Papa, and under the sea he created the great whirlpool Te Waha-o-Te Parata. And then all of Io-rangi-matua-kore's work was completed. When he created the multitudes in the sea, there were seven score twice-told, altogether divided up, that is 140 counted simply; in nature they were all deities. And at the time Io-rangi created Tāne-nui-a-rangi as their head. Io-rangi-matua-kore also gave Tāne a great knowledge of his works; and at the same time, Tāne-nui-a-rangi undertook his tasks.

Well then, while Tāne and his seven score twice told were living gathered together on Rangi that stands up there, they built their pā, Te Rauroha. When the house was erected and completed, Tāne named it Rangi-ātea.

At the same time, Io-rangi-matua-kore made Tāne decide to make a female, like them in appearance. She was formed by them from the sands at Kurawaka; when she was finished, it was Hine-hau-one. When Tāne mounted Hine-hau-one, well Tāne could not do it properly. His first children were creatures created in an outlandish way by Tāne.

These are their names: Te Taniwha, Te Pūtoto, Te Para-whenua, Te Pokiki, and Hore-roa. Five children were made by Tāne in this outlandish way. Just at that time, his older brothers called down from the second sky created by Ro-iho and Ro-eke, 'O, Tāne!'

Tāne called back, 'What?'

They called down, 'You mistook the way to the female; the entrance is down below.'

So then Tiki thought, 'Oh yes it was wrong.' So then Tiki's fire was kindled; Tiki-matua mounted, withdrew, and was exhausted. So then the ancient one of Tāne came down opposite Hine-hau-one's mons veneris.

Hine became pregnant, and when their child was born, Tāne named his child Hine-tītama; a female. Tāne took his daughter Hine-tītama as his wife. Now when Hine-tītama was swelling with his child, Tāne went and climbed to the twelfth heaven and stopped there. When he arrived at the last heaven, to stop there, Paia went back down into their pā, Te Rauroha. Later, Hine-tītama said to Paia, 'I keep trying to discover which of you fathered me.'

Paia said, 'You had better look at the ridge pole of the house fixed there, and count the rafters, the battens, and the posts at the back, the pou-toko-manawa, the posts by the doorway, the poupou of the paepae outside and the poupou of the side walls.'

Hine-tītama asked Paia, 'Is he really my father, the man who built this house that stands here?'

Paia replied, 'Yes, he is the man you were sleeping with. It is obvious that he is your father.'

Well, Hine-tītama was ashamed at this. She was overwhelmed with shame, and she fled from the sky and settled on the plain at Whiti-a-naunau. The people of Hono-i-wairua saw her, and asked, 'Where are you from?'

She told them she came down from the sky, from Tikitiki-o-rangi that stands up there.

The people asked another question, 'What is your name?'

She said, 'My name is Hine-nui-te-pō.'

Māui-pōtiki, the one who fished up Papa-tūā-whenua, heard of this and set out to slay Hine-nui-te-pō. She and Māui-potiki fought, and he was the one who died. This is how he died: through his head being trapped in Hine-nui-te-pō's vagina. So after this Māui was of no consequence and his story has been passed down as something for the descendants of Hine-nui-te-pō to belittle Māui with.

After Tāne-nui-a-rangi had finished at Tikitiki-o-rangi (this was the last of the twelve skies which had been made by Tāne and his seven score), he returned to Matangi-nui-a-rangi and to their pā, Te Rauroha. Then Tāne asked the people guarding their pā, 'Where is my wife?'

The people guarding the pā said, 'We don't know. We thought she had gone up to you.'

Tāne was bereft at the loss of his wife. He went to the sacred place at Kauahoaho-te-ata ['radiant light of dawn'], and drew to himself the winds of the skies which he had created. Then Tāne discovered the pathway that Hine-tītama had taken: she had gone on the whirlwind.

Well, Tāne went down into Koroirangi, a spirit house, and he came to Motu-tapu at Hawaiki-nui-a-Ruamatua.

Tāne saw Hine-tītama, and he greeted his wife. Well, Hine-tītama did not recognise him, for his appearance was strange when he arrived there. When the night came Tāne revealed his signs to his wife. She realised that this was Tāne, and they slept together.

Then Hine-tītama said to Tāne, 'The people who live here are evil, they are cannibals; I have come across them eating each other.'

Tāne said, 'They will never again eat man while we are living here.'

Hine-tītama said to Tāne, 'When I came down here these people asked my name, and I told them my name was Hine-nui-te-pō. They asked me, "Where do you come from?" I told these people, "I come from above, from Tikitiki-o-rangi that stands up there." Well, they were afraid of me. and the name they call me is Hine-ariki-rangi.'

Tāne said to Hine-tītama, 'You had better tell your people to stop calling you by that name they have given you. They must call you by the name you gave them; your name is Hine-nui-te-pō.' And so this was the permanent name of this woman.

At that time their child was born; she was given the names Hine-rau-whārangi, Hine-ahu-rangi, Hine-puarangi, Tangihia-ariki. After this others of their children were born – after Hine-rau-whārangi, the first child of Tāne and Hine-nui-te-pō. And at that time Tāne displayed his great signs at Hawaiki-nui, the separation of Te Hono-ki-wairua ['meeting place of the spirits']. And at that time the people living at Te Hono-ki-wairua came to realise that the person married to Hine-nui-te-pō was Tāne himself, and fear fell upon the people living there at Te Hono-ki-wairua.

Then they all came together as one people under Tāne-nui-a-rangi, and they were cared for by Tāne.

After that Tāne climbed up into Koroirangi. When he arrived up there, on Tikitiki that stands here, Tāne brought down here the sacred knowledge and the sacred place (that is, kauahoaho [shrine]), and two precious red stones. That is why people speak of the rolling stones of Io-matua-te-kore, and of the garments that were wrapped around him (that is to say, around these stones), and of Whare-kura [house of knowledge].

When Tāne went down to Motu-tapu, Te Hono-ki-wairua and Hawaiki, he erected a whare-kura as a house for the sacred knowledge; he went to Rangi-ata-mata to fetch some timber, and the posts, rafters and battens of this house arrived to be carved all over. This house had a shrine and a sacred place – that is to say, Io-matua-kore had them. This house stands at Hawaiki-nui-a-Rua-matua; Io-matua put his treasures inside Whare-kura for safe keeping. There was Kauahoaho-te-ata, that was a shrine, there were the rolling red stones of Io-matua, and there was sacred knowledge. The sacred knowledge was sought after; its descent came down through the human lineage – that is to say, through Tāne, our original source. Here it is.

Ko Tāne-nui-a-rangi = Hine-nui-te-pō
Ko Hine-rau-whārangi = Kawe-kai-rangi
Ko Te Kuku = Hine-i-te-ana-nui
Ko Tū-whakaheke-nuku = Puau
Ko Rua-taratara = Tū-te-amoamo
Ko Ruamano = Whare-i-kura
Ko Uenuku = Rongo-mai-taka-nui
Ko Paikea = Hutu-mahana
Ko Whatu-i-ata-marae = Te Au-ripo
Ko Ue-te-koroheke = Nanaia
  1 Ko Porourangi
  2 Ko Tahu-nui
  3 Ko Tahu-pōtiki

Then the origin of the younger brother of Tū-whakaheke-nuku was explained. This is his lineage:

Ko Tū-whakaheke-rangi = Punga-toroa
Ko Pito = Ngā-tai-āio
Ko Rere = Tua-ngahuru
Ko Karotai = Tato
Ko Rongo-kako = H[M]uri-whenua
1. Ko Kahukura-kōtore
2. Ko Rongo-rongo
3. Ko Tamatea
4. Ko Ūhenga-ariki
Ko Porou-rangi, Ko Tahu-makakā-nui, Ko Tahu-pōtiki, Ko Taewa-rangi, Ko Ruawhar[o].

After the generations of our ancestors whose names are given above, they migrated here from Tawhiti-nui, Tawhiti-roa, Tawhiti-pāmamao, Motu-tapu, Whare-kura, Hawaiki-nui and Te Hono-ki-wairua. The canoe on which they came here to Aotearoa was Tākitimu.

The fish hook of Māui, Muri-ranga-whenua's jawbone, was caught on the bargeboard of the house of his ancestor Tonganui. After Tāne and his seven score men had propped up Rangi, while they were living together there at their pā, Te Rauroha of Tikitiki-o-rangi, at that very time Papa-tūā-whenua went below. It was the pillars that had been created by Tāne as props to hold up Rangi which broke up Papa. Papa-tūā-whenua was all broken up, and went down to the depths of the ocean, to the great whirlpool Te Waha-o-Te Parata. Afterwards, Māui-pōtiki and his younger brother, who were at Tikitiki-o-rangi, were inspired by Io-matua, and they took up Papa with their hooks so that night was to one side and day was on the other.

Their canoe from which they fished up Papa was Nuku-tai-memeha. They cast their hooks belonging to Māui-pōtiki so that the day would be on one side – that is to say, they did so with Muri-ranga-whenua's jawbone; Māui-pōtiki was amidships, pulling up his line, when the ocean curled, the lightning flashed, and Papa-tūā-whenua's thunder crashed in the ocean. Māui-pōtiki saw that Papa-tūā-whenua was ascending and breaking up, and that their canoe was spinning around in the swirling current of the sea. Then Māui-tikitiki-o-rangi was afraid, and he called to his brother, Māui-pōtiki, 'Cut your line, that is not a fish which has taken your hook! We must return to shore, we will be killed!'

Māui-pōtiki told his older brother, 'No! When the head of the fish that has taken my hook comes right up, and we can see what it looks like, then we will return to shore.'

When Māui-pōtiki's fish had surfaced, it was a head of land: Papa-tūā-whenua was held by the bow of the canoe of their ancestor, Tonga-nui. Then they and their canoe returned to the mainland, to Hono-ki-wairua.

At the very time that they reached Motu-tapu of Hono-ki-wairua, Io-matua drew the light very tightly together inside very dark clouds. For four nights, Rangi who stands up there was in darkness. Then Io-rangi jerked away the dark clouds, and light came down onto Tikitiki-o-rangi, which stands up there.

At that very time, Tāne-nui-a-rangi climbed up onto the hill of Hikurangi, and found that the separation of Papa-tūā-whenua was fully achieved; there were props in every area of the sea, and all over the world. So Tāne went back down to Hawaiki-nui-a-Ruamatua and Motu-tapu, to his sacred house Whare-kura, and he stayed there right down until the generation of Tū-whakaheke-nuku and his younger brother Tū-whakaheke-rangi.

When the time of their generation came, the Nuku-tai-memeha canoe was passed down to them by their ancestor Tāne-nui-a-rangi. This was the canoe in which Māui had fished up Papa-tūā-whenua. The canoe was passed down from Tū-whakaheke-nuku to his grandson, Ruamano; he passed it down to his son Uenuku. This canoe stayed permanently with Uenuku.

Then later when his descendants were living together, Ruatapu stole the comb of his father, Uenuku. Uenuku asked his eldest son, Kahutia-te-rangi about it. 'It is with that illegitimate thief, that bastard conceived in the wind. Your comb is hidden away with Ruatapu.'

Then Uenuku was angry with Ruatapu. Uenuku said he was a no-account son of his, the son of his slave wife Pai-māhu-taka. Then Ruatapu was filled with shame, and he demanded that his father's canoe return him to the village from which his mother, Pai-māhu-taka, had been taken away captive after the defeats at Rā-kumia, Wai-kokopu and Te Whiri-pūreia. So Uenuku gave his canoe Nuku-tai-memeha to Ruatapu.

After that, Ruatapu told his older brother Kahutia-te-rangi (that is, Paikea) to return him to his village, Te Raukumia. Paikea and Ruatapu paddled out into the great ocean of Kiwa. The mainland became lost to view, and the canoe kept moving over the ocean in the darkness. Ruatapu pulled out the plug of their canoe, that is the bung of the canoe. The canoe then descended to the depths of the ocean, and Ruatapu killed Mahina's seven score men, that is to say the people of Paikea. All of them died.

Only Tama-rereti and Paikea survived. Ruatapu was absorbed in the pursuit of Paikea. But he could not catch him. When dawn came up, Ruatapu called to his older brother Paikea, 'Oh come here, you must go. When you come to land, the season of the year of our mother, Wehi-nui-mamao will be spread abroad. In the long nights of the winter, that is when I will come ashore, and Hikurangi will be the place where the people crowd together.'

So much for Ruatapu, he was absorbed in chasing Paikea and trying to kill him.

The canoe was carried off by Tama-rereti and the canoe, Nuku-tai-memeha, landed on the East Coast, the place where the sun comes up. Tama-rereti became the permanent owner of the canoe.

Ruatapu went off for good across the [ ] of the Great Ocean of Kiwa; he would not return to this mainland because he was ashamed of his murder of the seven score of Tū-mahina (that is to say, the tribe of his older brother Kahutia-te-rangi, otherwise known as Paikea). But, when the canoe was paddled across the depths of the ocean, Ruatapu changed its name to Tū-te-pewa-a-rangi. Ruatapu thought that his canoe, Nuku-tai-memeha, would continue to belong to him, but no, it was carried off by Tama-rereti. His companion who carried off the Nuku-tai-memeha was Ngahuru-ma-ru[a] of Matariki. The canoe finished up above with Rangi-nui-a-tamaku, who stands up there.

The hill in the centre is Horehore pā, Takapau. Photo by the author

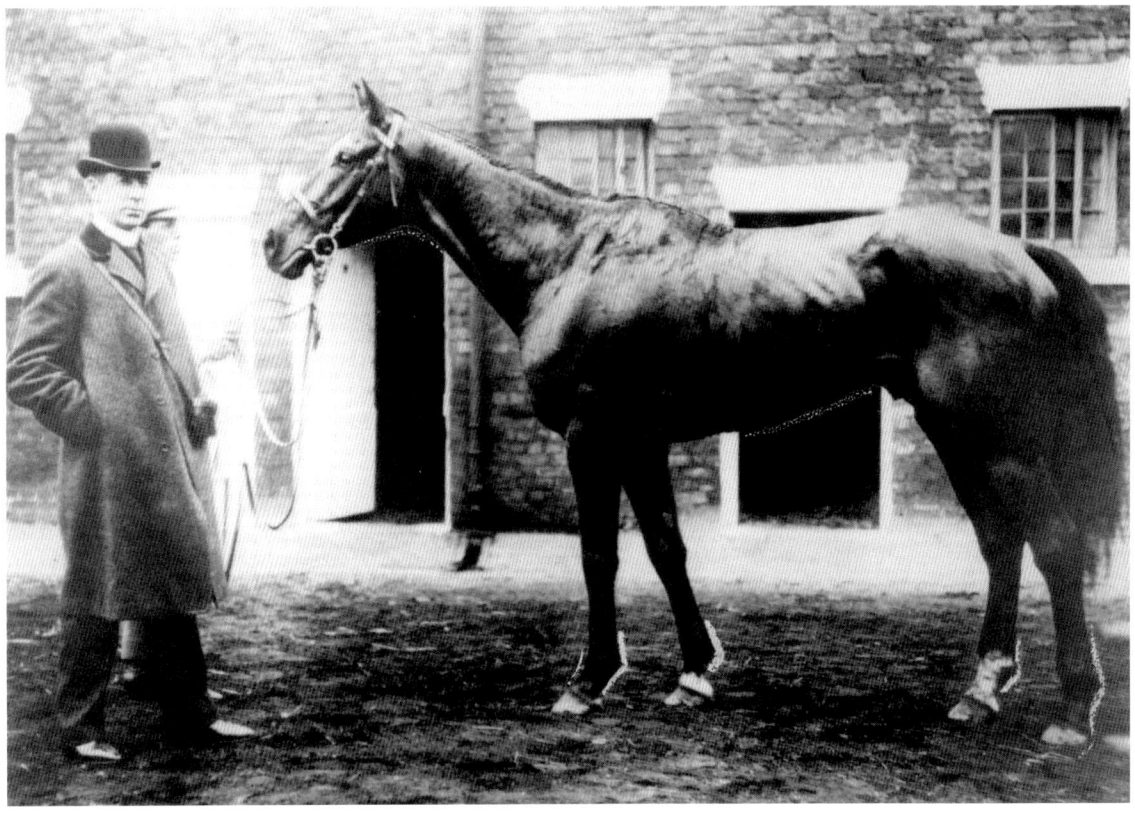

Moifaa, the New Zealand-bred winner of the Grand National steeplechase at Liverpool in 1904. Making New Zealand Collection, F-2354-1/2-MNZ, Alexander Turnbull Library

Apapa
April 18th 1934

Kia Maaka

Tēnā koe

ahoa ana nga tamariki atē riangi Koianake
akitea iho ana iroto i enei whakapapa

Rangi Koi anake = ngauao

Hineikakea = tamai awhitia = Reungaiterangi

Kuimate = ? Rangi Koi anake - 2   Kokiritangahoe

Hapuku = Hei poua   Hawaikerangi

Rangi Koi anake = wakiterangi
        Tepakaru (a toa)

Rangi Koi anake = Kaihou
  Kikiri (1)   Hawea (2)   Kaiaha (3)   Waymarama
                 Whakatoo   cos.

Kanohitulanga Karawa   Tiakitai
    Te Wrike   Hone Hoone
    Arihi   Tera Te Moana nui
    Maaka

Rangi Koi anake = maotaiterangi

        Hineirawaiterangi

mau pea Hoki awhaka puta puta Haere Hui Katoa
awha nga wahine atē rangiKoianake Te ahua o
Hineikakea raua Ko Reungaiterangi He puna rua na
tamai awhitia Ko wakiterangi to mua Koté Kaihou to mui
moe Katoa raua ia te rangiKoianake Kitaku rongo
Koenei wahine atē Puuru nei note Kaumatua Tanga
Koinei ranei tau apirangi ana pewhea ke ranei Hioi ana
            H Tupaea

A letter written by Hōri Tūpaea to Aritaku Maaka.
Maaka Collection

Aritaku Maaka.
Maaka Collection

CHAPTER SIX

HE PURUNGA RĀTAKA
KEEPING A DIARY

From the 1840s, many Māori used writing to record domestic matters, details of family life, their income and spending, and accounts of their travels in diary form. This chapter delves into the daily diary entries of Annie Maaka in autumn 1902, when she and her family were taking part in the annual cultural harvest of the tītī (mutton-bird).

Annie Haberfield Maaka 1882–1947

Annie Haberfield was a daughter of John Haberfield and Elizabeth Noki Honor, from the Otago and Murihiku districts of the South Island. Her paternal grandparents were William Isaac Haberfield, the well-known whaler from Bristol who settled at Moeraki, and Meriana Tete (Teitei), a daughter of Piki, the sister of the Ngāi Tahu ariki Tama-i-hara-nui. Annie's maternal grandparents were Joseph Honor and Popoia, who lived on Whenuahou (Codfish) and Ruapuke islands.[290]

Annie was born on 18 April 1882 at Mokomoko, near Ōmaui, on the southern side of the New River Estuary near Foveaux Strait.[291] The youngest of five children, she was brought up at Greenhills, a community on the main road between Invercargill and Bluff. Here Annie's section of the Haberfield family became almost part of the landscape. The family lived on a block of land beside the local church. The homestead situated about 100 metres from the road was originally surrounded by a high macrocarpa hedge which sheltered a garden and orchard.[292]

As a young woman Annie visited her brother William, a shearer who was then working at Takapau. Here she met William's best friend, Aritaku Maaka. On 28 October 1903 the couple were married at Takapau, where they lived during the early years of their marriage. Annie's Pākehā-style upbringing was reflected in many of her mannerisms and habits, while Aritaku and his people were still very community-based, with their Māori language and customs very much intact. This sometimes led to friction with Annie, who was branded as 'that woman from the south' by the local people.

James Belich has summed up the situation of many Ngāi Tahu in this period:

> in the late nineteenth century … [the old whalers'] European-Maori descendants were linked to, yet separate from, both mainstream Pakeha and mainstream Ngai Tahu. They saw themselves as, and were seen as, a little different from either; they were more landless than Ngai Tahu proper; and they were more prone to urbanising and the acquisition of European skills. Many 'lived as Europeans' according to the census definition.[293]

Annie worked hard alongside her husband on farms around Takapau and Waimārama, where the Māori community was also still very traditional. On one occasion she took her three children, Golan, Victor and Aritaku (Markie) to see the sights around Waimārama. On their return the elders doused them in water and recited karakia to cleanse them from the effects of traversing 'tapu' ground. Such differences saw Annie return often to her own people for periods of time.[294] Despite this, she became a prominent figure in the communities where she lived. Around 1910 Annie and Aritaku returned to Takapau, where they were eventually to raise ten children. In 1919 the family shifted to Rotorua and lived amongst the Arawa people at Ōhinemutu, where Annie set up a shop. From about 1922 the couple ran a farm at Te Kōpua, just south of Takapau.

Annie always found time to visit Wellington and the South Island to attend Ngāi Tahu functions and land meetings. One of her achievements was to win an appeal to the Native Land Appellate Court in 1926 to have the names of a number of her kaumatua entered on the list of elders living within the boundary of 'Kemp's purchase' of 1848. This entitled them to inclusion in the Ngāi Tahu claim as beneficiaries.[295] As well as fighting for her South Island family's land rights, she helped with the affairs of her husband's family and those of other Takapau residents. Annie was also determined that her children would be well educated. All ten passed the proficiency examination, which was very unusual for a family from a rural district such as Takapau.

After Aritaku's death in 1936, Annie established one of the first Māori-run businesses in Hastings, a fish and chips shop. She lived above the shop, and was often visited by kuia from Waimārama and

Takapau. Stock drovers often stayed the night before continuing their journeys. Eventually the business failed because of the unwillingness of local firms to supply it.[296] Annie eventually shifted back to the family home at Takapau, where she died on 3 September 1947.[297] One of her children wrote on the last page of one of Annie's diaries, 'Mum died at 8 a.m. Vic was present, while Tot and I held her hand as she went to Pup.'[298] She was taken to Taupunga marae at Waimārama, where the tangi was presided over by Bishop F. A. Bennett, Reverend Dan Kaa, Reverend Sam Rangiihu, and Reverend Huata. On 5 September Annie was buried next to Aritaku in the local cemetery.

Ngā rātaka a Annie
Annie's diaries

Annie made daily diary entries from her early teens until after she married. Especially after the birth of her children, her diary writing seems to have become more sporadic, and there appear to be no surviving diaries from the later period of her life. However, she continued to write letters to family members, and a few tattered pages of genealogy still exist. Her habit of diary writing must have continued for some time after she became a mother, as her three eldest sons all followed her example.[299]

Annie's diaries for 1899, 1902, 1915, and 1920 have survived, as has an exercise book containing newspaper clippings, certificates of registration, and handwritten copies of letters and replies concerning Ngāi Tahu land claim issues.[300] This book also contained lists of her shares in Ngāi Tahu lands, genealogies, recipes, and a few photos. Annie was an active participant in Ngāi Tahu land claim hearings, and spent a great deal of time in Wellington, Kaiapoi and Southland, where many of her relatives lived.

The activities regarding land issues recorded in this book arose from a 1920 Commission of Inquiry's recommendation that Ngāi Tahu receive £354,000 in compensation for breaches of the terms of 'Kemp's purchase' of 1848.[301] Hui were held to ascertain who should benefit from any compensation. At Tuahiwi on 12 March 1925, Judge R. N. Jones ruled on who was 'entitled to any relief that might be granted under the Ngāi Tahu claim.'[302] While Annie's grandmother Tete was allotted eighteen shares, Tete's siblings Hine-awhitia, Ruakaio, Horomona Mauhe and Tipoa were omitted from the list.

Although Annie's appeal to the court for the inclusion of these kaumatua was successful, this was not without cost, as she noted in her diary:

> Tete was granted 18 shares and her sisters and brothers were omitted and when I appealed, I won my appeal and then shares were taken off Tete. Not fair!

It was not until 1944 that the first Labour government passed the Ngaitahu Claim Settlement Act, which provided for compensation of £300,000 to be paid in 30 annual instalments. Harry Evison has argued that this act 'did not purport to satisfy the terms of the Treaty of Waitangi with regard to Kemp's purchase or the other nine official Ngai Tahu purchases'. In 1946 an act was passed setting up a Ngaitahu Trust Board to administer this fund.[303]

While Annie's lists of genealogies in this book validated her right to shares in land, they also reveal her adherence to an aspect of the Māori world that was commonplace at this time. People held tightly to their genealogical links and often kept their elders' whakapapa books close to them. I am privileged to have read many books in which South Island families have preserved their genealogies and traditional texts. Among the whakapapa books I have seen are those of Matiaha Tira-morehu, Herewini Erai, Wi Pōkuku, Kaiparahou Bragg, Horomona Pōhio, Kingi Rehu, Norman Bradshaw, and Hoani Maaka.

In this chapter I have concentrated on Annie's daily diary entries. Personal diaries were kept during the Reformation period in Europe. Written primarily within a religious framework, the diary was 'a spiritual balance sheet, showing whether and how far over a given period the individual had moved closer to or further away from God by practising certain religious virtues and vices.'[304] This process soon became secularised, and by Annie's era diary writing was particularly common among the social elite. In early New Zealand settler society, physical work, gardening, reading, writing and keeping diaries provided relief from boredom and loneliness. Sarah Courage described her diary as a 'confidential friend, wherein I could describe my pleasures and sorrows, with observations on my friends and acquaintances'.[305]

It is not known why Annie wrote a diary. Was it to preserve her actions and thoughts for her descendants, to keep herself occupied, or to follow the example of her forebears? Perhaps a little of all three? The entries are very repetitive; every day seems the same. Each entry begins with the date and a description of the weather, followed by an account of the day's activities, usually ending with 'went to bed'. Annie often mentions cleaning the house, washing floors, cooking dinner and making scones. Recipes written by hand or clipped from newspapers can be found throughout the diaries. In the 1915 and 1920 diaries, daily routines – washing, visiting the neighbours – continue to be recorded. Little else of Annie's family life is evident, with the exception of birthdays and the dates of the deaths of her children and parents.

I have chosen to transcribe Annie's diary entries for the period 4 April to 11 May 1902. Autumn is the season for the harvesting of the mutton-bird or tītī (*Puffinus griseus*), in which Annie took part. These entries record more activity than any other section of her diaries, and this was perhaps the most culturally Māori part of her life in Southland.

Hīkoi-tītī
Mutton-birding

At the time these entries were written, mutton-birding (hīkoi-tītī) and other customary food-gathering traditions were still important to southern Māori families. Food gathering was perhaps the most traditional part of Southland Māori life to survive assimilation into Pākehā ways. The tītī season is one of the last remaining customary harvesting traditions:

> Mutton-birding is the only modern survival of native enterprise ... which has withstood the destructive competition of the scientific and progressive undertakings introduced by the white man. But it has not only persisted ... it has ... expanded.[306]

During the season the 'beneficial owners' of the islands, or Rakiura Māori, return from all over the country to join their relations in carrying on the tradition of collecting tītī. Annie's beneficial rights to the tītī islands entitled her to set foot on Poutama, Pohowaitai and Pikomamaku.[307] However, it appears that in this period she was living on Tiā (Entrance Island), a small island at the entrance to Port Adventure on Stewart Island. While she does not name the island, it can be deduced from the places mentioned – which include Abraham's Bosom, The Arm, Back Beach and Owen's Island – that it is Tiā. While Annie's daily notes on island life are neither elaborate nor extensive, they outline the routines of mutton-birding from a young woman's point of view, as well as illustrating the constant movement of people between the islands.

Her writings also hint at the recreational activities of both young people and adults on the island. The belief in those days was that you created your own fun. Here living was close to nature, and amusements included playing cards, swimming, smoking (discreetly – it was prohibited on the islands) and fishing, while food-gathering, cleaning and cooking were chores. Storytelling was also common. This has been a Māori custom from time immemorial, and fables, ghost stories and the tikanga of birding are still told on the islands. Another form of recreation transferred from the mainland was organised dances in the evenings. The role these 'socials' played in the life of small Southland communities is outlined by James Bremer of Greenhills:

> The evening usually started with a square dance 'the first set' and was followed by the 'three steps', 'two steps', 'circular waltzes', 'polka Mazurkas', 'Boston two steps' 'The Lancers,' 'Highland Schottisches' etc ... At these they welcomed newcomers to the district and farewelled those that were leaving. There were wedding dances and dances to congratulate those who became engaged, sports club dances and dances to raise money for all sorts of local efforts.[308]

Annie sometimes reveals her emotions, using terms like 'feeling blue' and 'beastly down hearted'. She felt this way more often at the end of the birding season, when people were returning home to normal life. She records her feelings about being separated from close friends and relatives, and the lifestyle on the island. Similar emotions are still felt by modern mutton-birders on their return home. This annual gathering helped renew and strengthen friendships and family ties, which reached a degree of 'cohesion and communal sympathy' that was very uncommon among Pākehā groups.[309]

The people mentioned in these diary entries were friends and relatives among the major Māori families of the district, including the Gilroy, West, Bragg, Anglem, Skerritt, Spencer, Kihau, and

Marshall families; 'Beaut' and 'Hannah' are other relatives. Other old Murihiku identities are also mentioned.

Perhaps the only important element missing from Annie's diary is the techniques of mutton-birding. She probably felt no need to mention such a common practice. The process is outlined here to give the reader a sense of the harshness of the work, which may not be evident from the diary entries.

Each April, beneficial owners of the mutton-bird islands, which were termed by the old Māori 'ngā moutere tītī', travel to them to take tītī, originally for winter food stores but now as a commercial venture. In Annie's time 'poha-tītī' (kelp bags) were used. The process of making poha-tītī usually began after New Year with the collection of harakeke (flax), which was woven into kete (kits) to hold the poha-tītī together. Large strips of rimu (kelp) were carefully selected, prised open by hand, inflated into something resembling a hot-water bottle, and then dried. (If the rimu got wet, it would perish.) These bags were then softened like chamois leather. Kiri-tōtara (tōtara bark) was gathered from one side of selected trees to be used to protect the filled poha. When these preparations had been made and the food and other stores were ready, families sailed to the islands to begin their hunt for the birds, which had returned to lay their eggs and rear their young (pī-tītī). The old people say that the tītī migrates from, not to, the islands.[310]

The hunters seek the young tītī in their rua (burrows); the act of pulling the bird out of the hole was called nanao. One way to kill the tītī is to bite the crown of the bird's head while the body is still inside the rua. The tītī is then pulled from the hole, held down and gently squeezed to expel the ruaki (stomach contents) in a process known as whakaruaruakakata. Great care is taken to ensure that this fluid does not soil any portion of the bird's body, as it would then be impossible to pluck the feathers and the bird would have to be disposed of. Later in the season the birds emerge from their rua to 'taka-huruhuru' (shake the down from their bodies to let their feathers grow); this is a good time to stalk them at night using a rama (torch).[311]

After the feathers were plucked, the birds were cleaned with boiling salt water to remove their down. They were tied with flax in sets of ten called hui, then hung overnight on a stage (whata) erected for the purpose. At dawn the head, wings, legs and kumu (tail) were cut off, after which the birds were partially split and gutted. After the fat from inside the bird was cleaned, boiled and strained, the birds were cooked in this fat and placed on pūnui leaves until they were ready to be packed into the rimu. This process was known as tītī tahu. Other birds were completely split, salted and placed in large barrels. Later they were packed into the poha; the breastbones were kept away from the kelp, lest this split. At this stage the birds were counted, and then the poha were secured by flax laces (the tā process). The kiri-tōtara strips were used to line the outside of the poha, and the whole package was placed in a kōnae (woven kit) ready to be packed away. These poha contained between 20 and 80 birds, with 40 usually considered to be a large poha.[312] Edward Shortland described a poha as 'a sort of cask shaped like a sugar loaf, constructed from the air bladder of a species of sea-weed, strengthened outside by layers of the bark of the "totara", and kept firmly together by means of stakes tied with flax. "He poha titi," a cask of preserved birds called "titi".'[313]

Today the cultural harvesting of tītī has changed greatly with the use of modern technology. Travel by faster boats or helicopters is easier, if more costly, but landing and transporting gear are still arduous and sometimes dangerous. Techniques of hunting and preparing tītī have changed little over the years, but the birds have been stored in barrels and latterly in plastic buckets. However, some families still use poha-tītī to store their tītī.

Greenhills, 4 April – 11 May 1902

Friday April 4

A wet morning cleaned out the house got ready for the Island of Dreams.[314] Left Bay about 8 a.m. in Huia[315] Had a good sail down. a little sick reached the I'd[316] about 1 fixed up a bit went to bed.

Saturday April 5

Rained a little. scrubbed out. had a yarn with the girls over old huies.[317] had a feed of mutton birds. boys went out fishing got a few. went over to the other house had a game of euchre. Cara & I got a growling from Bragg for laughing

Sunday April 6

A lovely morning. "Despatch"[318] came in with a big crowd aboard Ciss and Mrs Buller[319] came over left again about 2. All went up the arm got some oysters had a good time went to bed.

Monday April 7

Another lovely day. Ciss & I baked all the morning. "Raven" came in anchored. Abraham's Bosom[320] boat came ashore with a crowd on her. Cara,[321] Ciss, Beaut[322] & I went round the Id for a walk Cooked apple pudding for tea. had fun on the [?] Beaut, Ciss & I played Dit[?] Charlie and John a [?] euchre We won, had … pers went to bed.

Tuesday April 8

Boat came ashore for Mrs Buller and Ciss left about 6 a lovely day. Gannet[323] passed with some mutton birders baked a few doughnuts and a loaf. Had a feed of titis and pumpkins. went round the ID cut bracks[324] had a game of euchre & a feed of chocolate.

Wednesday April 9

A misty kind of day, went out birding caught 76 came home about half past 12. finished plucking at ½ past 3 and cleaning about 6. Cooked tea washed up went up to Gilroy's Beaut and I played Charlie and Tod Lost. went to bed Cara scalded arm.

Thursday April 10

Went out to work caught 40 birds came home about 11 am. finished plucking and cleaning about 4. boys all went up the bosom. made some pancakes for tea. played Charlie – lost again. Had a feed of kaka's stew went to bed.

Friday April 11

Stopped home and cut up a hundred odd birds "Huia" and Rosey[325] came down Tom[326] brought me a letter from Ned. such a relief. J. Marshall[327] [Nay?] came ashore had dinner and went up to the bosom to anchor went to the back beach[328] wrote 3 letters.

Saturday April 12

Had chops for breakfast packed two bag's one 49 & the other 61.[329] went over to the other house had a yarn Huia took the birds to the bay Bob came ashore. Beaut, Cara and I went up the bush for a walk had a game of cards.

Sunday April 13

Got breakfast went around for some water, roasted some mutton for dinner "Rosey" went away the boys went up the arm[330] baked all the afternoon went over to the other house had a sing-song

Monday April 14

Went out to work caught 30 birds came home early a big shower come on got wet through. finished plucking and cleaning about 2 O'clock went over to the other house had a yarn John in bed not well went up to Gilroy's Tod playing some music. all hands dancing & growling[331] had supper went to bed.

Tuesday April 15

Got up about nine still raining washed some of the clothes went round for water. finished started cutting up. finished early. made a heart stew[332] for tea Cara and I had a box with the gloves Beaut & I had a walk yarn over old huies.

Wednesday April 16

Rained hard, stopped home made two plum puddings boys went round the Island stewed my pinny,[333] made a cake boys went fishing brought up a jelly fish and had a bit of fun pelting one another with it then I went over to Hannahs had a dance and end up with a game outside. Had supper went to bed.

Thursday April 17

Got up about seven, went out to work all hands had a bit of a riff caught 40 odd birds came home cooked dinner. Billy Woodcock came ashore told us all the news finished cleaning about 5 oclock had a game went to bed.

Friday April 18

My birthday 20 today went out caught 50 odd birds Cara, Beaut & I had a bit of fun on the manu[334] screaming etc. had a row with Hannah. finished cleaning about 5 cooked some groper for tea. Cara. Beaut. & I played John Tod and Charlie euchre. Beaut and I went in for a wade had a good swim

Saturday April 19

Packed a "poha" 30 birds then cut up 90 finished about 12. scrubbed out the house baked some scones & pancakes. Cara came over had a yarn. boys went over to other side got 24 woodhens.[335] had a game of euchre (won).

Sunday April 20

Had a feed of woodhens. "Hananui"[336] came in. all hands came ashore. M C.B. & I went for a walk got the sulks with the boys not letting us go in the boat. had a fit of the blues went up to Gil's went to bed.

Monday April 21

A beastly wet morning packed 2 bags 1 50 & 38. finished early Beaut came over and had a yarn baked some buns and a loaf made some doughboys[337] for tea "Huia" came in brought papers in wrote a letter home. got a packet of lollies from Joosks G. Marshall, Tom, Taff all came ashore had a game outside.

Tuesday April 22

Ground a bit damp boys went out to work. Cara & Beaut came over sat down and had a yarn over old times. helped the boys to clean went down beach and cleaned a groper "Huia" went home washed a few things and then had a game of euchre and all ended up in the tent. went to bed.

Wednesday April 23

Went out worked Cov's point got 50 odd birds 'Despatch' came from Owen's Island.[338] G.Cooper came ashore finished plucking and cleaning about 5 had a feed of groper wrote a couple of letters had a dance and a few games went to bed

Thursday April 24

Cut up about 40 birds finished early "Despatch" came down from bosom. send some birds home and to K.Kihau and 3 letters "Huia" came in boys went aboard got a letter from Jim. none from Ned. made some pancakes for tea had a read went up to Gils had a dance.

Friday April 25

A lovely morning went out to work the fern "manu" caught 40 odd birds Beaut & I came home first had a feed of apples finished cleaning about 5 "Gannet" came in Mrs Hansen[339] etc aboard boiled some rice for tea went up to Gils had a few laughs came home went to bed.

Saturday April 26

Went out to work caught 20 birds Cara Beaut & I came home had such fun played a few tricks on the boys clothes & fired off the guns then went poha-ra-ing,[340] caught another 20 Beaut caught a white tete.[341] washed me head and went to bed.

Sunday April 27

A lovely morning. All us girls went round back beach for a swim beastly cold had a good time had dinner Hinks Cara, Beaut & I went round to the "Parira" Id had a read after tea went down to the beach boys came down had a few yarns went to bed.

Monday April 28

Another fine day, cut up 30 odd birds finished about twelve cooked dinner and then scrubbed Beaut and I went to Well Point for some water boys went round for a swim and about 5 Beaut Hink and I stripped I had Charly Skerretts trousers Beaut. Sonny's and we went in for a dip. "Rosey" and "Huia" anchored at back beach all hands came ashore. had a dance up at Gils. Beaut, Bill Anglem, H.Sylvester went out to "Rosy" in dinghy stole some pudding.

Tuesday April 29

A light northerly wind went out Pahu[342] rang caught 60 odd birds and then Cara, Beaut, Dorcas and I sat down had a yarn Sonny Gilroy caught a pie ball [piebald] mutton bird.[343] came home had dinner finished plucking went down carried two bins water for cleaning made some doughnuts for tea fried some fish, had a game of cards went to bed.

Wednesday April 30

A fine day, had a couple of showers. "Huia" came down about 6 in the morning then came ashore with news that Jim was very ill Bragg left I'd for Dunedin Packed two bags one 70 + 45 cut up 60 odd birds Beaut and Hink came over had a feed of apples Tod got drunk Cara and Beaut slept over had the good time, up all night boys wouldn't let us go to sleep till 3 o'clock.

Thursday May 1

A lovely morning Sarah Gilroy came in early in morning caught us all in bed all hands went out to work I stopped home got up about 8. Saw the "Rosy" coming i fired of[f] the gun to let boys know. Bob came ashore Packed a poha 59 in it. Tom etc came ashore, brought a letter from 'Ned' news from Jim a little better went to bed.

Friday May 2

A dull sort of a day went out to work caught 30 odd birds had such fun on the manu smoking fags etc climbing trees came home plucked and cleaned finished about 5 had a few laughs. All hands of the "Huia" and "Rosey" came ashore played a few games of euchre had a dance and supper went to bed.

Saturday May 3

Such a lovely morning cut up 30 odd birds swept up. Bob made some doughboys went round to back beach for swim Bob, Charly and John came in with us water dead cold Felt awfully bad went to bed about 7 had no tea.

Sunday May 4

Didn't' get up till 11 made a woodend [woodhen] stew. Bob and Hannah made a pudding had a read & Beaut & Hink came to tea wrote a few poetry's had a laugh turned in about 12.

Monday May 5

A fine morning blew hard at night went out caught 30 odd birds finished about 5 "Huia" came Tom came ashore slept made some doughnuts for tea wrote a letter to "Ned" All hands playing euchre went to bed. but forgot to post it.

Tuesday May 6

A fine day Cara and I didn't get up till late went out caught 50 odd birds finished about 6 went up to Gilroy's had a game of cards All us girls & kids went round to back beach with lanterns had quite a giddy time John and Charlie came along the road and frightened us went to bed had supper.

Wednesday May 7

Stopped home calm dull day. Cut up thirty birds Beaut and I went to Well point and washed "Rosy" just out fishing. Came home made a torch. Cooked some titis All hands of the Rosy came ashore to torch.[344]

Charly & I played Beaut and Bob cards John and I went out and caught 100 odd birds. "Huia" came down. news Jim very ill slept over at Gilroys brought some cake and pudding from home.

Thursday May 8

A lovely morning Bob and Tom left on Rosy to go to bay & then to Dunedin. cut up 50 birds Bill Anglem helped boys with birds felt beastly down hearted all day Huia came in Marshall and Taff came ashore boys all went torching got about 80 birds plucked went to bed.

Friday May 9

A lovely morning got up about ten packed about two pohas one 45 + 34 Cara helped me packed the things to come home Beaut and I went round back beach road for last time had some tea at Gilroys and then left Oh how bitter was the parting waved till we got out of sight dead sick Got at bay about 8 pm Tod Taff and I pulled in from mouth … [illegible]

Saturday May 10

A glorious morning felt beastly down hearted. "Ah sweet memories" fixed up a bit. Sat down had a yarn and then had a bath went over to Dodd's in evening came home went to bed. Taff slept at house … [illegible]

Sunday May 11

Rained a little "Rosy" brought rest of birds from the Id Charlie came ashore. John came into the room, wouldn't go out sat down in afternoon and read C.Swain came down to tea, went to church. C.S. came down to house. All had a feed of mutton birds went to bed.

Annie Maaka (née Haberfield). Maaka Collection

The Haberfield family of Moeraki and Greenhills, Southland. Back row: John Kerle Haberfield and daughter Lydia. Centre: daughters Annie and Caroline, Mrs Elizabeth Noki Haberfield, and daughter Elizabeth. Front: son William Isaac Haberfield. Maaka Collection

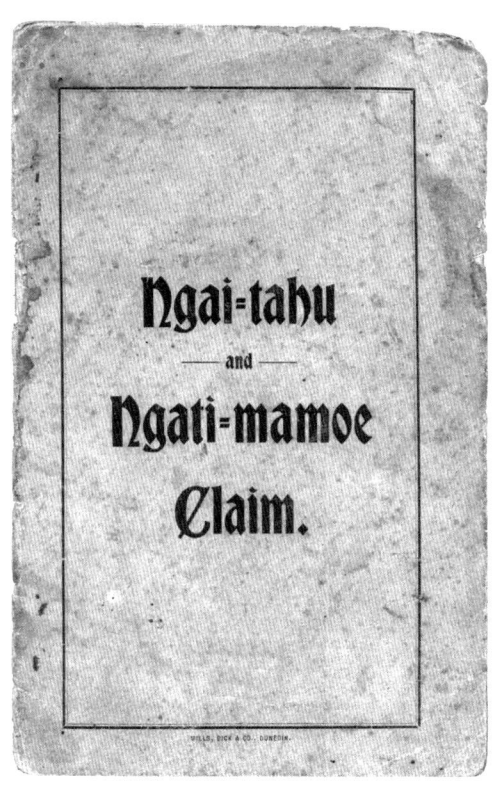

The cover of an early booklet about the Ngāi Tahu claim. Maaka Collection

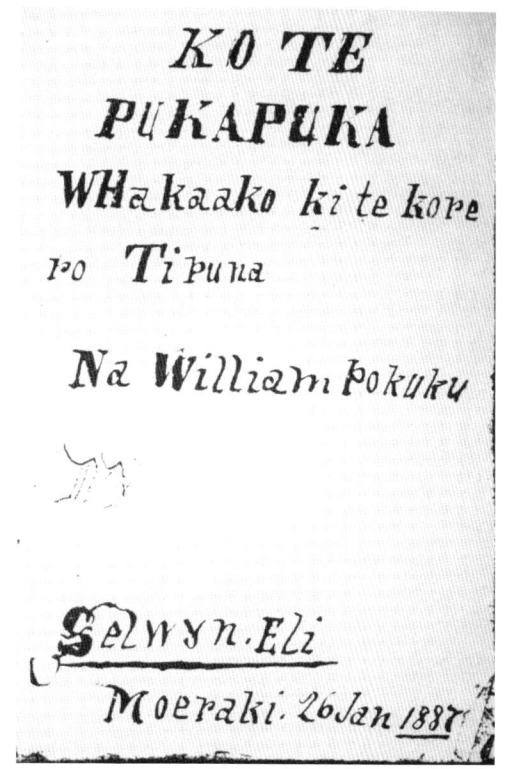

The cover of a whakapapa book written by Herewini Erai entitled 'The Teaching Book of Ancestral History by William Pokuku'. Photo by the author

Best friends and relations: Maria, Hannah and Annie on the 'Island of Dreams', c. 1902. Maaka Collection

A poha. Photo by the author

Annie Maaka. Maaka Collection

1902   **3** THURSDAY 93—272   **April**

Got up about 5 made
etc left about 6
packed up the things
for the Island.
Had a feed of pears
Huia out fishing. came
on to rain. did a
bit of mending went to
bed.

4 FRIDAY 94—271

A wet morning cleaned
out the house got
ready for the Island
of to Jack's. left Bay about
8 AM too Huia had a
good sail down. a little
got reached the Id about 1p
fixed up a bit went to bed.

5 SATURDAY 95—270

Raained a little. scrubbed
out. had a yarn with the
girls over old times. had
a feed of mutton birds.
boys went out fishing
got a few went over to

6 SUNDAY 96—269
Low Sunday—1st Sunday after Easter

A lovely morning "Despatch" came
in & with a big crowd aboard
Ciss & Mrs Buller came over
left again about 2. All went up
the arm got some oysters. had
a good time went to bed.

A page of Annie's diary. Maaka Collection

CHAPTER SEVEN

Te ara tika o te kupu
The pathway of the written word

Golan Maaka regarded his ancestors' writings as tapu; he was their guardian. For him, as for his forebears, the written word was very important. He wrote the material discussed in this chapter during his academic studies, for pleasure, and to keep a tribal record for the next generation.

Te Kōrana Golan Haberfield Maaka 1904–1978

Golan Haberfield Maaka was born to Aritaku Maaka and Annie Haberfield in 1904 at Ōruawharo, Takapau. Early in his life the family moved to Waimārama, where he attended the Waimarama Native School before being sent to Heretaunga School in Hastings. The family moved back to Takapau around 1910, and in 1915, at the age of ten, Golan was sent to Te Aute College, where he was educated until 1922. Becoming disillusioned with Te Aute, he transferred to Dannevirke High School, from which he matriculated in 1924. He attended the University of Otago Medical School, and was awarded an MB ChB in 1937 after completing a thesis entitled 'Ratana Pa: A General Survey of Conditions at Ratana from a Public Health Perspective'. After doing his internship at Wellington Hospital, he was a house surgeon at Napier Hospital for seven years, and helped victims of the 1931 earthquake.

Golan was among the New Zealand doctors who volunteered for the Far East Relief team which served in central China during the Sino-Japanese war in 1937-8. He was stationed at I-ch'ang on the Yangtze River for many months, mostly treating army personnel serving on Chinese munitions ships and helping disease-ravaged villages. After a long journey through central China to Chungking and on to India, Golan eventually returned to the medical base at Hong Kong. His experiences in China were to have a great impact on his view of the world. His mind was opened to both the vastness of knowledge and the perils of life overseas.

Golan returned to New Zealand at the end of 1938 after being officially honoured by Chiang Kai-shek's government. Following a break from medical life, he volunteered unsuccessfully for the Maori Battalion in 1939 before joining the Health Department as a venereologist at Tāneatua. It was here that Golan met Florence Ramari Stewart, whom he married in 1941. By 1944 Dr Maaka had become a medical practitioner in Whakatāne; he is thought to have been the first Māori to establish a full-time general practice in New Zealand. Golan was to practise in Whakatāne amongst the Tūhoe and Ngāti Awa people for nearly 35 years, becoming well known for not charging his patients and for his accuracy in diagnosing skin complaints. Because of their religious beliefs, many Māori people would allow only Golan to examine them. Suspicion of Western medicine and medical practitioners was still very much alive.

Dr Maaka's interests included socialising and rugby, but his greatest passion was Māori history. He was an avid reader, recorder, researcher, and writer of Māori language, tikanga and tradition, world politics, astronomy, philosophy, European history and English literature. He also loved 'cowboys and Indians' comics.[345] Current affairs were important to him: no one ever read the newspaper before Golan.[346] His thirst for all types of knowledge – especially Māori knowledge – was unquenchable. Many people of the Mataatua district believed that Golan, an outsider from Ngāti Kahungunu, came to know more about the Māori history of the Bay of Plenty than anyone else of the time.[347] As a medical practitioner, he not only treated people for their ailments but befriended them and made them feel comfortable enough to talk to him.

It was well known that before undertaking a consultation with a new patient, Dr Maaka would seek common ground by linking himself to them through history and genealogy. He spent each night writing in his scrapbooks many of the stories he had heard during the day. Golan relished his talks with Māori elders, especially those of Tūhoe who still 'lived Māori history' in their daily lives. One indication of the regard people had for his knowledge of things Māori, especially genealogy, is the large number of letters he received requesting family lineages.

Golan was influenced greatly by the fact that his elders had written down their own histories and genealogies. His mother's insistence on the value of education and her keeping of a daily diary made a deep impression on him. The family whakapapa books of which he became the custodian were blueprints for his own recording style. Better transport, more opportunity to socialise with people, and his own enthusiasm for research and love of Māoritanga enabled him to supplement his ancestors' writings.

Golan regarded Māori knowledge as a taonga that should be kept and talked about, so it would stay alive in the minds of the people. This was why he transcribed much material and wrote copious notes. He saw many elders go to the grave without passing on their knowledge, perhaps because of the low regard for things Māori and the lack of interest shown by the next generation in an era when Western values seemed to have prevailed. 'He believed Māori history had lost its place in small-town New Zealand in the mid-twentieth century – it had no place in people's lives.'[348]

In the 1950s Golan, his father-in-law Albert Te Tawhero Stewart, and George Koea, the editor of the *Bay of Plenty Beacon*, resolved to collaborate to write a Māori tribal history. They felt they could produce a better account than any that had been published.[349] However, with the death of Albert Stewart in 1958 the drive to accomplish this task waned. Golan always intended to write a book 'when he found the time'. Instead, time caught up with him, and Dr Maaka passed away on 17 May 1978 at Whakatāne, where he was buried. He was survived by his wife, three daughters, and his whānau.

Te ngākau nui ake a Te Kōrana
Golan's private passion

Dr Maaka's passion for the written record spanned his whole life. His writings in the Maaka Collection take many forms: letters, academic papers, whakapapa books (including traditional narratives, notes and songs), and school notebooks and diaries. He annotated books, made voluminous notes, and wrote papers summarising human history.

As a pupil at Te Aute College, Golan recorded every day of his school life from the age of thirteen in a diary, as well as writing numerous letters to friends and his mother back in Takapau. During his years of study at the University of Otago he continued to fill diaries and books with his daily routines, rugby scores, exam results, historical information, and his opinions on issues affecting New Zealand and Māori people. His habit of diary writing continued even in China, although quite sporadically because of his workload and the dangers he faced. Unfortunately much of the material from his Chinese excursion has been lost. One book that has survived contains hundreds of Chinese words and phrases, their meanings, and information about grammar, as well as notes on Chinese philosophy, traditions, and food, and letters from Chinese acquaintances.

Golan kept a daily diary into the 1940s. These entries record his comments on current events during the Second World War:

> May 8, 1940 – Vote Of No Conf in Chamberlain Following Norwegian Debacle
> May 10, 1940 – Germany Invades Holland, Belgium, Luxembourg. Winston Churchill new P. Min. Chamberlain Resigns
> June 5, 1940 – 350,000 Brit & Fn Troops Get back to Engl from Dunkirk – 30,000 Killed & 1000 guns lost. Paris Bombed – 250 killed.
> June 10, 1940 – Enormous Battle For France 'Cobber' Kain Killed – N.Z. – 40 Planes

After 1941 Golan's diary writing declined, probably because of his heavy medical commitments. Nevertheless, he continued to note important dates and events in his historical writings and elsewhere. He published only one paper during his career as a medical practitioner, on 'Health Trends in the Maori Today', which appeared in the proceedings of the 1959 Young Maori Leaders' Conference and later in the Maori Affairs Department magazine *Te Ao Hou*.[350] Golan's writing became more focused on history, especially that of his tribes of Ngāi Tahu and Ngāti Kahungunu, as well as Ngā Puhi, Waikato and Mataatua. These writings include cosmogonies, songs, histories, genealogies, proverbs, and lists of place names.

Golan loved to summarise the content of books and add corrections and comments. One of his whakapapa books is a 94-page ledger book, 33 × 29 cm, filled with writings on Māori history, including a 17,000-word history of southern Ngāti Kahungunu from the tribe's origin to the 1860s. This was Golan's revision of W. T. Prentice's 'Maori history' of Hawke's Bay,[351] to which he added notes on family history and personal comments over the years. The scribbled corrections and additional information became so extensive that this section was almost unreadable by anyone else. This whakapapa book also included a seventeen-page history of Ngā Puhi, with notes from Percy Smith's *Wars of the Northern Against the Southern Tribes of New Zealand in the Nineteenth Century*;

numerous waiata; whakapapa of Ngāti Kahungunu, Ngāti Awa, Rongowhakaata, Waikato, Rangi-tāne, Waitaha, and Ngāi Tahu; notes on family history; and lists of pā in the Ōhiwa and Manawatū districts.

His collection of published books was extensive. Māori tribal history, English, Russian, American Indian, Byzantine, Jewish, Tibetan, Chinese, Melanesian, Inca, African, Easter Island, Greek and Roman history, science, astronomy, medicine, politics, rugby, transport, poetry, theatre and languages were among the subjects he read and talked about often. It was very rare to find a book of his that he had not written on and filed relevant newspaper clippings in. For example, at the top of page 149 of his copy of Pei Te Hurinui Jones' *King Potatau*,[352] where the death of the Ngā Puhi warlord Pōmare in 1826 at Te Rore on the banks of the Waipā River is recounted, Golan wrote, 'Maize grown at Waikato first came from the seeds found in Pomares stomach.'

Most of his books had comments written inside their covers. In Bertrand Russell's *History of Western Philosophy*, Golan wrote: 'The Russians say "Russell is a philosophising wolf whose dinner jacket conceals the brutal instincts of the beast."' In A. L. Krobber's *Anthropology*, he recorded: 'Jan - 1956 – Dr Konrad Lorenz, & Zoologist USA – I believe I've found the missing link between animal & civilised man – it is us.'

In his copy of George Gamow's *One, Two Three … Infinity: Facts and Speculations of Science*, Golan described the effects of the atomic bomb as he understood them in 1948:

> Atomic bombs can be exploded in the air, under water or at ground level. In the moment of explosion nuclear fission produces a ball of fire which may grow to a diameter of 900' and a temperature of 7000 degrees C. Then comes the blast at a speed of 800 miles per hour and then a counterblast from the opposite direction. The bombs energy is released as radiation – heat – light – which are produced a fraction of a second after the explosion. Five miles away the 'light' is equivalent to that of 100 suns. Following the light (greyish-green) come the gamma rays which have immense power of penetration and are deadly to life … the bomb can flatten 30,000 houses in one smack.[353]

Below this statement Golan wrote, 'Einstein died today – 19-4-55.' Similarly, Golan noted a number of sayings that appealed to him on the inside cover of his copy of T. Sharper Knowlson's *Put on Your Thinking Cap* (a collection of sayings and pithy anecdotes from throughout the ages).

People and relationships were important to him, and he often recorded the names of those he met. On the inside jacket of his copies of Warren Bayliss's *Takapau* he noted all the community's leading families and individuals. He recorded on a large envelope the names of all the Mataatua elders aged 60 and over whom he served as a doctor.

Golan's appetite for knowledge was insatiable. Anything interesting was worth recording. People remember him sitting in his car after attending hui jotting down the speeches and proverbial sayings he had heard on any piece of paper he could find.[354] Golan drew maps and sketches and wrote whakapapa and personal notes on hundreds of scraps of paper, prescription pads, cigarette boxes, envelopes and anything else he could lay his hands on at the time. One such note, headed 'he tino tapu rawa tenei korero; this is very sacred', recorded a series of taiaha movements entitled 'He whakapapa mau rakau' that had been recited to him by an elder in 1927. This information was tapu because an enemy who knew the sequence of your fighting movements could defeat you. Golan believed that if certain people knew he possessed this information, they would 'hit the roof'.[355]

Two of the most moving notes written on his prescription pad paper relate to the diagnosis of his terminal illness and the accidental death of one of his grandsons. On other scraps of paper he noted less important matters that were dear to his heart, such as buying a new car:[356]

> I got a near new Falcon 500 last month, but didn't trade in my rambler which is still a good car – so I will be trying out the falcon on those Taupo-Napier hills.

Golan often used symbols and his own form of shorthand to speed up his note-taking, and perhaps to conserve space. This practice probably began when he took notes at university. He used symbols for the length, pitch and value of the words in waiata, enabling him to remember the contours of songs.

Golan kept his most precious notebook in the top inside pocket of his suit jacket. He wrote in this small (13 × 20 cm) notebook only in Māori. It contains whai-kōrero by prominent people, waiata, letters, the names of stars and phases of the moon, whakapapa, cartoons, Māori war-casualty figures, grammar, lists of words, and hundreds of whakataukī. Much of the material written in this notebook came from personal comments or old articles in Māori newspapers and magazines.

Eventually Dr Maaka's family noticed that their household belongings were slowly being overwhelmed by his notes and books: 'they were piled to the roof'.[357] As his youngest daughter Sandra wrote for his biography:

> Next to eating, Dad loved to read. I would say he bordered on being a genius, Dad was an erudite man; extremely learned … General knowledge was his forté. There was nothing he didn't know. He had a photographic memory, a mind for detail, a thirst for knowledge. Not one newspaper or magazine ever got chucked out. The garage didn't hold the car, it held newspapers and books to the brim. There was nowhere to put anything in our house as it was overflowing with books, newspapers and food. … He knew the history of every country in the world. He studied books on science, medicine, stars and space, but his greatest love was Māori. He studied Māori history, Māori wars, genealogy and Māori language. Every patient who came in he'd ask who they were then proceed to tell them about themselves, or else he would jot down notes of what he didn't know.[358]

Golan's writings show that he had a good grasp of Māori language and tikanga. People seldom heard him speak Māori in public or as a doctor; he felt his professionalism might be questioned if he made a mistake. However, according to his family, he had a genuine passion for the language. Every night Golan studied his father's Māori Bible, not only for its content but to examine its grammar.[359] He was fascinated by the language and its use of metaphor. His writings include compilations of both commonly used words and terms and those of more ancient origin.

To Golan's family, his writings and whakapapa books were tapu. Unlike his grandmother Miriama and aunt Te Rina, he considered Māori knowledge, including his own, to be the domain of men, and would not allow his wife or daughters to have access to this material. Yet it seemed that this privilege was extended to any man. When his nephews visited him in his last years, he saw the chance to impart what he knew. However, there was not enough time for them to absorb such a volume of information. After he became aware that his days were numbered, he relented and began to talk seriously with his daughters. When he was on his deathbed many people asked what would happen to his writings, and advised the family that they should be stored safely. During his tangi, some of his papers were found scattered along the passage of his home, and it became clear that some books and papers had been stolen.[360] Similar incidents have occurred in other Māori families.

While the opportunity to pass down aspects of Golan's life and other knowledge orally was lost, his genealogies, histories and notebooks, as well as those of his parents, grandparents and great-grandparents, were stored in a large suitcase that remained hidden in an inaccessible cupboard for eighteen years. The contents of this book are drawn from this material.

The following extracts from Dr Maaka's diaries, whakapapa books and papers show the progression of his writing. The first, an example of his earliest form of recording, is a sequence of entries from the diary he kept at Te Aute College in 1920. The second piece is an excerpt from his medical thesis on health conditions at Rātana Pā. This is followed by examples of his lists of Ngāti Kahungunu and South Island Ngāi Tahu whakapapa. These selections from his writings give an indication of the path on which his passion for writing took him, from recording daily life in diaries to academic writing and then to keeping tribal knowledge alive.

Te kuratanga

School days

Golan's earliest known writings are the diaries he kept at Te Aute College between 1918 and 1922. It is obvious that his introduction to the world of writing was greatly influenced by his mother Annie. Golan's earliest diary entries are written in a similar style, beginning with a description of the weather and including brief notes on the day's events. This pattern is also evident in the writings of Golan's younger brother, Victor.[361] Boys at the school may have been encouraged to write diaries and memoirs as part of their studies, but it appears this was not usual.

The history of Te Aute College begins in 1847, when the government enacted an Education Ordinance providing funding for Māori schools. Governor Grey persuaded Reverend Samuel Williams of Ōtaki to move to Hawke's Bay to open a school by promising him a 4000-acre endowment of Crown land, a matching gift from local Māori, and an annual grant of £300. Te Hāpuku and other Ngāti Whatu-i-āpiti chiefs duly promised 4000 acres at Pukehou. When the school opened in 1854, boys and girls were taught reading, writing, arithmetic, and the gospel in raupō huts. In 1878 John Thornton was appointed headmaster. Thornton looked forward to the day when Māori would have their own clergymen, doctors and lawyers.[362] The standards he set at Te Aute produced young men who went into offices, the clergy, and interpreting, and others who went on to university. Under Thornton's leadership, the school produced men of the calibre of Sir Āpirana Ngata, Sir Peter Buck, Sir Māui Pōmare, Reverend Reweti Kohere, and Dr Tutere Wīrepa. They and many others worked to improve the situation of Māori, and Te Aute became as well known for its old boys as for its exploits on the rugby field.

When Golan attended Te Aute College, between 1915 and 1922, its headmasters were first Reverend J. A. McNickle, and from 1920 Reverend E. G. Loten. Golan was sent to Te Aute aged ten for disciplinary reasons after being caught committing petty crimes and getting up to other mischief around Takapau.[363] Te Aute was only about 25 miles from his home, but to Golan it seemed like a distant land. He remembered his college years well – for the great comradeship amongst the boys, the rugby, and also the hard times.

As will be seen in the following diary extracts, tending the gardens and milking cows on frosty mornings were daily duties for the boys. 'Elementary practical agriculture' and woodwork were among the most favoured areas of study for Māori boys. John Porteous, the Senior Inspector of Native Schools, noted the importance of agriculture:

> In every school there should be a garden, quite apart from the teacher's own garden, where experimental work is carried out, and where crops suitable for food are grown ... Occasional visits by the teachers to the homes of the children would do much to make the home garden a success, and [be] a means of adding variety to the food-supply of the family.[364]

These sentiments were supported by Loten, who 'proposed to give agricultural training a prominent place in the school curriculum'.[365]

One of Golan's earliest memories of Te Aute was of sitting at his desk next to a 'man'.[366] It was often said of Te Aute pupils in those days that they were 'men', not boys. His desk-mate in 1915 was George Finau, an eighteen year old Samoan.[367] Golan told his family how he was once hung up on a hook in the cloakroom for 'narking' to the masters that one of the elder boys had eaten his porridge. He was not found until the end of the day, almost unconscious and blue from lack of oxygen. Drill and cadet training were part of school life at this time, and Golan remembered having to carry a rifle whose stock made a permanent dent in his shoulder. As a youngster, he often became so tired that older boys carried him on their shoulders.[368]

Many of Golan's memories of his time at Te Aute were not happy ones. He always resented the fact that he was sent away from home at such a young age, and that he was reminded in later years how several families went without to pay for his education.[369] The school was hit by several tragedies while Golan was there. After fires ravaged it in both 1918 and 1919, the boys lived in canvas tents. In November 1918 the influenza pandemic swept through the school. He often found the teachers, Ernest Loten (the headmaster from 1920 to 1951) in particular, to be both cruel and not challenging enough. After trying to win a place at Palmerston North High School, he attended Dannevirke High School from 1922. His disillusionment is obvious in a letter he wrote to his mother:

> My opinion [of this place] is that it's going to blazes ... At present I am having to learn myself English, physiology, geography and history. How am I going to pass if I have to teach myself everything? Besides, I'm wild at Mr Loten, because he jumped down my throat ... So I want to leave this term and I'm going to. It wouldn't be so bad if he spoke to me a bit more civil, but I'm not going to have a little devil like him talking to me like a kid ... If I do leave it will be hard on the boys.[370]

Although his college days brought both hardship and rivalry, it was at Te Aute that his love for recording and writing developed. In addition to his school routines and studies, Golan began to record daily events in a personal diary, a discipline that he continued throughout his secondary and tertiary education. His earliest diary entries show considerable maturity for someone so young. He also began to write letters regularly, perhaps because he felt so far away from family. In his diary he mentions writing to and replying to letters from his brother Vic, his mother, and other close friends and relations. As the years passed his view of the world broadened, and so did his appetite for recording more than just daily activities.

Six of the diaries written while Golan was at school and university have survived, along with three other books that contain lecture notes on Latin, French, physics, anatomy, and medical history and practice. The example which follows is part of his diary for 1920, which was an eventful year for

Golan. Because his father was very sick, his family had shifted to Rotorua and he was alone in Hawke's Bay; yet his school days seem to have been full of important experiences. During the year Golan was promoted to lance-corporal in the cadets, passed his Standard Public Service Entrance exam, and captained the third XV football team which won the Ransom Cup. Perhaps the most significant event was a school trip to Rotorua in April, during the visit of the Prince of Wales. There were also numerous rugby games and many social occasions with the girls of Hukarere College. Golan summed up the year in his diary as 'on the whole … a very pleasant one'.

This diary is an 'Eclipse Day Book', 12 × 30 cm with ruled pages. In addition to daily entries it contains the names of every Te Aute College boy while he was at the school; newspaper clippings about important New Zealand sports events; scores and lists of team members for local, national and international matches; genealogies of the English royal family; the dates of 130 important events in European history, beginning with Julius Caesar's invasion of Britain; poems and songs in Māori and English; lists of the books he read and movies of the time; Māori words and grammar; haka; quotations from *Macbeth* and *Hamlet*; and musical theory. The diary thus gives a snapshot of what Golan was taught as well as of other things that interested him and his peers.

Lists of names – of people he attended school with, played sports with, or met – are an important feature of Golan's writings. He made an effort to show his relationship to each of the names he listed, a practice he was to keep up all his life. While his love of whakapapa was not yet apparent in these early years, his interest in Māori history and language was clear. Golan's diaries are also filled with colourful cartoons of historical characters or images of icons that Golan loved. There are drawings of historical characters such as Genghis Khan, Tāmati Waka Nene, Horomona the blind chief of Waikato, 'Mustapha', Tū-hawaiki, Te Rauparaha, national and international sportspeople, and illustrations of songs and plays, Māori battle scenes, warriors, and war canoes. Newspaper photos of famous Hollywood actors and boxing heroes like Jack Dempsey, Jimmy Wilde and Bombardier Wells are pasted into the pages.

Sport was a major activity amongst Māori people of his day, especially team sports like rugby, hockey and basketball, and also tennis. Games were played in school tournaments and between tribes. Golan's diaries are full of stories about Te Aute old boys and other Māori who excelled at rugby, team lists, and the scores of numerous games played during his school days. For the rest of his life Golan recorded countless team plays and formations of New Zealand All Black, New Zealand Māori and rugby league teams. Many team formations (complete with the weights of players in stones and pounds) and scores appear in the diary.

Te Aute Seniors 1922

Chesley 12.2
Ruru 11.6   Ihaia 10.2   Anaru 10.2
Akuira 11.6   Leach 10
Drummond 10
Forbes 11.10   Tibble 12
Tibble 12.8   Dooley 12.6   Maaka 12
Ruawai 11.10   Wiremu 11.10
Morete 12.6 (Capt)

Te Aute's rugby history was all-important to the boys, who spent hours discussing Māori rugby. Sometimes the school was visited by old boys and other Māori players who had had national or international rugby success – men such as Alex Takarangi and Dawson Nīkera, both New Zealand Māori representatives – who talked to and coached them. Golan chronicled noteworthy Te Aute players – including himself and his brother Victor, whose future feats he humorously predicted:

1880-90	Goldsmith, Wynyards, Ellison, Gage, Paul, Wihapi, Hiroa old Te Aute players who went England in Maori team
1902	R[K]atene a great player & also the greatest pole vault jumper in Australasia. Noted for right angular running
1917–20	Peina Taituha Brilliant 5/8's. Also represented Wanganui Reps and S Maoris & Parata's rugby team 1922
1915, 20	Patana Wihapi a fast wing 3/4 Played for H.B. 1915 and for NZAD in '19 '20. Represented Bay of Plenty Reps. Picked for Parata's team 1922
1924-25	V. Maaka great 'All Black' forward.

1915-22   G. Maaka – Worlds most brilliant 3/4 Go like a Greyhound, nippiest, trickiest, softest, greatest strategist ever seen in shorts – indomitable tackler like a brick wall – very dangerous fend – can side step his way thro' a whole team – his feinting passes too wonderful to describe – fools them every time – lost count of all the points he has scored – very dangerous when aroused – played for All Blacks, Spring Boks, Wallabies & Barleycorns (& Takapau) – also world XV.

Golan's diaries are filled with the names of great boxers and accounts of fights. Māori and Pākehā had sometimes fought each other in country areas like Waimārama.[371] Two cups from Golan's period are still competed for at the school, the Te Aute College Boxing Competition Cup, presented by Tuahine Rēnata, which was first won by Pine Taiapa in 1920, and the T. Kuru and Son Challenge Cup.[372] Golan's love of boxing later widened to include wrestling, and he became the doctor on hand at all the boxing and wrestling bouts held around Whakatāne.

At university Golan continued to write in his diary each day, but after he married and became a full-time doctor this practice waned. In his later years, Golan's Te Aute diaries were one of his most precious possessions. He delighted in reflecting on his school days, and often sat around the fire with his daughters reminiscing.[373]

A transcription of selected diary entries for 1920 follows. Where possible, boys mentioned in the text are identified in footnotes.

Te Aute College Days
Diary entries for 1920

March 18th	Plenty work all day. Flue 25 boys in bed.
March 19th	Caught flue Stayed in bed. Wills h.
March 20th	Shifted into No.2[374] Got letter from Tu & P
March 21st	About 40 boys in bed.
March 22nd	Still bad. Mum went through to Napier £5. Mr Bennett.[375]
March 23rd	Removed into tent.
March 24th	Nice day. Had kai in tent got parcel.
March 25th	Raided chapel – hill Apples.[376]
March 26th	Had last feed in tent Removed. 1st footy meeting.
March 27th	Started work. Built fence for Mr Scully.[377]
March 28th	Walk. Took apples from village church yard.
March 29th	Had school. Received uniforms. Game 1st season.
March 30th	Practice, run, shower, Game. T. Tibble[378] dislocated his arm.
March 31st	Practice Searched lockers.
Thursday April 1st	Had no fun like 1917 Nice day.
April 2nd	Huiki's birthday.
April 3rd	Picnic Easter Same gang Good feed Dance.
April 4th	I am 16 years to-day. Chapel Nice day.
April 5th	No school Nice day Easter Monday Peeling fruit.
April 6th	Game School Nice day. Practising Chaddo's box[379]
April 7th	TeK Practising. School Letter from Mum & 1 from Vic.[380]
April 8th	Wet day Practising. Wrote letter to Mum.
April 9th	Uniforms Drill.
April 10th	Work. Dance theory on music Dance.
April 11th	Sunday. Chapel Nice walk Night service chapel.
April 12th	In wash Recieved letter from Mum & Vic Game.
April 13th	Eric Cambell[381] came. Training and game. Cold day.
April 14th	Cold day. TeK
April 15th	Fine day. Inspected for sores.
April 16th	Drill. Hot day. Test on all subjects. Came 4th – 71.7.
April 17th	Beaten by Pirates 42 to 5. They had tea here. Dance
April 18th	Chapel as usual. Went out on trolleys 5 miles. Night service.
April 19th	Drizzly day. Recieved news about Prince's visit.[382] Music lesson.
April 20th	Fine day. Practise. Matamua etc came back.[383] News about Rotorua Only 40 allowed.[384]
April 21st	Packed up TeK. Hair cut. Cold day.

April 22nd	Left Pukehou, Huks[385] Slept on train.
Friday April 23rd	Arrived at Rotorua Had great reception. Haka by old men. Frosty morning Carried luggage around found tent Dance. Met Narty Wemyss. Nice girl. Saw Ngahuia & Harriet.[386] Footy. Beat old boys 3-0.
April 24th	Went home.[387] Waerenga[388] boys came Visited home. Morning bath. Saw Mum in Wanganui tent. Narty & I went out.
April 25th	Service in open air. Parade. Went around Ohinemutu. Work. Saw Tuhaka. Waerengahika blokes beat 3rds by 8 to 5.
April 26th	Work. Concert in large marquee. Dance Olga Nicholson sang.
April 27th	Y.M.C.A boxing etc. Plenty work. Plenty old boys Nice day. Went home. Narty Fred Horrie & I went out.
April 28th	Rainy day. Prince's visit postponed. Football. Wanganui Maori practice. Dance. Narty and I went to Ohinemutu
April 29th	Prince visited us, inspected us, Hakas, pois etc Addresses. Kiwis entertained us in Y.M.C.A. Thousands of Maoris.
April 30th	Loafed around pah. Practised football went home to Ohinemutu. Dance in marquee. Saw Harriet Haenga Mick & I went for bath.
May 1st	Had our photo taken on aeroplane Narty, Thompson free pictures in marquee. Dance. Mr Bennet[389] took us around Ohinemutu. Wanganui v. Ngapuhi. Narty & I went to pictures. Thompson & Lora.
May 2nd	Tommy Wakarua[390] & I went to sanatorium. Went home. Concert and dance. Lecture on football by Takarangi[391] Mr Loten[392] with us & Huks. Mr Bennett took us around Whakarewa Ancient pah. Free pictures.
May 3rd	Packed up Said Goodbye to Narty. Left with South Maoris. 4 p.m Rain Saw Mum & Pup[393] on station. Nice trip. Huks came with us Chocs from Hara.
May 4th	Arrived at Palm.[394] 9 a.m. Saw Prince Left 2 p.m. Paul B & I bought stuff. Saw Jimmie Heperi Arrived Home 7.15 pm. Goodbye to Huks school.
May 5th	Cold day Digging spuds.[395] Boys went to Waipuk.[396] Jun v Sen
May 6th	Cold morn. Training. Started school. Game. Letter from Harriet.
June 15	Nice day. Practice down field. Memorable evening, 5 old boys, Mr Tomoana, Nikera etc singing and hakaing etc.[397] Came down to coach team. Eric Hemi and I went – over Pukenui.
June 16	Teck, Dodged in loft with Bill Waka.[398] Letter from Tuhaka.
June 17	First Term Exam English, Dict & arith. 3rd and 4th had game.
June 18	Cadet test – Made lance corp. Contin of exam. Science, Latin Nice day.
June 19	Dull day. Seniors beat H.S.O.B 9 to 3, Juniors drew with Pirates 3 to 3 – at Napier. Thirds had practice downfield. Hemi & I went over to Mr Warrens. Had fun with an inebriate.
June 20	About 20 boys at communion this morn. Hemi, Peter & I went to lake on trolley.[399] Service at night by Rev. Bennett.
June 21	Cold day. Continued our exam. Plenty cars came up. Including Tira Went over Pukenui Boys picked for Palmeston Swagger died in station Allan Davidson visited boys
June 22	Drizzly day. Went on to milking. Peter gave me 21 – Boys went on to Palmerston North. Hulton[400] & I carted luggage down. Did a bit of work.
June 23	Another wet day We had some fun down field. Seniors beat Wanganui 14 to 8 Had game of cards etc in Mr Hamlin's. Juniors drew with Wanganui 6 all.[401] Had Autumn dinner Boxing etc.
June 24	Milked cows late Got out of bed at 8.30 Had plenty of work. Dull day. Killed 8 hens Boys came back. No dance.
June 25	Wet day Got out 8.30. No school Fooled around doing nothing.
June 26	Chaddy and I went home to Tak[402] Saw Pup, Rina & Phoebe, Vic & Marky. Bill Wakarua went past on express. Saw Reihana, Pene, came on express from Hikurangi.[403] Went to pictures, slept with Chaddy.
June 27	Went over to Pup[404] & co. Wet day. Stayed at Rongo played cards etc Vic and I had some fun Met Rangi Ellis, saw old Peggy. Sam told us some yarns etc Slept with Chaddy again.

June 28	Came back to school Drizzly day Said au revoir to Vic & Pup and Marky Vic and Marky went back to Rotorua Letter from Ila Barret sessions on plant pathology. Had practice
June 29	Nice day Swept school room. No school this morning Architestariast came down and made plan of building. Bought pies Shifted on to Peter's table Letter to Ila Barrett.
June 30th	Pup went past but I didn't see him Milked cows etc Thirds beat Waipawa N.S. by 35 to 0 Nice day No prep Wrote to Harriet.
July 1st	No school Frosty morning We went down to the wool shed to clean it. Mr Loten gave us lessons on pruning Thirds and juniors had a pretty good game.
July 2nd	Dull day. Left the 3rd team. Motor lorry capsized. Practice as usual. Pup left for Rotorua from Takapau Prefects dance down wool shed, played a few tunes.
July 3rd	Hot day. 9 boys came back. Lorry, Holton & I worked a lot this morning Had a feed with priests Seniors beaten by Pirates 11 to 8, Juniors beat Napier High 23 to 3. Thirds played 1st game for Ransom Cup. Thirds beat Hastings High 35 to 3.
July 4th	Rotten day. Service in chapel. New boy Jury Ron came yesterday. Wrote to Victor returned to 3rds Went for walk milked cows. Mr Spencer took service at village church.
July 5th	Went out training Very foggy day gardening. Began school work again. Had practice down field Watson & Tareha came back fog all day. Letter from Ila Barret.
July 6th	Dull day Worked on pots this morning Edmonds, Knock, Mataku came back Mr Spencer came to school for the last day Received lollies from Vic. Had nice game tonite.
July 7th	Teck. this morn. Wakarua, Hemi & I dodged in loft. Cleaned bloomin pots. Practice this morning Davey came back. Did a bit of sewing Nice day Practice this afternoon.
July 8th	Foggy day. Played against juniors tough game. Beaten 20 to nil. Saw Mick Pup got pneumonia again. Had first bath for about a fortnight. Lollies stolen.
July 9th	Another drizzly day Drill tday We were introduced to Rev Simpkins & his wife. Reverend Arthur Williams took us for scripture. To meeting of 3rd team. Received our pugarers.
July 10th	Wet day HS teams didn't come down. Did nothing in. Juniors went to Takapau & played Dannevirke High School. They beat Dann. 18 to 6. Went for mail with Chambers.
July 11th	Fair day. Chapel service taken by Rev Arthur Will' Ihaia Katene Chaddy & I went for walk. Served at village church.
July 12th	Nice day Went home to Takapau Nice day. Pup was very ill. Slept with him at home. Bloomin' dry show now.
July 13th	Windy day. Mum, Marky, Henry & Nancy arrived 9 a.m. Victor stayed at Rotorua Pup much better Slept in front room. Saw J...[illegible]
July 14th	Said goodbye to Pup. Mrs Hapuku went to Opapa Came back to school Marky & Froggie went to Waipuk Thirds beat Napier High 11 to 3 A tough go.
July 15th	Nice day Had school Worked off black mark[405] Helped matron to pack up. Clothes sent into the wash Peter Ihaia broke his collar bone
July 16th	Drill today Lovely day Rev, Arthur Williams to scripture. Matron left school after being 7 years on staff Gave speech Had a bit of practice. Meeting in Mr Hamlins. Shop 2/6.
July 17th	Gardening this morning dug up at the rear garden Thirds beat Waipawa High 12 to 3 Hang of a tough go. Juniors beaten. M.B.O.B. 18 to 0 Seniors beaten by A.S.O.B 19 to 15.
July 18th	Chapel service taken by Deane Mayne very interesting. Went for a walk bloomin cold day Village church tonight Fred & I went for a walk down South Road.
July 19th	Rīwai[406] & I worked at the front of matrons Nice day Practice as usual Gardening this afternoon Was sis had a sqrint around Mr Takarangi arrived.
July 20th	Paul B[407] & I finished in front of matrons Nice day Had practice downfield Letter from Victor Had a nice game, Received clothes.
July 21st	Very important event happened today Civil service class planted trees down football ground Received a letter from old Piripi Nearly broke my arm today TecK

July 22nd	Hang of a cold day Walker,[408] Matamua, Thompson & I dug spuds down field Thirds beat Juniors by 29 to 14 Seniors left for Gisborne for King's Cup
July 23rd	Cold morning Tipi[409] & I did a bit of planting Drill Had good fun Sports etc. Did nothing in afternoon but had a game
July 24th (Saturday)[410]	New boy came Shop Letter to Vic & Piripi Seniors beat Gisborne High by 11 to 3 Thirds & Juniors had a rough game...
July 25th	Village church this morning Mr Hamlin on duty Peter Ihaia & I bought apples etc Nice day Mr Bennett took night service in chapel
July 26th	Had a hang of a boil on my jaw Thirds and juniors had game also some relay races etc School around oven Nice day.
July 27th	Lovely day Training this morn Removed piano into Scullys Relay races down field FIRST TIME AEROPLANE FLEW OVER T.A.C.
September 9th	P Service class. Had communion in chapel with ministers. Pine Tamahori[411] gave us a private talk in the school Men to be proud of Had music lesson Had a hit of cricket Service.
September 10th	Nice day No school this afternoon Boys had photos taken on top lawn Thompson, Leach and us did some snap shots Ministers were over here staying with us. Saw Pirihira – got 5/-
September 11th	Worked this morning Dull day Julian and I went to shop Huiki & Hemi went to Hastings Played Cricket & Tennis all afternoon Polish gone Had dance tonight in school room
September 12th	Another dull day Service in chapel Hemi, Mc & I finished pears. McPherson, Paul & I cooked eggs in kitchen Nearly caught Service at village church at night
September 13th	Rained today Huiki came back Started to study for exam Old Scott Stewart went back to Otago Pirates won H.B. sheild Received a letter from Piripi Gardening, gravelling road, Peina & I
September 14th	Another wet day Got up pretty early to study Clothes from wash arrived Gave out clothes Juniors didn't play High School Had a snorter bath. Mr Loten gave us poetry books.
September 15th	Hang of a cold afternoon Found my lost ypres brooch in loft Sent in clothes to be washed Wood work Atkins & I dodged Received my shorts from nurse.
September 16th	Nice day Built a hut over the bank Got another boil on my jaw Juniors went down – practicing for their game against High School next week Sent a letter to Victor.
September 17th	Very nice day Worked on top Tennis lawn. Jack Bennett gave us instructions on musketry. Marked out the lines on the lawn Choir practice tonight Boys got a bit rowdy.
September 18th	Stayed back. Nothing unusual happened Funny day Cleaned dormitories Boys went out eeling Timihou & Buller got into a row[412] Tennis season opened.
September 19th	Nice day Chapel Went up to communion, unshaven & shorn Peter, Katene, Chaddy & I had feed of biscuits from priests Service in chapel, South Road. Had a good time there
September 20th	Dull day Gained a bit this afternoon Tennis, Gardening Had some fun during prep. Pine gave us a lecture of his trip through Africa etc! Practiced on bar.[413]
September 21st	Another dull & wet day Had a nice bath Peter & I went for a walk down to Priests Standard 7 had cricket this afternoon Practised some stunts on the bar
November 1st	One of the coldest days Very windy Boys went to Otane selling tickets Did nothing of any importance Studied a bit Practise for concert
November 2nd	Nice day Had some fun in dormitory. pillow fighting boys Concert went and gave performance at Otane Waikau & I had a game of tennis Girl died at Hukarere.
November 3rd	No early school this morning Had good old fat for Tea Blokes except for Public Service had tech Letter from Vic. Funny bloomin day Did a bit of studying.
November 4th	Had a nice bath Stunner day Shooting pretty good So far Mackey = 101 out 115.[414] Chaps played tennis as usual. Mosquitoes galore hanging around.
November 5th	Nice day Pretty tired after days work Guy Fawkes day Cadets school & 3 teams had photos taken Had shooting for marksmens badge

November 6th	Another nice day Worked black mark off this afternoon Sparks had a row Sam Ruawai.[415] Dancing abolished Had tennis this afternoon & school & prep tonight.
November 7th	Dull day Chapel this morn Evensong village church Two eggs each Hulton Katene & I went for a walk. Peter Barn & Chaddy also came. Hemi Winters[416] & I went & pinched some oranges from Williams
November 8th	Dull day Had game of tennis Rangi Rupuha[417] went on car Sent clothes into wash Bloomin mosquitoes still going strong Sent letter to mum. Lost my key
November 9th	School this morning as usual Sam Ruawai & I to Dr Jarvis Had a nice bath Bloomin mosquitoes on offensive Tennis all this afternoon
November 10th	Nice day School as usual Stole back my belt Mr Loten was doing planting spuds Chaps had tech. P.S.E. chaps worked by themselves
November 11th	ARMISTICE DAY. 2nd Anniversary Marched and saluted flag 12 of us attended Mrs Hedleys funeral 2 min silence Nice day Aspinall & co gave us an exhibition on muscles.
November 12th	Nice day No. 4 or 5 dorm had practise In strong for team 4, 5,6, details finished shooting Shooting was very nice Made highest marks in school (105 out of 115) Nice Prep.

Rapu mātauranga

Academic study

This example of Golan's writing was motivated by his need to reach the high level of knowledge and understanding that was required to qualify as a doctor. Golan studied medicine at his father's wish; it was not his preferred vocation. He attended the University of Otago from 1925 until 1932, when he completed his studies. He received his MB ChB degrees in 1937. While Golan was at Otago, he wrote mainly academic papers, and eventually completed a thesis, 'Ratana Pa: A General Survey of Conditions at Ratana from a Public Health Perspective', as part of his medical degree.

The Rātana movement was well-established by Golan's university years. His family attended the celebrations and hui at Rātana Pā for many years, for both political and religious reasons. The movement had begun after Tahupotiki Wiremu Rātana had a vision in November 1918 in which the 'Wairua Tapu' (Holy Ghost) appointed him as the 'Mangai' ('Mouthpiece of God') to unite the Māori people and turn them to Jehovah. Later Rātana had a vision in which an angel repeated this message and added that he should 'destroy the power of the *tohunga* and … cure the spirits and bodies of his people'.[418] His reputation as a prophetic leader and faith healer rose, and Māori and Pākehā alike began referring to him as the 'Maori miracle man'. People travelled from all over the country to hear him preach. Tents and shacks proliferated at what became Rātana Pā, between Turakina and Whangaehu in the lower Rangitīkei district. By 1921, Rātana had 19,000 followers.[419] After establishing his church, Rātana became involved in politics, eventually cementing a strong liaison with the Labour Party.

At the time Golan wrote his thesis, many within the movement distrusted outsiders:

> Comradeship is one of the features of Ratana life – everybody being hail-fellow well-met and that sort of thing, although black sheep or outsiders (like myself) were viewed with a certain amount of suspicion. Though never with ill feeling.[420]

Because Wiremu Rātana and his people shunned publicity, it was difficult to observe or criticise the movement. According to family tradition, Golan asked a close relative who was a Rātana adherent to help him with his research. The pair attended hui at Rātana Pā, and Golan's relative also told him about the workings of the community. The two often rode a motorcycle around the area to see the sights and discuss health-related issues. By gathering information in this unusual manner as well as through family visits, Golan acquired enough material to write his thesis. In later years he told his whānau that he had seen many people restored to health, and believed in Rātana's healing powers.[421]

Family sources say that after he had finished writing his thesis, Golan asked his medical supervisors for a private audience, rather than making his findings public in the usual way. He realised that there might be repercussions for both himself and his whānau if the Rātana movement discovered that he had made this study without their permission. It is believed that his supervisors agreed to this request.

Parts of the thesis were published in Golan's biography. The following extract, from pages 50 to 53 of the thesis, outlines his observations on the general cleanliness of the people and the diseases that were prevalent at Rātana Pā.

An extract from 'Ratana Pa: A General Survey of Conditions at Ratana from a Public Health Perspective'

General Cleanliness and Habits of the people and diseases.

Clothing:- On the subject of clothing one cannot make any dogmatic statements. Some of the people are very clean and neat and pay particular attention to their general appearance. This applies more especially to the more educated. On the other hand, many of the people just wander around in any old thing – especially the men. Weather conditions hardly seems to concern them at all. Many of the younger men are particularly careless in this respect. On a very cold day they may be seen wandering around quite happily in a pair of old dungarees and a football jersey. In warm weather they are swathed up to the neck in singlets, cardigans and other apparel. Many pay the penalty by acquiring various chest complaints especially bronchitis. Their taste in colour and the cut of their clothing leans towards the bizarre, as a rule.

Most of the older women wear loosely fitting garments, consisting of a long skirt and a blouse. Many do not wear boots or shoes but tramp around barefooted. A handkerchief tied over the head serves as a sort of bonnet. The colours of these garments are bright and manifold.

The younger women are very particular about their attire and in general, dress very well and sensibly.

The general standard of cleanliness is high and the women spend a good deal of time at the wash tub. The children are well cared for, in fact too well cared for.

The question of bed clothing and mattresses is important. The people use too many blankets and fur rugs. Far more than is needed. They sleep huddled together in the one room, this providing an excellent opportunity for the spread of the different afflictions that exist amongst them – especially hakihaki and tuberculosis. This overcrowding probably accounts for the high incidence of tuberculosis amongst the Maori people. Other factors such as a hereditary weakness, also seems to play a part, although some authorities assert that the people are very resistant to tuberculosis, being immunised by sub minimal dosage. I saw one very bad case of acute pulmonary T.B. there. The patient (a young man in his twenties) was very ill but continued to move about amongst the people, coughing huge lumps of phlegm everywhere and eating out of the same utensils. Many had other TB lesions but the figures would be difficult to ascertain unless a medical man were stationed there.

Various dermatatic diseases are seen – especially the skin diseases scabies or hakihaki. It consists of a popular and vesicular eruption which commences between the fingers, in front of the wrist and other parts of the body within easy reach of the hands and is due to an itch acarus. Great itching is caused especially at night. By their mode of living, it can easily spread at Ratana but little can be done in the line of treatment due to the lack of baths. It can be prevented by the adoption of the ordinary measures of personal hygiene i.e. the wearing of clean clothes and using one's own bed clothes and towel.

Sulphur baths and the free use of sulphur ointment and washing this off in the mornings and then donning clean clothing – these precautions soon cure it. Proper disinfection of the bed clothes and ordinary clothes could be carried out by washing in hot water (120°F) with soft soap and leaving them to soak for three hours or so in some disinfectant (1.1000 Mercury Perchlor). The old Maori cure for it was the use of an infusion from leaves of the ngaio tree.

Such diseases as Typhoid and Dysentery are quite rare at Ratana. Typhoid caused great mortality amongst the people once but the breaking up of the old pahs and the better standard of living have greatly reduced the incidence of this disease. The people cannot spend too much attention on such matters as proper disposal and destruction of rubbish and drainage. Inoculation with T.A.B. vaccine has also reduced the prevalence of typhoid. The old Maori remedy was to drink flax juice, with disastrous results.

Eye diseases (especially a variety of Trachoma) and goitre and other diseases are quite common. The latter being more common amongst the inland people. The eating of seaweed (or Karengo) by the coastal tribes must have some effect in keeping down the incidence of goitre there.

With regard to trachoma it is very prevalent. One Maori doctor goes so far as to say two thirds of the population have some form or other of Trachoma or Conjunctivitis. The conjunctiva becomes red and inflamed and in more severe cases there is a muco purulent discharge. It is a noticeable disease. The people just do not bother about it and just let it go on from bad to worse. The ordinary method of dissolving a teaspoon of boracic acid powder in a cup of hot water and then leaving this to cool and later using it as an eyewash is the most practicable method if dealing with it.

Combined with this, the people should avoid sitting in stuffy and smoke filled rooms and avoid using other people's towels.

The various bronchitic and rheumatic diseases are also frequently seen – all due to their careless and happy go lucky style of living.

Regarding the old Maori methods of dealing with disease, this was left to the hands of the 'tohunga' – a combined priest and doctor and his method of treatment was purely empirical. His business was to expel the evil spirit or atua. This was done by reciting magic incantations and the use of various herbs and concoctions.

Ngā Whakapapa
The genealogies

Dr Maaka's greatest love was whakapapa. Having seen the richness of the written whakapapa that were handed down to Golan and others of his generation, we can understand why he would carry on the tradition. Many of the genealogies he wrote down were copied from books or committed to memory in conversations with elders. Many are written in one of the styles used by his elders – tāhū, whakamoe or karapitipiti. However, he also used Pākehā-style charting, perhaps to enable him to explain relationships more clearly to others.[422] Setting out ancestral relationships in family trees and charts took much less time than the old way of discussing them for hours or days.

Whenever Golan heard kōrero about ancestors or links that were unknown to him, he would rush home to record this information and compare it with what he already knew. The same genealogical lines are written down in books and on pieces of paper umpteen times. The act of writing down the same lineage many times, while compiling information or during explanatory conversations with his family, helped keep the material alive and accurate.

Golan's writings are full of lineages from many tribes which trace the lines to people with whom he was personally acquainted. He habitually wrote the genealogies of people mentioned in the text inside his books of Māori history. For example, Golan's copy of Jack Mitchell's *Takitimu* is almost completely covered in whakapapa showing his genealogical connections to specific stories in this book. His treasured first edition copies of *Nga Moteatea*, *The Life and Times of Patuone*, *Old Wairoa*, *Tuhoe: The Children of the Mist*, and *Takapau: The Sovereign Years* are filled with notes recording his genealogical ties to people and subjects mentioned in these books. Later in life Golan began to compile whakapapa in large scrapbooks. Hundreds of pieces of paper with whakapapa notes scribbled on them were found in his collection. Eventually he filled four scrapbooks with genealogies and hundreds of short notes which had not been organised when he died.

The lists which follow are randomly chosen examples of genealogical tables pertaining to his Ngāti Kahungunu and Ngāi Tahu (Southland) lines, and those of his wife. These tables have been transcribed exactly as they were written. Abbreviated words are explained in footnotes, while my additions or corrections appear inside square brackets. Names indented from the left-hand margin are those of children of the ancestor(s) named on the previous line. Symbols such as 'm', '-', '=' and 'm-' all mean 'married'.

A Ngāi Tangimoana line

Te Rupepae
Pekapekaiharorangi
Tukauika
Tane Mahuta
Tokerautawhiri
Rata
Ratawhare
Hotunuku
Hoturangi
Hotuariki
Hotupotae
Hoea
Maira
Whakarongo
1　Tangimoana
Moeahu
Tuhoropunga
2　Tangimoana
Parari
Te Rangiapu
Te Aketahi
Te Uinga
Tohungaio
Whanga-taua
Maaka
Aritaku
Te Korana
Na Te Aomatarahi
Ko Rongomairaukura raua ko tona teina ko Te Aowhakaari he whanautahi enei
Na Te Rongomairaukura
Ko Tuterangikapake
Ko Hinetapuharau
Ko Hinekatonga
Ko Te Mahaki
Ko Ngahu = Pango
Ko Turaki = Wharemau
Ko Ataneta Matariki = Whangataua
Ko Maaka
Ko Aritaku
Ko Te Korana

Ngāti Kahungunu lines

Hinetahurangi – Pungatoroa
Pito – Ngaitaiaio
Rere – Tuangahuru
Karotai – Tato

Rongokako – Muriwhenua

Kahukurakotore	Rongorongo	Tamateakaiariki	Uhengaariki ara ko Tamateaurehaea

Whakamarama i nga wahine a o tatou tupuna me nga tamariki matamua a
ia wahine Ko Tamatea e ono ana wahine i whai uri katoa:

1 Onoonoiwaho
    Whaene male – lived at Mangatawa (Tauranga)
2 Ihuparapara
3 Moanaikauia
    1 Ranginui
    2 Kino
    3 Haumanga
4 Iwi-pupu
    Kahu-ngunu
5 Tanewhare
    Tamakopiri
6 Kahuhokere
    Ruaehu

Ko Kahungunu e whitu ana wahine
    1 Ko Hinetapu
    2 Ko Hinepuariari
    3 ko Kahukurawaiari
    4 Ko Te Hautaruke
    5 Ko Ruareretai
    6 Ko Pouwharekura
    7 Ko Rongomaiwahine

[Na Rongomaiwahine
Ko Kahukuranui]
Ko Rakai-hiku-roa
E wha nga wahine a Rakaihikuroa
1 Papauma
    Ko Hineraumoa
2 Ruarauhanga
Ko Hineteraraku
3 Turoimata
    Ko Tuwhakawhiurangi
4 Kaahu
    Kaore he uri
Ko [Tu]Whakawhiu-rangi – Hinekura
Ko Te Rangitahia – Te Haukakawa
Hinearorangi – Rakaunui
1 Ko Tamaru
2 Ko Hineiri
3 Ko Tumurirangi
1 Ko Tamaru moe i a Heitaramea
Ko Te Kekehu – nohomaiterangi
Ko Te Kaiopetaua – Whakaangi
Ko Ngaoko – Parahouhou
Ko Tuhua – Hinewaoriki
Ko Hiraka – Arihia etc

3   Ko Tumurirangi moe i a Whakatopa
Ko Te Matehaunganui – Te Rangikawhiua (he mokopuna na Te Whatuiapiti)
Ko Te [E]kitea – Te Urungapaewai
   1   Ko Te Rangipupuonuku
   2   Ko Te Pataoterangi
1   Ko Te Rangipupuonuku moe i a Te Opekai
   1   Ko Te Iwikaingata (Tiro)[423]
   2   Ko Parahouhou
   3   Ko Ngapuoterangi
1   Ko Te Iwikaingata moe i a Tohungaio
   1   Ko Ngahoka
   2   Ko Whangataua
1   Ko Ngahoka – Pipi
Ko Potau – Hipora
Ko Ataneta – Hohepa
Manahi Paewai etc

2   Na Whangataua moe i a Ataneta Matariki
1   Te Rangiwhaiata[424]
2   Ko Inia Whanga-taua
3   Maaka – Miriama

Aritaku

Kahungunu
Kahukuranui
Rakaihikuroa
Rangitawhiao
Paero
Tamateuru
Te Rautuotawhaki
Kahuturoa
Te Rangitekahutia
Tataku
Rangiwhitiki (Rangihoutihi)
Tohungaio
Whangataua
Maaka
Aritaku
Te Korana

Kahungunu
Kahukuranui
Hinemanuhiri
Tamaterangi
Rakaihakeke
Okuratawhiti
Tapuwae
Rangituanui
Rangikawhiua
Kautuku
Hineaka
Te Arahe
Tira
Herapohue – Hakaraia
Miriama
Aritaku
Te Korana

Na Tapuwae
Matakaingaitetihi
Kahuoterangi
Wairau – Ngete
Te Paihau – Inumia
Te Heiwaiarangitoheriri
Te Paihau
Hiria
Adeline
Ramari = Te Korana

Ko Tapuwae
Matakaingaitetihi
Te Kahuoterangi
Wainoho[u]
Ngapotakirau
Te Aotarewha
Mawete
Te Kitea
Parikoau
Te Iwikaingata
Whangataua
Maaka Whanga-taua
Aritaku Maaka
Te Korana

A Te Arawa line

Tamatekapua
Kahumatamomoe
Takotomoetaharangi
Uenuku – Punehu
Rangitihi – Papawharanui
Tuhourangi – Rongomaipapa[425]
Hapuriri – Tamahineterangi
Hapokerekere – Te Kuramaringi
Haumanga – Hineteuira
Houmearoa – Te Aomatarahi
Rongomaipureora
   1 Ko Hinengaki
   2 Ko Te Ikaraeroa
2 Te Ikaraeroa m Rakaitekura
Tumapuhiarangi & Te Angiangi
Hikatoa
Ruatotara
Mauriuri m – Utamoana
Te Puha m – Matioro
Hakaraia = m Hera
Miriama
Aritaku

Southern Ngāi Tahu whakapapa

Rongokako
Tamatea
Kahungunu
Kahukuranui
Rakaihikuroa
Tamanuhiri
Tamawhakatina
Tamaihuporo
Rakaitekura = Te Aohikuraki
Tuahuriri

Na Tutekawa

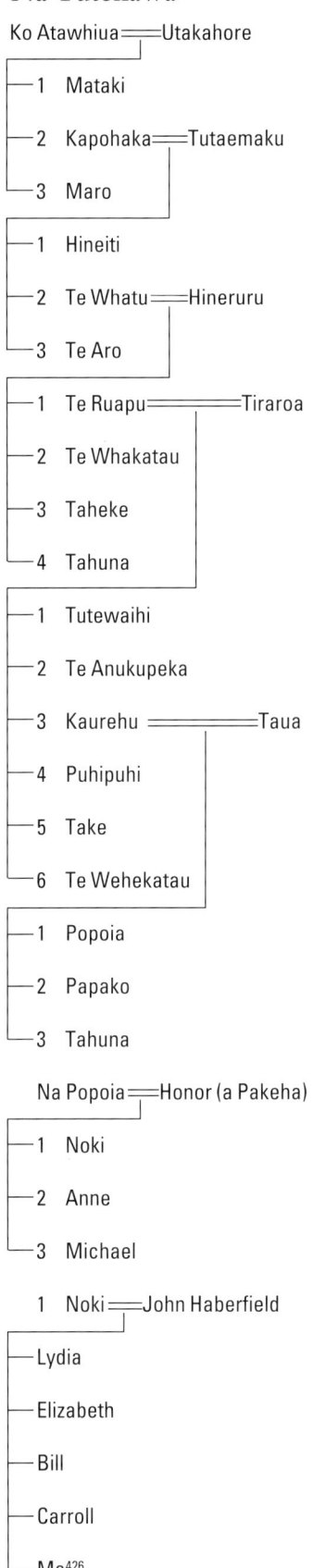

Ko Atawhiua ══ Utakahore
— 1 Mataki
— 2 Kapohaka ══ Tutaemaku
— 3 Maro
— 1 Hineiti
— 2 Te Whatu ══ Hineruru
— 3 Te Aro
— 1 Te Ruapu ══ Tiraroa
— 2 Te Whakatau
— 3 Taheke
— 4 Tahuna
— 1 Tutewaihi
— 2 Te Anukupeka
— 3 Kaurehu ══ Taua
— 4 Puhipuhi
— 5 Take
— 6 Te Wehekatau
— 1 Popoia
— 2 Papako
— 3 Tahuna

Na Popoia ══ Honor (a Pakeha)
— 1 Noki
— 2 Anne
— 3 Michael

1 Noki ══ John Haberfield
— Lydia
— Elizabeth
— Bill
— Carroll
— Ma[426]

Na Atawhiua = Tupuku
Kopiri
Takaoteraki
Pitorua
Waipunahau
Tutu
Whakatitiro
Piki
Tete
John
Ani
Korana

Na Paikea
Tahupotiki
Iraatahu
Rakatehurumanu
Nukuroa
Tamateakaimatua
Toiteuatahi
Te Waiwai
Ruakaito
Tamawhakatina
Tamaihuporo
Rakaitekura
Tuahuriri = Hinetewai
Turakautahi = Hinekakai
Urihia = Hineari
Tamaio = Hinewaitutu
Whakaro = Nuku
Mumuhako = Whakaka
Paahi = Piki
Tete[427]

Ko Turakautahi = Tawharepapa
Rakiamoa
Tupai
Tutu
Whakatitiro
Piki
Tete

Na Tutemanatia
Maika
Tutekawa
Te Atawhiua
Kopiri
Takaoteraki
Pitorua
Te Waipunahau
Tutu
Whakatitiro
Piki
Tete

Na Tutemanatia
Paerata
Kohairua
Rakaihoropito
Whaki
Hineumutahi
Korehore
Tutemakohu
Nuku
Mumuhako
Paahi
Tete

Na Tuahuriri
Turakautahi
[Nā] Turakautahi = Hinekakai
   1 Urihia
   2 Kaweriri
1 Ko Urihia = Hineari
Tamaio = Hinewaitutu
   1 Te Hikutu
   2 Hinutere
   3 Whakaaro
3 Ko Whakaaro
Mumuhako
Paahi
Tete
John
Ani
Golan

2 Ko Kaweriri
Te Wera
Te Puhiarakaiora
Maka
Whakaka
Paahi
Tete
John
Ani[428]
Golan

A cartoon drawn and sent to Dr Maaka by Mr Haeusler of Whakatāne. Maaka Collection

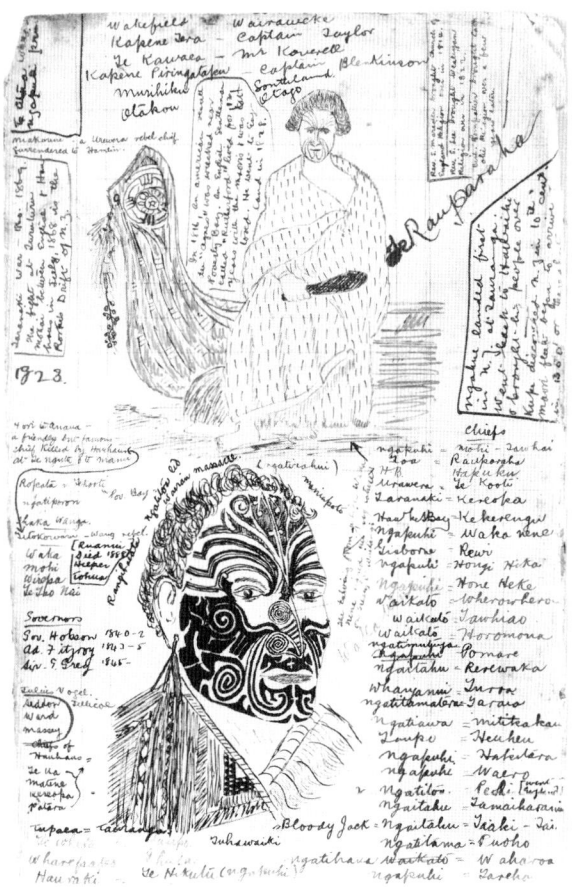

A section of Golan Maaka's notebook. Maaka Collection

Doctor Golan Haberfield Maaka. Maaka Collection

Te Aute College songs recorded in Golan's diary.
Maaka Collection

A page of Golan's diary for 1920. Maaka Collection

Golan Maaka at Te Aute College, about 1920.
Maaka Collection

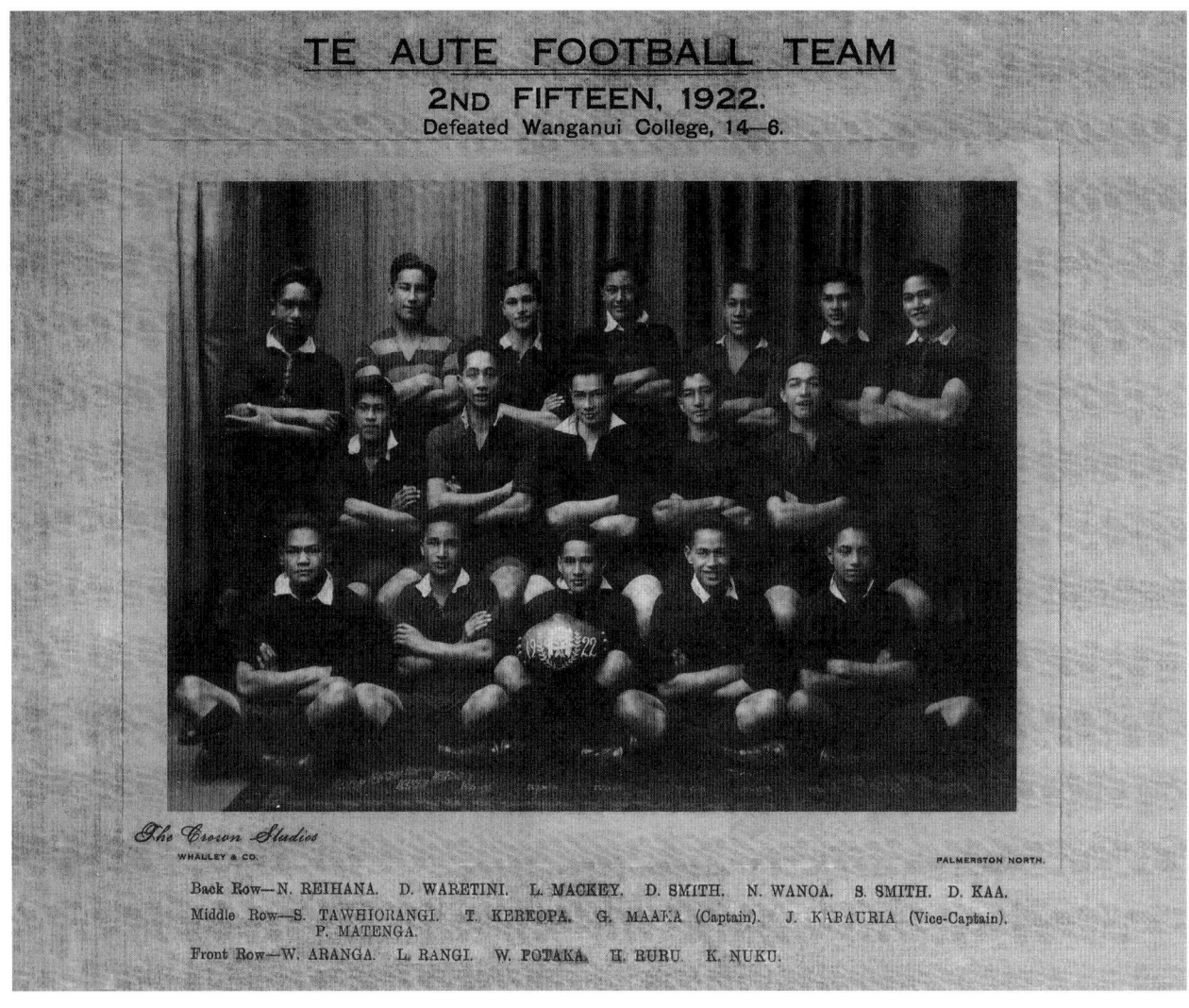

Golan Maaka captained Te Aute College's second XV rugby team in 1922. Maaka Collection

An example of Golan's written memoirs. Maaka Collection

A Te Aute College old boys' reunion in 1945 celebrating the 25th anniversary of Reverend Loten becoming headmaster. Golan is seated in the centre, in front of Loten. Maaka Collection

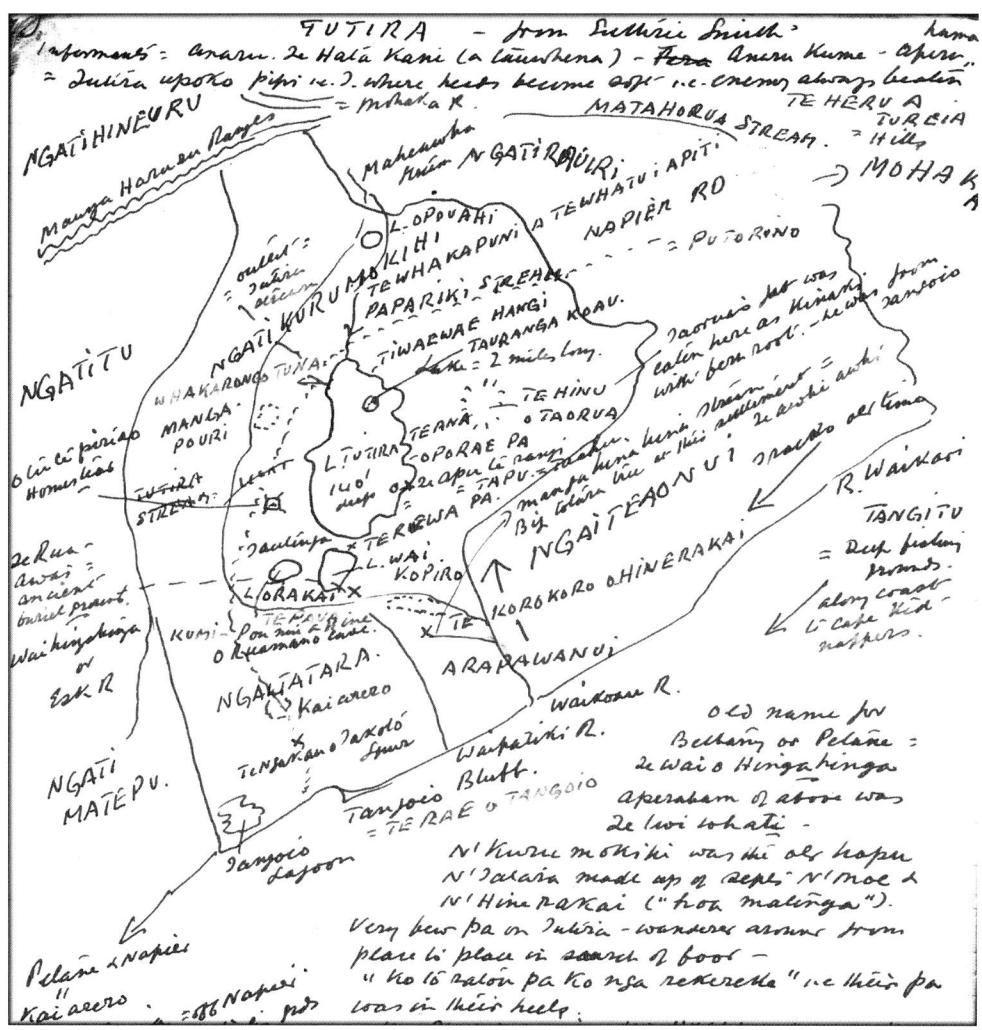

A map of Lake Tutira and related historical notes in one of Golan's whakapapa books. Maaka Collection

117

The Duke and Duchess of York were welcomed by large crowds at Rotorua in April 1920. S. P. Andrew Collection, F-19963-1/4, Alexander Turnbull Library

A section of Golan's whakapapa book recording the history of his Ngāti Kahungunu people.
Maaka Collection

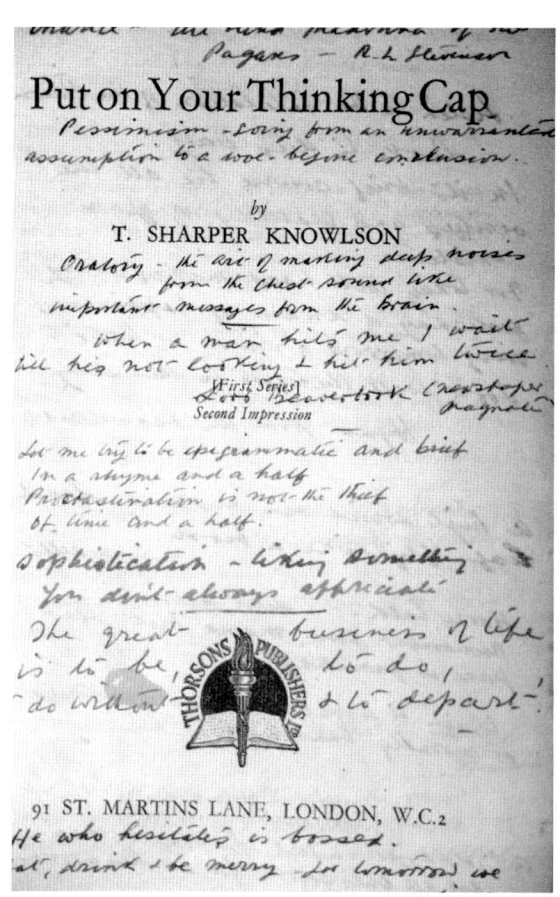

Almost all Golan's books were annotated with personal comments or related information. Here he has scribbled pithy sayings on the front cover of T. Sharper Knowlson's Put on Your Thinking Cap. Photo by the author

A single sheet of paper records the story of Hatupatu in note form. Maaka Collection

Golan's father-in-law, Albert Te Tawhero Stewart.
Both men were interested in history and writing.
Maaka Collection

Golan used a form of notation to record the tune of an old waiata. Maaka Collection

Dr Golan Maaka in his characteristic reading position,
not long before his death in 1978. Maaka Collection

The Ratana Church's temple at Rātana Pā, c. 1930.
A. P. Godber Collection, G-18648-1/2, Alexander Turnbull Library

A section of Golan's Ngāi Tahu whakapapa charts. Maaka Collection

CHAPTER EIGHT

He kupu whakamutunga
Conclusion

I count myself privileged to have access to the written records of my ancestors that have been spared from fire or burial. The process of gathering, collating and analysing these writings has focused my attention on issues concerning research, ownership, the use of te reo, publishing and kaitiakitanga – all hot topics in Māori circles. I would like to conclude with some thoughts on these issues.

Kaupapa Māori
A Māori research strategy

My plan for undertaking this project included what is termed today a kaupapa Māori framework as the research strategy. Kathy Irwin has described this approach as 'research which is "culturally safe", ... involves the "mentorship" of elders ... is culturally relevant and appropriate while satisfying the rigour of research, and ... is undertaken by a Maori researcher, not a researcher who happens to be Maori'. A Māori researcher in this sense is someone skilled in Māori tikanga whose work 'stems from a Maori worldview',[429] and who accepts that Māori should empower themselves by asserting their control of the study of Māori people's lives.[430] Central to this, Irwin and Russell Bishop argue, is 'the importance of the concept of *whanau* as a supervisory and organizational structure for handling research'.[431] From this perspective, knowledge is owned collectively by tribes, hapū and whānau, and should be used for purposes determined by or in conjunction with these groups.

At the beginning of this project, my whānau decided whether my idea was acceptable, and which material could be published. Discussions were held with the 'hunga mōhio' (those deemed to have mana in the family) to ensure that appropriate decisions were made. Many Māori believe that no written work is ever created in isolation by a single 'author'. They hold that works of Māori history are derived from information about historical events, tribal ideas and concepts that was once known and owned collectively and transmitted orally between generations. I consider myself an author only in the sense that I have compiled and interpreted whānau- and hapū-derived information.

Ngā take
Some issues

Characteristically, writing is an individualistic act that allows an author to gain kudos and mana as the 'owner' of the fruits of their intellectual labours.[432] Depending on the quality of the work and its presentation, the author may be recognised as an expert in their field and receive benefits such as an enhanced reputation, formal tertiary qualifications, or payment. This is of concern to some Māori.

In the nineteenth and early twentieth centuries, Māori history was almost entirely written by Pākehā, sometimes in ways which ignored Māori realities and failed to acknowledge either their contributions or their authority. Tribal control of traditional knowledge was lost when it appeared in the much more accessible print medium.[433] Māori have sought to remedy this by writing works from a Māori perspective.

Fear of commercialisation is perhaps the most intense Māori anxiety about making tribal information accessible.[434] The commercialisation of the written word has a long history. As printing presses proliferated and the making of multiple copies for publication became widespread, the concept of protecting the property rights of creators of a 'permanent form' of information was promulgated in the Statute of Anne of 1710. This gave priority to the 'encouragement of learning by visiting the copies of printed books in the authors'. The public interest was seen to be supported by the commercial dissemination of knowledge in books, and this view became stronger in subsequent centuries.[435] Jim Traue argues that information has become a resource, 'the driving power of the modern information economy':

> no matter what format it happens to be in it is information capable of being sliced into measurable pieces and priced for sale, the vast accumulations of books, periodicals, archives and manuscripts in our publicly funded libraries and archives look like gold mines ripe for exploitation.[436]

The exploitation of indigenous peoples' knowledge as a commodity has had disastrous results, including the distortion and standardisation of that knowledge to make it fit marketing requirements. Mita Carter believed strongly that Māori history has been recorded by the ignorant and analysed by the uninitiated:

> all that was cherished, revered and tapu has come under academic scrutiny. When Te Whatahoro recorded the recitals of Te Pohuhu, Te Matorohanga and others, a new era had begun, an era of misinterpretation, of misunderstanding, of tribal assessment and, sadly, ridicule. The ancestor has been dismembered, his recitals trespassed upon.[437]

In a world of huge publishing companies, insatiable demand for books and knowledge, microfiche, rapid advances in the film, television and video industries, CD-ROMs and the Internet, Māori information is becoming more readily accessible. Technological advances are both profitable and enlightening, but they can sometimes cut across Māori protocols. Some believe that the 'homogenising influence of technological civilization' contributes to the 'suffocating' of Māori culture.[438]

For these reasons, Māori have been cautious about allowing their stories and histories to be recorded for public dissemination. The people usually ask, 'For what purpose is this being done?' History need not be the work of outsiders, but can and should be undertaken by the whānau or iwi concerned. For example, a Māori pharmacist believed it to be imperative that her people's use of medicinal plants was written down so that this family knowledge could be retained for successive generations:

> While Maori talk about intellectual property rights, they say nothing can be written down. I've changed that now because these people want to die, with their word living. I was honest and up front with them and I said, 'This knowledge, I'll write it down, it will be printed so when you're dead and gone, you have left your taonga and your mokopuna will know your gift.' Because that's what the big cry of Maoridom is, it's not being passed on. So who's going to do that for them? These Maori are happy as their word will live like that of the Paipera Tapu [Bible] and they have honoured these tupuna and/or tohunga who had the gift to heal them.[439]

Today Māori seek to control the methodologies that are used to record, protect, enhance and transmit traditional information.

Poor scholarship has brought much Māori knowledge and heritage into disrepute. Māori tradition and history have sometimes been seen, both outside and within the Māori world, through mystical, romantic or cynical eyes. The danger is that traditional Māori scholarship is thereby devalued and inadequately understood. After two generations of carefully scrutinising and untangling early ethnologists' interpretations of Māori tradition,[440] it is imperative that Māori do not continue to allow misconceptions to be promulgated without tautohetohe (debate and discussion).

Māori have sought to control authorship and creative expression in the arts on the grounds that, if Māori concepts and ideas are to be utilised, this should be done correctly and within Māori parameters which fully recognise cultural values and the original sources, lest their history and kōrero take on a life independent of the people who created and maintained it.[441] One way to ensure this has been to establish tribal archives.

He pātaka iringa kōrero
Tribal archives

In recent years many tribal groups, including Ngāti Awa, Ngāi Tahu and Tainui, have created regional or tribal research and archives institutions to secure control over their whakapapa, written traditions, land claims research, and census records. Some of these regional archival units have developed relationships with local museums, libraries and educational institutions to achieve their goals. These units are designed to help re-establish self-esteem and pride of culture in the tribe and its people by increasing their knowledge of tikanga Māori and tribal tradition.[442]

Tribal research has the potential to deepen the knowledge of all members of the iwi. At the individual level, researchers become better informed. Through tribal archives 'it is possible to lift the educational level of the people, improve tribal morale and produce a more positive self-image of being Maori'. The tribal archive's role is to establish a 'knowledge base at home' and provide 'a pool of resources such as computer disks, audio tapes, video tapes, whakapapa tables and so on'.[443] The information is made available to the people, under terms set by the tribal organisation to safeguard the knowledge resource.

Hirini Mead believes that every tribal group should 'have control over what information should be gathered, who does the gathering and storing of the information, and in determining the terms of access to the information'. As he notes, 'immense pleasure is enjoyed by researchers in doing something for their people and in being able to make a contribution to the iwi'.[444] But the 'pleasure' of working for one's people for aroha (love) should not be the only incentive for young tribally-orientated researchers. Expert research takes time and money, and it should be paid for. In the past a person's specific skills were recognised, and culturally appropriate payment was made by the recipients of their expertise. This principle should still apply today.

Competence in Māori history and local tikanga, and a wider understanding of the traditional rules that apply to their study, should help create communities that are 'better placed to manage their cultural heritage in a wider New Zealand context'.[445]

Mātau ki te kupu tuhi

Being literate

Literacy in both Māori and English is an essential prerequisite for researching Māori history today. Literacy does not mean just the ability to read and write a language, but has a number of broader meanings. The adult literacy organisation Literacy Aotearoa sees it as 'a crucial tool for accessing the opportunities, choices and rights that society has to offer'.[446] In a survey of adult literacy in New Zealand, literacy was defined as 'using printed and written information to function in society, to achieve one's goals and to develop one's knowledge and potential'.[447]

Literacy can be understood as 'a process which: is a creative set of social practices … has meaning; integrates language skills (reading, writing, speaking and listening) with thinking; is a political process, which empowers people; is inextricably linked to the ways people live their lives'. Literacy also enables learners to 'participate in the meanings of text'; to 'use texts functionally'; and to 'analyse texts critically'.[448] Applying all these meanings to both Māori and English will lead to a greater understanding of both tikanga Māori and tikanga Pākehā, and ease movement between languages, social customs, and political and bureaucratic systems. The need for 'literacy' in using information technology is also becoming inescapable.

Literacy in all these contexts is necessary for those seeking to understand history through texts and maunscripts. Being literate in Māori social customs, and of course in te reo, will stand you in better stead when working with whānau oral histories and manuscripts. Gaining access to publications and manuscripts held in institutions requires a knowledge of search and retrieval systems, cataloguing and referencing. Having the literacy skills to understand and analyse historical manuscripts allows us to research, reconstruct and reinterpret documents in ways that are more meaningful for ourselves and our culture.

Kuni Jenkins has emphasised the need to be literate in both Māori and English:

> Maori growth of critical [rather than merely functional] literacy is incomplete without learning both Maori and English literacies. It is therefore a paramount consideration to engage our learning of both in order to establish more meaningful political and social relationships between the two groups. The strength of one's literacy is then left open to the challenge of knowing how to maintain one's cultural roots within the dual relationship and working out a strategy of resistance to any attempts by one of the groups to undermine or corrupt the other.[449]

Whakatakoto tikanga-ā-tuhi

Setting conventions

In this information-based society, Māori have established conventions and standards not only to control tribal information but also to validate and transmit it in tikanga-appropriate ways. While the printed word can never replace speech, it does play a role in keeping the language alive.[450] It is therefore important to formulate standards and conventions to ensure accuracy in the written form of the language. The orthography of the language was developed by missionaries in the north to help translate it into a written form. Two hundred years later, ways are still being found to improve these conventions, taking into account changes in both the language and technology. This has meant finding the best way to depict the value of stressed vowels, break up or hyphenate proper names, create new words or word combinations for new concepts, and show dialectal nuances.

Recently, attempts have been made to revitalise the use of tribal dialects in published works. The introduction of the alphabet is thought to have obscured dialectal subtleties and thereby 'masked tribal identity in the oral traditions', at least until the late twentieth century, when Māori began to undertake their own writing and publishing.[451] An undeniable dialectal difference was revealed when scriptures written in Māori by northern missionaries were not understood by James Watkin's communicants at Waikouaiti in the South Island in 1840. Watkin's attempts to remedy this problem led eventually to changes in the Māori alphabet to allow the expression of southern vocalisations.[452] Today dialectal differences are a source of pride for local tribes and hapū, and they should be reproduced in print. For example, in the photographer Justin Spiers' publication *Moeraki*, Huata Holmes gives an account of the voyage of the Araiteuru canoe and the formation of the Moeraki boulders using a phonetic alphabet for southern vernacular Māori.[453]

In 1840 Watkin observed that there had already been great changes to the Māori language through the introduction of foreign words, a process which continues to accelerate:

> some of them have been superseded by English curses and phrases … the language is a good deal corrupted by [the] introduction of foreign terms, some the slang of sailors … others belonging to I know not what language.[454]

Attempts to turn back the tide of transliteration are assisted by *Te Matatiki*, a publication of Te Taura Whiri i te Reo Māori, which strives to 'extend the linguistic range of Māori by weaving together into new combinations current speech, and words and phrases which have fallen out of every day use'.[455] The missionary-created alphabet was also considered deficient by Bruce Biggs, who advocated the use of the doubled vowel to mark distinctions of pronunciation and meaning.[456] Others have supported the macron, which has emerged victorious thanks to the introduction of computer software that allows it to be used readily.

New conventions and standards for Māori-language publishing are essential if te reo is to survive in the new technological age. The four-column page convention demonstrated in chapter 4 may serve as a prototype for others to develop. It is based on the assumption that is necessary both to see the original document rather than just a transcript, and to translate it into modern Māori and English. Improvements and additions to the conventions for printed Māori will undoubtedly emerge along with new technologies. Some of the above matters have been addressed in this book.

Tiaki taonga
Safekeeping

One important topic remains to be discussed. Sometimes the significance of the manuscript's content and historical context may overshadow its safekeeping. Probably the most important issue for families and tribal archives which hold ancestral whakapapa books and records is ensuring their protection. Fifteen years ago the manuscript material in the Maaka Collection was in a poor condition, scattered around the country and disorganised. Some of it was locked in suitcases, old boxes and tins, and stored in damp places. These conditions caused some papers to perish, while other material stored in a shed was eaten by silverfish. Over the years as the material was collected it became clear that better forms of protection were needed. There were two choices: place the collection in an institution, or carry out some simple processes to preserve the documents and keep them at home. The family decided on the latter. For those who make the same choice, I provide here some techniques to help safeguard these taonga which have been suggested by the conservators of Archives New Zealand and the National Library.[457]

Where possible, material should be photocopied and at least two copies made; but be aware that repeated photocopying of original documents can discolour them and make them brittle. Originals and photocopies should be kept in different locations as a precaution against fire or other disaster. Use the photocopied version for reference and teaching purposes to keep the original from deteriorating. The more handling there is of manuscripts, the greater the risk of wear and tear on the edges of the pages which can slowly spread across the whole document. To prevent oils and perspiration from hands damaging the paper, wear cotton gloves.

It is essential to store manuscripts in a relatively dry place and package them properly. Make sure they are stored flat, unfolded and bound with flat cotton tape tied loosely. Refrain from using rubber bands, which will become brittle; paper clips or staples, which rust; or Sellotape, which damages paper as it ages. Keep documents in acid-free cardboard folders or plastic sleeves, but do not use PVC plastic. Damaged acid-free documents should not be repaired inappropriately but kept in separate folders. Avoid unnecessary folding of letters and papers, which will compromise their longevity. Keep the original manuscripts free from dust or dampness, which can encourage a build-up of mould, and check for possible infestation by insects. Store these taonga in dark and fairly dry environments. Do not leave them near heating systems or water pipes, and avoid garages, sheds, cellars and other places which are poorly ventilated. Make sure that you regularly clean, dust and maintain your storage area. By taking these steps you will prolong the life of your documents.

The National Preservation Office Te Tari Tohu Taonga, in partnership with Te Papa National Services and the National Library's Takawaenga-a-rohe (Māori Liaison Librarians), runs workshops for iwi and hapū on the care and preservation of documentary heritage, textiles, wood and stone. These workshops are for individuals and groups who are interested in or responsible for the care of historical records, photographs or Māori textiles. Whānau are invited to bring along any form of taonga (including artifacts, manuscripts, paintings, photographs, carvings, kakahu and piupiu). They are given advice on how to prevent the deterioration of this material, and where and how to store it in their homes. Presentations are also given on the choices available to Māori in relation to setting up whare taonga (archival units) and/or tribal museums. These hui also discuss wider iwi and hapū aspirations and policies, who should be involved in setting up such institutions, the costs, and sources of funding.[458]

If they are well looked after, these taonga can continue to inspire many interesting and enlightening journeys. This study has been a kind of journey, but it is by no means the full story of the writings of this whānau, some of which have been withheld for various reasons. Ensuring the safety and integrity of the mana of the whānau and hapū is important. One way to accomplish this is to leave more 'sacred' and personal information in the hands of the hunga mōhio, to be revealed at an appropriate time. 'It is my blanket, and if I give it away, how can I keep warm?'[459] Another proverb spoken by Paraire Tōmoana at Waitōtara in 1936 also conveys this message:

Me tuha anake? Kahore! Me horo anō rā tētahi wāhi.
Should it be spit alone? No! We must swallow some of it![460]

Ngā Āpitiranga
Notes

Introduction

1 Edward Shortland, *The Southern Districts of New Zealand*, Longman, Brown, Green & Longmans, London, 1851, p. 95, cited in A. Salmond, *Eruera: The Teachings of a Maori Elder*, Oxford University Press, Auckland, 1980, p. 248.
2 Roger Maaka, interview, Christchurch, 1996.
3 *The Bible – The Classic Text: Traditions and Interpretations*, www.uwm.edu/Dept/Library/special/exhibits/clastext/c lspg006.htm, University of Wisconsin, Milwaukee, 1997.
4 A. T. Ngata, *The Price of Citizenship*, Whitcombe & Tombs, Wellington, 1943, p. 5, cited in Salmond, *Eruera*, p. 251.

Chapter 1

5 K. Jenkins, 'Te Ihi, Te Mana, Te Wehi o Te Ao Tuhi: Maori Print Literacy from 1814–1855: Literacy, Power and Colonisation', MA thesis, University of Auckland, 1991, p. 38; Henry Williams, 'log-book', 27 Jan 1832, cited in Hugh Carleton, *The Life of Henry Williams: Archdeacon of Waimate*, Reed, Wellington, 1948, p. 158.
6 Jenkins, 'Te Ihi', p. 11.
7 Jan Vansina, *Oral Tradition as History*, University of Wisconsin Press, Madison, 1985, p. xi.
8 David Riesman, 'The Oral and Written Traditions', in Edmund Carpenter & Marshall McLuhan (eds), *Explorations in Communications*, Beacon Press, Boston, 1960, pp. 110–11, cited in M. Jackson, 'Literacy, Communications and Social Change: The Maori Case, 1830–1870', MA thesis, University of Auckland, 1967, pp. 104–5.
9 Karen Sinclair, *Prophetic Histories: The People of the Māramatanga*, Bridget Williams Books, Wellington, 2002, pp. 6–7.
10 Te Maire Tau, 'Mātauranga Māori as an Epistemology', *Te Pouhere Korero*, vol. 1, no. 1, 1999, p. 15.
11 M. Orbell, *Maori Poetry: An Introductory Anthology*, Heinemann Educational Books, Auckland, 1983, p. 6.
12 M. Marsden & T. A. Henare, 'Kaitiakitanga: A Definitive Introduction to the Holistic World View of the Maori', paper prepared for the Ministry for the Environment, Nov 1992, pp. 5–6.
13 H. T. Rikihana, *Te Ao Tūroa: Science*, vol. 1, Auckland College of Education, Auckland, 1992, part 4, proverb 10, p. 44.
14 Tipene O'Regan, 'Old Myths and New Politics: Some Contemporary Uses of Traditional History', *New Zealand Journal of History (NZJH)*, vol. 26, no. 1, 1992, p. 25. See also D. R. Simmons, *The Great New Zealand Myth: A Study of the Discovery and Origin Traditions of the Maori*, Reed, Wellington, 1976, p. 237.
15 Pei Te Hurinui, *King Potatau: An Account of the Life of Potatau Te Wherowhero, the First Maori King*, Polynesian Society, Wellington, 1959, p. 35.
16 Roma Mere Roberts & Peter R. Wills, 'Understanding Maori Epistemology: A Scientific Perspective', in H. Wautischer (ed.), *Tribal Epistemologies: Essays in the Philosophy of Anthropology*, Ashgate, 1998, p. 45.
17 Tau, 'Mātauranga Māori', p. 14.
18 Roberts & Wills, 'Understanding Maori Epistemology', p. 54.
19 E. Tregear, *The Maori Race*, A. D. Willis, Wanganui, 1904, pp. 383–4.
20 Maori Purposes Fund Board papers, MS papers 0189, folder 87, Alexander Turnbull Library (ATL).
21 Marsden & Henare, 'Kaitiakitanga', p. 3.
22 Ranginui Walker, 'The Relevance of Maori Myth and Tradition,' in Michael King (ed.), *Te Ao Hurihuri: Aspects of Maoritanga*, Reed, Auckland, 1992, p. 182.
23 Orbell, *Maori Poetry*, p. 7.
24 A. T. Ngata, *Nga Moteatea*, Part 1, Polynesian Society, Wellington, 1959, p. xv.
25 Ibid., pp. xvii–xix.
26 Walter J. Ong, *Orality and Literacy: The Technologizing of the Word*, Methuen, London, 1982, p. 67.
27 Pei Te Hurinui, *King Potatau*, p. 35.
28 Jenkins, 'Te Ihi', p. 8.
29 C. Winitana, 'From Words to Wood,' *Mana*, no. 6, Jul–Sep 1994, p. 14.
30 Hirini Moko Mead, *Te Toi Whakairo: The Art of Maori Carving*, Reed, Auckland, 1986, pp. 10–11.
31 Tau, 'Mātauranga Māori', p. 16.
32 *Tanenuiarangi*, University of Auckland, Auckland, 1988, p. 24. See also I. Zaczek & J. O. Westwood, *The Art of Illuminated Manuscripts: Illustrated Sacred Writings*, Studio Editions, 1996, p. 19.
33 T. W. Downes, 'History of Ngati-Kahu-ngunu; Chapter I – Continued', *Journal of the Polynesian Society (JPS)*, vol. 23, 1914, p. 112.
34 H. T. Whatahoro & S. Percy Smith, 'Te Kauwae-raro: The Lore of the Whare-Wānanga, Part II, Chapter X, The Coming of "Takitimu" Canoe to New Zealand', *JPS*, vol. 24, 1915, p. 16.
35 Pei Te Hurinui, *King Potatau*, pp. 33–7.
36 E. Dieffenbach, *Travels in New Zealand*, vol. 2, John Murray, London, 1843, Capper Press reprint, Christchurch, 1974, p. 164.
37 Jenkins, 'Te Ihi', p. 36.
38 Ibid., p. 27.
39 J. Binney, *The Legacy of Guilt: A Life of Thomas Kendall*, Oxford University Press, Auckland, 1968, p. 9.
40 W. P. Reeves, *The Long White Cloud: Ao Tea Roa*, Golden Press reprint, Auckland, 1973, p. 101.
41 Thomas Kendall, *A Korao no New Zealand; or, the New Zealander's First Book; Being an Attempt to Compose some Lessons for the Instruction of the Natives*, G. Howe, Sydney, 1815.
42 P. Bawden, *The Years Before Waitangi: A Story of Early Maori European Contact in New Zealand*, author, Auckland, 1989, p. 120.
43 Peter Lineham, 'To Make a People of the Book', in R. Glen (ed.), *Mission and Moko: Aspects of the Work of the Church Missionary Society in New Zealand, 1814–1882*, Latimer Fellowship of New Zealand, Christchurch, c. 1992, p. 153.
44 J. McRae, 'Maori Literature: A Survey', in Terry Sturm (ed.), *The Oxford History of New Zealand Literature*, Oxford University Press, Auckland, 1991, p. 4.
45 Lineham, 'To Make a People', p. 153.
46 A. G. Bagnall & G. C. Petersen, *William Colenso, Printer, Missionary, Botanist, Explorer, Politician: His Life and Journeys*, Reed, Wellington, 1948, p. 54.
47 C. J. Parr, 'A Missionary Library: Printed Attempts to Instruct the Maori, 1815–1845', *JPS*, vol. 70, 1961, p. 445.
48 Ibid., p.446.
49 J. McRae, 'From Māori Oral Traditions to Print', in P. Griffiths, R. Harvey & K. Maslen (eds), *Book and Print in New Zealand: A Guide to Print Culture in Aotearoa*, Victoria University Press, Wellington, 1997, p. 30.
50 L. Head & B. Mikaere, 'Was 19th Century Maori Society Literate?', *Archifacts*, Jun 1988, p. 17.
51 Raymond Firth, *Economics of the New Zealand Maori*, 2nd edition, Government Printer, Wellington, 1959, p. 247.
52 Maori Marsden, 'God, Man and the Universe: A Maori View', in King (ed.), *Te Ao Hurihuri*, p. 119.
53 Evidence to Select Committee of the House of Commons, 12 Feb 1836, Journal of William Yate, 1833–1845, cited in J. Binney, 'Christianity and the Maoris to 1840: A Comment', *NZJH*, vol. 3, no. 2, 1969, p. 151.

54 Paki Harrison, in B. Haami (director), 'Tapu', *Waka Huia*, Television New Zealand, 1989.

55 Peter J. Lineham, *Bible and Society: A Sesquicentennial History of the Bible Society in New Zealand*, Bible Society in New Zealand/Daphne Brasell Associates, Wellington, 1996, pp. 19–20.

56 P. Lineham, 'This is my Weapon: Maori Response to the Maori Bible', in Glen (ed.), *Mission and Moko*, p. 178.

57 K. R. Howe, 'Missionaries, Maoris and "Civilization" in the Upper Waikato, 1833–1863', MA thesis, University of Auckland, 1970, p. 62, cited in Valerie Carson, 'Submitting to Great Inconvenience: Early Missionary Education for Maori Women and Girls', in Glen (ed.), ibid., p. 72.

58 Harrison M. Wright, *New Zealand, 1769–1840: Early Years of Western Contact*, Harvard University Press, Cambridge, Massachusetts, 1959, p. 174.

59 Parr, 'Missionary Library', p. 437.

60 Ibid., pp. 433–4, 439.

61 R. Taylor, *The Past and Present of New Zealand*, London/Wanganui, 1868, p. 20, cited in Jenny Murray, 'Tenei ano Taku Korero: Here is My Report', *Te Pae Tawhito o te Wā/History Now*, vol. 2, no. 1, May 1996, p. 35.

62 A. T. Ngata, 'The Maori and Printed Matter', in R. A. Mckay (ed.), *A History of Printing in New Zealand, 1830–1940*, Wellington Club of Printing House Craftsmen, Wellington, 1940, p. 48.

63 J. B. F. Pompallier, *Early History of the Catholic Church in Oceania*, H. Brett, Auckland, 1888, p. 47.

64 Parr, 'Missionary Library', p. 439.

65 D. F. McKenzie, *Oral Culture, Literacy and Print in Early New Zealand: The Treaty of Waitangi*, Victoria University Press, Wellington, 1985, pp. 16–17.

66 Tipene Ngata (Āpirana Ngata's son), interview, Waiōmatatini, 1989. See also Ranginui Walker, *He Tipua: The Life and Times of Sir Āpirana Ngata*, Viking, Auckland, 2001, p. 65.

67 Parr, 'Missionary Library', p. 438.

68 E. Markham, *New Zealand or Recollection of It*, Government Printer, Wellington, 1963, p. 66.

69 W. Wade, *A Journey in the Northern Island of New Zealand*, George Rolwegan, Hobart, 1842, Capper Press reprint, Christchurch, 1977, p. 184.

70 Wright, *Early Years of Western Contact*, p. 175.

71 W. Colenso, Journals 1846–8, vol. 1, entry for 23 Apr 1846, cited in Angela Ballara, 'The Origins of Ngati Kahungunu', PhD thesis, Victoria University of Wellington, 1991, p. 471.

72 Reverend [Alfred] Brown's Journals, 2 Dec 1845, transcript held at Waikato University.

73 J. Binney, *Redemption Songs: A Life of Te Kooti Arikirangi Te Turuki*, Auckland University Press/Bridget Williams Books, Auckland, 1995, p. 16.

74 Felix M. Keesing, *The Changing Maori, Memoirs of the Board of Maori Ethnological Research*, vol. 4, Thomas Avery & Sons, New Plymouth, 1928, p. 58.

75 C. J. Parr, 'Maori Literacy 1843–1867', *JPS*, vol. 72, 1963, p. 219.

76 Jackson, 'Literacy, Communications and Social Change', p. 180.

77 Markham, *New Zealand*, p. 55, entry for 16 Mar 1834.

78 William Brown, *New Zealand and its Aborigines: Being an Account of the Aborigines, Trade, and Resources of the Colony, and the Advantages it now Presents as a Field for Emigration and the Investment of Capital*, Smith, Elder & Co., London, 1845, pp. 98–9.

79 Parr, 'Missionary Library', p. 438.

80 Parr, 'Maori Literacy', p. 219.

81 Parr, 'Missionary Library', p. 438.

82 Head & Mikaere, 'Was 19th Century Maori Society Literate?', p. 17.

83 Parr, 'Maori Literacy', pp. 212–13, 222.

84 J. M. R. Owens, 'Christianity and the Maoris to 1840', *NZJH*, vol. 2, no.1, 1968, p. 39.

85 Head & Mikaere, 'Was 19th Century Maori Society Literate?', p. 19.

86 Jackson, 'Literacy, Communications and Social Change', p. 178.

87 I. Illich & B. Sanders, *ABC: The Alphabetization of the Popular Mind*, North Point Press, San Francisco, 1988, pp. 32, 43.

88 R. S. Milne, 'The Inevitability of Administrative Discretion', in R. S. Milne (ed.) *Bureaucracy in New Zealand*, New Zealand Institute of Public Administration/Oxford University Press, Wellington/London, 1957, p. 8.

89 Jenkins, 'Te Ihi', p. 10.

90 C. Orange, *The Treaty of Waitangi*, Allen and Unwin/Port Nicholson Press, Wellington, 1987, p. 79.

91 Alan Ward, *A Show of Justice*, Oxford University Press/Auckland University Press, Auckland, 1974, p. 72.

92 G. V. Butterworth & H. R. Young, *Maori Affairs*, GP Books, Wellington, 1990, p. 23.

93 The Maori Land Courts, Report of the Royal Commission of Inquiry, 1980, *Appendix to the Journals of the House of Representatives (AJHR)*, 1980, H-3, p. 7.

94 Vincent O'Malley, *Agents of Autonomy: Maori Committees in the Nineteenth Century*, Huia, Wellington, 1998, p. 32.

95 *AJHR*, 1980, H-3, p. 11.

96 The author has seen minute books of this kind that belong to Ngāti Kahungunu and Whakatohea people.

97 The Maaka Collection contains a number of letters sent to relatives which include details of whakapapa or oral tradition that contradicts or supports the evidence of claimants or witnesses.

98 I. H. Kawharu, *Maori Land Tenure: Studies of a Changing Institution*, Clarendon Press, Oxford/New York, 1977, p. 41.

99 Ruka Broughton, 'The Origins of Ngaa Rauru Kiitahi', MA thesis, Victoria University of Wellington, 1979, pp. 47–8.

100 Letter from T. Tarakawa to S. P. Smith, 17 Oct 1894 , Polynesian Society papers, MS Papers 1187, folder 178, ATL.

101 Anne Salmond, 'Maori Epistemologies', in Joanna Overing (ed.), *Reason and Morality*, Tavistock Publications, London, p. 250.

102 Walker, 'The Relevance of Maori Myth and Tradition', p. 182.

103 George Graham, 'The Origin and Meanings of Maori Placenames', typescript, MS 120, M 54, p. 17, Auckland War Memorial Museum Library (AM).

104 *He Kōrero Pūrākau mo Ngā Taunahanahatanga a Ngā Tupuna*, New Zealand Geographic Board, Wellington, 1990, p. xiii.

105 Danny Keenan, 'Aversion To Print? Māori Resistance to the Written Word', in P. Griffith, P. Hughes & A. Loney (eds), *A Book in the Hand: Essays on the History of the Book in New Zealand*, Auckland University Press, Auckland, 2000, pp. 26–7.

106 Ibid., p. 24.

107 Ibid., p. 25.

108 Ibid., p. 26.

109 O'Malley, *Agents of Autonomy*, p. 12.

110 Keith Sinclair, *Kinds of Peace: Maori People After the Wars, 1870–85*, Auckland University Press, Auckland, 1991, p. 101.

111 Jane McRae, 'Transitions', in Griffith et al. (eds) *Book and Print in New Zealand*, p. 27.

112 Murray, 'Tenei ano Taku Korero', p. 35.

113 Bruce Biggs, 'The Oral Literature of the Polynesians', *Te Ao Hou*, no. 49, 1964, p. 24.

114 Toon Van Meijl, 'Historicising Maoritanga: Colonial Ethnography and the Reification of Maori Traditions,' *JPS*, vol. 105, no. 3, 1996, pp. 322–3.

115 Quoted in T. Simpson, *Te Riri Pakeha/The White Man's Anger*, Hodder & Stoughton, Auckland, 1986, p. 99.

116 Quoted in I. L. G. Sutherland (ed.), *The Maori People Today: A General Survey*, Whitcombe & Tombs, Christchurch, 1940, p. 28.

117 Bill Solomon, interview, Kaikoura, June 1997. He told me that his tupuna in the mid-nineteenth century had written down an enormous amount of local Māori history in the Māori language, purely for the love of writing and to preserve this history.

118 Many Māori religious sects, including Ringa-tū, Rātana and Māramatanga, had scribes who wrote down their leaders' prophecies. Sinclair, *Prophetic Histories*, pp. 7, 214–15.

119 McRae, 'Maori Literature', in Sturm (ed.), *The Oxford History of New Zealand Literature*, p. 9.

120 J. Metge, *The Maoris of New Zealand*, Routledge and Kegan Paul, London, 1967, p. 120.

121 Sinclair, *Prophetic Histories*, p. 7.

122 Walter Lorne Campbell, Journals, 5 Nov 1870, Micro Ms Copy 0001, reel 2, ATL.

123 Renata Tamakihikurangi to the Superintendent of Hawke's Bay, Feb 1861, cited in John Caselberg (ed.), *Maori is my Name: Historical Maori Writings in Translation*, John McIndoe, Dunedin, 1975, p. 95.

124 Brown, *New Zealand and its Aborigines*, p. 98.

125 Head & Mikaere, 'Was 19th Century Maori Society Literate?', p. 19.

126 Hori Te Aroatua to the editor, *Huia Tangata Kotahi*, 8 Sep 1894, p. 3.

127 See the famous letter of Tamehana Te Waharoa to Donald McLean, 23 May 1861, *AJHR*, 1861, E-1B, no. 18, pp. 13–17.

128 See, for example, Chris Pugsley, 'Walking the Taranaki Wars: Maori Defeat at Mahoetahi, 6 November 1860', *New Zealand Defence Quarterly*, no. 11, 1995, p. 33.

129 Charles Royal, interview, Otaki, Nov 1996.

130 Examples can be seen in J. H. Mitchell, *Takitimu*, Reed, Wellington, 1944, genealogical tables ix, x, xi, xii, xx. These show Mitchell's Ngāti Kahungunu connections to important people such as Wiremu Pōtae, Te Kani a Takirau, the Ngarimu family, Rongowhakaata Halbert, Āpirana Ngata, Te Apatu, and King Koroki.

131 M. P. Shirres, *Te Tangata / The Human Person*, Accent Publications, Auckland, 1997, p. 98.

132 Richard Taylor, 'Manuscript Notes on New Zealand and its Native Inhabitants', Part 2, c. 1854, p. 184, GNZMMSS 297/30, Auckland City Libraries.

133 F. E. Maning, *History of the War in the North*, in Caselberg (ed.), *Maori is My Name*, p. 60.

134 Bruce Biggs, 'Knowledge as Allegory,' in John Morrison, Paul Geraghty & Linda Crowl (eds), *Science of Pacific Island Peoples*, Volume Four, Education, Language, Patterns and Policy, Institute of Pacific Studies, University of the South Pacific, Suva, 1994, p. 2.

135 Rapata Wiri, interview, Auckland, Nov 1998. His family's whakapapa books were lost in this way.

136 Hikawera Wiremu Mahupuku, undated ms, M2942cop4MS29, copy held in Department of Anthropology, University of Auckland, p. 1, translation by Pat Hohepa.

137 Elsdon Best, *The Maori School of Learning: Its Objects, Methods, and Ceremonial*, Government Printer, Wellington, 1974, p. 23.

138 S. P. Smith, 'The Lore of the Whare-wananga: Part 1 – Te Kauwae-runga', *JPS*, vol. 22, 1913, pp. 104–5.

139 Wiremu Paratene Okawhare to Sir George Grey, 'He Pukapuka no Nga Tupuna', 17 Mar 1853, GNZMMSS 33, Auckland City Libraries.

140 Te Whatahoro Jury, Journals, 29 Jun 1863, MS Papers 0189-B054, ATL.

141 Samuel Locke, 'Historical Traditions of the Taupo and East Coast Tribes', *Transactions and Proceedings of the New Zealand Institute (TPNZI)*, vol. 15, 1882, p. 433.

142 Florence Keene, *Tai Tokerau*, author, Whāngārei, c. 1986, p. 100.

143 Sharon Dell, 'The Maori Book or the Book in Maori', *New Zealand Libraries*, vol. 45, no. 5, March 1987, p. 100.

144 Keenan, 'Aversion To Print?', p. 23.

145 O'Regan, 'Old Myths and New Politics', p. 25.

Chapter 2

146 J. McEwen, *Rangitāne: A Tribal History*, Reed Methuen, Auckland, 1986, p. 134.

147 William Colenso, Journal, 25 Apr 1851, cited in A. C. Bagnall & G. C. Petersen, *William Colenso*, Reed, Wellington, 1948, p. 462.

148 Napier Minute Book no.2, 20 Aug 1868, Māori Land Court, Hastings.

149 Walter Campbell, Journals 1868–1872, 26 Mar, 20 Jul 1869, Micro Copy MS 0001, Reel 2, ATL.

150 Napier Minute Book no. 7, 23 May 1884, Māori Land Court, Hastings.

151 Napier Minute Book 22 A (no. 2), p. 310. See also the 1886 succession application of Miriama, Boxes Waimarama V1 – NA.303–305, 1886–1905, Waipuka V1 -NA.330, Okaihau V1 – NA.173, Māori Land Court, Hastings.

152 Letters to William Colenso, c. 1844 – c. 1856, MLMSS.137, folder 4, Mitchell Library, State Library of New South Wales, Sydney, Australia.

153 His sister Erena Mekemeke was the wife of Tiakitai.

154 Miria Simpson, *Ngā Tohu o Te Tiriti: Making a Mark*, National Library of New Zealand, Wellington, 1990, p.78. Harawira Te Tātare Mahikai (Tiakitai's half-brother) signed the Treaty of Waitangi along with Te Hāpuku and Waikato on or after 24 June 1840.

155 William Colenso, Journal, copies at Berry Historical Library, Hawke's Bay Museum, Napier.

156 Harawira signed the Treaty of Waitangi.

157 Walter Campbell, Journals, 5 Nov 1870, 24 Nov 1870, 29 Jun 1871.

158 Apirana Ngata, 'Tribal Organization', in Sutherland (ed.), *The Maori People Today*, p. 160.

159 Ranginui Walker, *Ka Whawhai Tonu Matou: Struggle Without End*, Penguin, Auckland, 1990, p. 136.

160 O'Malley, *Agents of Autonomy*, p. 33.

161 Report of the Commission Appointed to Inquire into the Subject of the Native Land Laws, *AJHR*, 1891, Session II, G-1, p. vii.

162 Walker, *Ka Whawhai Tonu Matou*, p. 136.

163 Sydney Grant, *Waimarama*, Dunmore, Palmerston North, 1977, p. 31.

164 Reminiscences of Thomas Moore of Waimarama from 1845, qMS moo, 48040, ATL.

165 Grant, *Waimarama*, pp. 36, 47, 51.

166 Napier Minute Book no. 2, pp. 19–23. By this time Mukakai Maaka had died, but he was still registered as a shareholder. It is not until after this case that his kin succeeded to his estate. See succession application in Boxes Waimarama V1 – NA.303–305, 1886–1905, Waipuka NA.330 V1, and Okaihau V1 NA.173, Māori Land Court, Hastings.

167 Grant, *Waimarama*, p. 53.

168 Ibid., p. 54.

169 Napier Minute Book no. 7, 1884, esp. pp. 156–63.

170 Grant, *Waimarama*, p. 55.

171 Napier Minute Book no. 7, pp. 110, 143, 158. Maaka Mukakai, Hākaraia's son-in-law, was also named as a shareholder in Tiakitai's list, through his mother.

172 See evidence from Napier Minute Book no. 13, pp. 379–83, cited in Ballara, 'Ngati Kahungunu', pp. 336–40.

173 J. D. H. Buchanan (ed. D. R. Simmons), *The Maori History and Place Names of Hawke's Bay*, Reed, Wellington, 1973, p. 69. This boundary line consisting of 60 place names was recited to Buchanan by Ripeka Inia of Waimārama in 1947. See Buchanan Papers, Box 2, File 2, Berry Library, Hawke's Bay Museum.

174 Buchanan Papers, Box 2, File 2, Berry Historical Library, Hawke's Bay Museum. This boundary consists of 44 names.

175 Buchanan, *Maori History*, p. 200.

176 Kevin Jones, *Ngā Tohuwhenua Mai Te Rangi: A New Zealand Archaeology in Aerial Photographs*, Victoria University Press, Wellington, 1994, pp. 270–3.

177 *Ngā Tohu Pūmahara: The Survey Pegs of the Past*, New Zealand Geographic Board, Wellington, 1990, pp. 5–8.

178 Takirirangi Smith, 'Doing Research From Home: Tangata Whenua Issues and Māori Research', in Te Pūmanawa Hauora (ed.), *Proceedings of Te Oru Rangahau / Māori Research and Development Conference, 7–9 July, 1998*, 2nd edition, Te Putahi-a-Toi/School of Māori Studies, Massey University, Palmerston North, 1999, p. 247.

179 Angela Ballara, *Iwi: The Dynamics of Māori Tribal Organisation from c. 1769 to c. 1945*, Victoria University Press, Wellington, 1998, pp. 194–5.

180 Evidence in Te Whiti South hearing, Minute Book no. 8, p. 208, cited in A. G. Bagnall, *Wairarapa: An Historical Excursion, Masterton Trust Lands Trust, Masterton*, 1976, p. 9.

181 Evidence of Inia Whangataua, Waikopiro Minute Book, Māori language version, 1889, Maaka Collection.

182 Napier Minute Book no. 7, Waimarama subdivision, pp. 111–12.

183 Douglas Sinclair, 'Land: Maori View and European Response,' in King (ed.), *Te Ao Hurihuri*, p. 68.

184 Napier Minute Book no. 7, pp. 110–11. See also McEwen, *Rangitāne*, p. 43. Also mentioned in Mohi Te Atahikoia, typescript, pp. 9–10, MS Papers 1354, ATL.

185 Napier Minute Book no. 7, p. 148.

186 Ballara, 'Ngati Kahungunu', pp. 353–4.

187 Donald McLean, Diaries and notes, entry for 4 May 1848, cited in Ballara, *Iwi*, p. 353.

188 Ballara, *Iwi*, p. 197.

189 Ballara, 'Ngati Kahungunu', pp. 346–7.

190 Ballara, *Iwi*, p. 198.

191 Ballara, 'Ngati Kahungunu', p. 366.

192 Ballara, *Iwi*, p. 199.

193 Leslie G. Adkin, *Horowhenua: Its Maori Place-names and their Topographic and Historical Background*, Department of Internal Affairs, Wellington, 1948, pp. 19–20.

194 Elsdon Best, *Fishing Methods and Devices of the Maori*, Dominion Museum Bulletin no. 12, 1929, reprinted by Government Printer, Wellington, 1986, p. 145.

195 Napier Minute Book no. 7. Mohi could not name any places belonging or given to Tiopira as he believed the people lived communally.

196 Buchanan, *Maori History*, p. 165. Two sites are recorded for Te Pā-o-Ngāti Apa, one a pā near Waihekura in the northern part of Waimārama on the Waipuka Block at reference point N142 400045, the other at reference point N134 335111, beside the Tukituki River.

197 A place near the Waingongoro stream at Waimāmara. There are two ancestors named Manawa-kawa. The earlier ancestor is the son of Tapanga, a son-in-law of Hika-toa by his first wife Te Pīrau. The later and more illustrious Manawa-kawa was the brother of ‹pokoiri and father of Rangi-koia-anake I.

198 Mau is an abbreviation of Whare-mau.

199 Buchanan, *Maori History*, p.173. A pā on the south side of a peak located near the mouth of the Paparewa Stream – N142 402986. Some traces were still visible in 1952. See also map of Waimārama in Buchanan papers, Box 2, File 2, Berry Historical Library, Hawke's Bay Museum.

200 Hare Mātenga was a half-brother of Ataneta Matariki, Mukakai Maaka Whangataua's mother. Hare Mātenga died in December 1887 and Ataneta Matariki on 8 January 1886. Maori Land Court Succession Applications, Maori Land Court, Hastings, Boxes Waimarama V1 – NA.303–305; Okaihau V1 – NA.173; Waipuka V1 – NA.330.

Chapter 3

201 J. Binney, 'Some Observations on the Status of Māori Women', in Barbara Brookes, Charlotte Macdonald and Margaret Tennant (eds), *Women in History 2*, Bridget Williams Books, Wellington, 1992, p. 14.

202 M. Roberts & P. Wills, 'Understanding Maori Epistemology: A Scientific Perspective', in H. Wautischer (ed.), *Tribal Epistemologies: Essays in the Philosophy of Anthropology*, Ashgate, 1997, p. 46.

203 O'Regan, 'Old Myths and New Politics', p. 24.

204 Binney, 'Some Observations', pp. 19–20.

205 Roger Maaka, interview, Wellington, 1997. When Aritaku Maaka and others needed to refer to whakapapa, they always consulted Te Rina and other women of the family.

206 This was Irihapeti Whakamairu, a daughter of Retimana Te Korou.

207 Mohi Te Atahikoia, private MS, p.166, undated, copy held by author.

208 Patrick Geary, *Phantoms of Remembrance: Memory and Oblivion at the End of the First Millennium*, Princeton University Press, 1995, pp. 52, 63, 69–71, cited in David Lowenthal, 'History and Memory', *Public Historian*, vol. 19, no. 2, 1997, p. 38.

209 Lowenthal, 'History and Memory', p. 39.

210 See Angela Ballara, 'Wāhine Rangatira: Māori Women of Rank and their Role in the Women's Kotahitanga Movement of the 1890s', in Judith Binney (ed.), *The Shaping of History: Essays from the New Zealand Journal of History*, Bridget Williams Books, Wellington, 2001, p. 84.

211 Napier Minute Book no. 2, 20 August 1868.

212 Napier Minute Book 22a, no. 2, p. 310.

213 Golan Maaka, private MS, undated, Maaka Collection.

214 Napier Minute Book 22a, no. 2, p. 299.

215 Major Mason, interview, Mangakino, Oct 1996. Major often heard his mother, a niece of Te Rina's husband Pū-rākau Maika, talk of how Te Rina was kidnapped.

216 Ibid. Major Mason remembered being told that it was Ngāruma, a kuia from Tamaki-nui-a-rua (Dannevirke), who took Te Rina.

217 Matangihau Maaka (née Ellers), interview, Masterton, Apr 1996.

218 Angela Ballara, 'Maika, Purakau', in *Ngā Tāngata Taumata Rau, 1901–1920*, Auckland University Press/Te Tari Taiwhenua, Auckland/Wellington, 1996, p. 90.

219 See *Te Kopara*, 1 Dec 1917, for an invitation to attend the opening of this house.

220 Major Mason, interview, Mangakino, Oct 1996.

221 Ballara, 'Maika', p. 92.

222 Major Mason, interview, Oct 1996.

223 Max Mouatt, interview, Havelock North, Aug 1997.

224 Death register, Māori index, folio no. 1001/44, Auckland City Libraries. See also Ballara, 'Maika', p. 92.

225 Kupakupa was a brother of Hui-ariki and Hine-te-ao, and an uncle of Hika-toa.

226 A Waimārama chief.

227 Te Rina's grandmother.

228 Te Rina's father.

Chapter 4

229 Walter Lorne Campbell, Journals, 26 Mar 1869, Micro MS Copy 0001, reel 2, ATL.

230 Ibid.

231 See, for example, 'Panuitanga', *Te Wananga*, nos 33/34, 25 Aug 1877, p. 339.

232 According to Inia Whanga-taua's application of June 1884 for succession to his brother's Waimārama estate, Maaka Mukakai Whanga-taua died in December 1882. Māori Land Court, Hastings, boxes Waimarama V1 – NA.303–305, 1886–1905, Waipuka V1 – NA.330, and Okaihau V1 – NA.173.

233 Miriam Macgregor, *Pioneer Trails of Hawke's Bay*, Reed, Wellington, 1975, p. 38.

234 Alan Ward, *A Show of Justice: Racial 'Amalgamation' in Nineteenth Century New Zealand*, Auckland University Press, Auckland, 1983 reprint, p. 265.

235 *Te Wananga*, no. 20, 29 June 1876, p. 246, letter to the editor by Hemi Keepa, Hiraka Tuhua and Hori Te Aroatua regarding land disputes, fencing and farming.

236 W. Bayliss, *Takapau: The Sovereign Years, 1876–1976*, Hart Printing House, Hastings, 1975, p. 156.

237 Claudia Orange, 'Introduction', *The Turbulent Years, 1870–1900: The Māori Biographies from the Dictionary of New Zealand Biography Volume II*, Bridget Williams Books/ Department of Internal Affairs, Wellington, 1994, p. xviii.

238 Bayliss, *Takapau*, p. 44.

239 Macgregor, *Pioneer Trails*, p. 18.

240 Bayliss, *Takapau*, p. 45.

241 Probably F. H. Meinertzhagen, a Pākehā who leased land at Waimārama.

242 Minutes of Omahu meeting, 24 Dec 1876, *Te Wananga*, 13 Jan 1877.

243 See Te Whatahoro Jury manuscript books, Maori Purposes Fund Board series 189, B9, B18 and B63, ATL. Also mentioned in William Colenso's Native School notebooks, 1844–45, MS Papers 1408–1413a, ATL.

244 The children were Wikitōria, Irihāpeti, Ngāpera, Kāwana, Ānaru and Te Hikonga.
245 'He Korero Tatai Mo Horehore Pa, i Te Takapau', *JPS*, vol. 15, no. 58, Jun 1906, pp. 61–8.
246 Tunuiarangi manuscript, Polynesian Society Papers, MS Papers 1187, ATL.
247 Tuhua, 'He Korero Tatai Mo Horehore Pa', p. 64.
248 G. Maaka, genealogy book, undated, Maaka Collection.
249 Aritaku Maaka, genealogy book, undated, Maaka Collection.
250 Buchanan, *Maori History*, p. 152, topographical reference N134 c.327382, 'pa where Napier now stands'.
251 McEwen, *Rangitāne*, pp. 74–7.
252 G. Maaka, genealogy book.
253 McEwen, *Rangitāne*, p. 77.
254 A pā 5 kilometres south-west of Dannevirke. Ibid., p. 67.
255 Ballara, *Iwi*, p. 45.
256 Butterworth & Young, *Māori Affairs*, p. 23.
257 Ward, *Show of Justice*, p. 264.
258 Ibid., p. 205, citing S. Locke to D. McLean, 23 Jan 1865.
259 Ibid., p. 264.
260 Richard S. Hill, *Policing the Colonial Frontier: The Theory and Practice of Coercive Social and Racial Control in New Zealand, 1767–1867, Part Two*, Historical Publications Branch, Department of Internal Affairs, Wellington, 1986, p. 801.
261 Ibid., pp. 814–15.
262 Butterworth & Young, *Maori Affairs*, pp. 35–6.
263 Walker, *Ka Whawhai Tonu Matou*, pp. 154–5.
264 O'Malley, *Agents of Autonomy*, p. 50.
265 *New Zealand Parliamentary Debates*, 11 Oct 1872, vol. 13, p. 587, cited in ibid., pp. 52–3.
266 Ibid., pp. 53–7, 63.
267 Ibid., p. 259.
268 *Te Wananga*, 7 Jul 1877, p. 285.
269 O'Malley, *Agents of Autonomy*, pp. 65–6.
270 Sinclair, *Kinds of Peace*, p. 103.
271 O'Malley, *Agents of Autonomy*, pp. 72, 261.
272 See the very good biography of Mohi Te Atahikoia by A. Ballara in *The Turbulent Years, 1870–1900: The Maori Biographies from the Dictionary of New Zealand Biography, Volume Two*, Bridget Williams Books/Internal Affairs, Wellington, 1994, p. 153.
273 Hill, *Colonial Frontier*, p. 803.
274 Ibid., pp. 803–4.
275 Ward, *Show of Justice*, p. 98.
276 'This is the election of Ngāi Tahu, for Maaka Whanga-taua as the investigator, for Rāpana Whiuwhiu as a policeman, for Ānaru Tū-roa as a scribe. These are the names of the people.'

Chapter 5

277 His headstone at Waimārama records that he died in 1936 at the age of 70.
278 Roger Maaka, interview, Whakatāne, 1993. Golan Maaka wrote in his whakapapa book (held by the author): 'Whiu Carroll said, his family, ours (Te Rina, Mouru etc) and Karetu = N'Ura and N' Hikatoa lived for years at Matahiwi with Moana-nui – but had to return to Waimarama.' See also Bradford Haami, *Dr Golan Maaka: Māori Doctor*, Tandem, North Shore, 1995, p. 57.
279 M. M. Redwood, *Proud Silk: A New Zealand Racing History*, Reed, Wellington, 1979, pp. 190–1.
280 Roger Maaka, interview, Whakatāne, 1993. Old Te Meihana of Poroporo in Whakatāne told Golan that he had met Aritaku when they travelled to the opening of Te Tokanga-nui-a-Noho at Te Kuiti. See Binney, *Redemption Songs*, pp. 272–5.
281 Certificate held by Roger Maaka, Christchurch.
282 Hori Te Aroatua to editor, 23 Aug 1894, *Huia Tangata Kotahi*, 8 Sep 1894, p. 3.
283 Te Komiti o te Hahi o Te Takapau minute book, Jan 1922, Maaka Collection.
284 Date of death taken from his headstone at Waimārama. See also Death register, Māori index, folio no. 1413/36, Auckland City Libraries.
285 Roger Maaka, interview, Whakatāne, 1993.
286 Roger Maaka, email to author, 14 Aug 2003.

287 G. Maaka, genealogy book, undated, Maaka Collection.
288 A pā high on the ridge overlooking Takapau township.
289 Tanguru Tūhua, book dated 1906, Polynesian Society Papers, MS Papers 1187–187, ATL. Author's translation.

Chapter 6

290 For her whakapapa, see chapter 7.
291 Birth index, folio 2055, Auckland City Libraries. The small community here included the Rissetto family, who were closely related to Annie's family.
292 J. E. Bremer, *The History of Greenhills*, author, Greenhills, 1976, p. 51.
293 James Belich, *Making Peoples: A History of the New Zealanders from Polynesian Settlement to the End of the Nineteenth Century*, Penguin, Auckland, 1996, p. 256.
294 Koa Murdoch, interview, Whangarei, Jun 1997.
295 *Hawke's Bay Herald*, 16 Dec 1926.
296 Haami, *Dr Golan Maaka*, p. 90.
297 Date of death taken from headstone at Waimārama.
298 Annie Maaka, diary for 1915, Maaka Collection. The writer was probably either her daughter Nancy or her son Markie. 'Tot' was a nickname for her son Derek, while 'Pup' was the family name for Aritaku.
299 Interviews, Roger Maaka, Christchurch, 1996; Roseanne Jones, Waioeka, 1996. Their fathers both kept daily diaries in the manner of their mother Annie.
300 These books, tied with a blue ribbon, were found recently hidden in the garage at Dr Maaka's home at Whakatāne. This had been locked since his death in 1978.
301 *AJHR*, 1921–22, G-5, p. 40.
302 *Hawke's Bay Herald*, 30 Jun 1926.
303 Harry C. Evison, *The Long Dispute: Maori Land Rights and European Colonisation in Southern New Zealand*, Canterbury University Press, Christchurch, 1997, p. 345.
304 Miles Fairburn, *Nearly Out of Heart and Hope: The Puzzle of a Colonial Labourer's Diary*, Auckland University Press, Auckland, 1995, p. 4.
305 Ibid., pp. 200–1.
306 Basil Howard, *Rakiura: A History of Stewart Island, New Zealand*, Reed, Dunedin, 1940, p. 210.
307 *Kahiti o Niu Tireni*, no. 3, 24 Jan 1924. The list of beneficial owners was also published in Eva Wilson, *Titi Heritage*, Craig Printing Co., Invercargill, 1974, pp. 162, 163, 165.
308 Bremer, *Greenhills*, pp. 38–9.
309 Howard, *Rakiura*, p. 213.
310 Interview, Koa Murdoch, Whangarei, Jun 1997.
311 H. Beattie, *Traditional Lifeways of the Southern Maori: The Otago University Museum Ethnological Project, 1920* (ed. Atholl Anderson), University of Otago Press, Dunedin, 1994, pp. 178, 184.
312 The birding process outlined here was described to the author by Koa Murdoch, interview, Whangarei, Jun 1997.
313 Edward Shortland, *The Southern Districts of New Zealand*, London, 1851, Capper Press reprint, Christchurch, 1974, p. 312.
314 Stewart Island.
315 *Huia* was a sailing cutter belonging to Bob and Nay Bragg. O. Sansom, *The Stewart Islanders*, Reed, Wellington, 1970, pp. 105, 160.
316 Island.
317 'Huies' may refer to meetings, to 'old times', or to the mutton-birding term for carrying the birds on a length of flax.
318 *Despatch* was a steamer. Sansom, *The Stewart Islanders*, p. 54.
319 Mrs Buller's husband Barney Buller was the captain of the *Hinemoa*, which serviced all the lighthouses around the district. Murdoch, interview, 1997.
320 Abraham's Bosom is a sheltered bay at Port Adventure.
321 Cara Gilroy.
322 Cara Gilroy's sister Sarah.
323 *Gannet* was a cutter with a big gaff topsail. Sansom, *The Stewart Islanders*, p. 105.
324 Bracken.
325 *Rosetta* was a schooner belonging to Tom Bragg. Sansom, *The Stewart Islanders*, pp. 105, 160.

326 Tom Bragg.

327 'Old lady Marshall' ran the store at Halfmoon Bay.

328 'Back beach' was the generic term for a beach sheltered from the prevailing westerly wind. Murdoch, interview, 1997.

329 A packed bag is a kelp bag (poha-tītī) into which birds were packed.

330 A narrow strip of water at Port Adventure.

331 People would have been 'growling' because the rain had hindered the catching of birds. If it was absolutely necessary, birding continued in the rain – a muddy and dirty process. Murdoch, interview, 1997.

332 Tītī hearts had to be boiled for a long time as they were fairly tough. Sometimes they were pierced with a stick and roasted on a fire. They were a common meal here. Koa Murdoch, interview, 1997.

333 Perhaps a term for boiling underwear, handkerchiefs and whites.

334 The birding grounds.

335 Weka.

336 *Hananui* was a fishing boat skippered by Wallace Nilsen. Sansom, *The Stewart Islanders*, pp. 187, 230.

337 Dumplings, often roasted or boiled in camp ovens with mutton-birds.

338 Horomamae (Owen Island) is south of Tiā, off John Point at the entrance of Lords River.

339 Mrs Hansen ran the boarding house on Stewart Island.

340 Reworking rua that have already been worked over. Tiny Metzger, interview, Bluff, Feb 1998.

341 Koa Murdoch, interview, Whangarei, Dec 1996. Catching a white tete (tītī) was an aitua (bad omen); they were never killed or eaten. Koa remembered her father, William Haberfield, bringing one home and telling his children that they should never kill such a bird. He then returned it to its rua. Herries Beattie, in *Traditional Lifeways of the Southern Maori* (p. 179), noted that the white tītī was often called the 'jimmy-bird'. Jimmy is a southern term for a ghost.

342 A hollow log or tree trunk used as a gong to signal the start of work in the morning. The tītī islands may have been the last location where pahū remained in functional use. See Mervyn McLean, *Māori Music*, Auckland University Press, Auckland, 1996, p. 171.

343 A bird that is half white and half grey, or has white patches.

344 To torch (rama-tītī) is to collect tītī at night using lanterns and torches made of material found in the bush.

Chapter 7

345 Sandra Maaka, interview, Whakatāne, 1995.

346 Florence Maaka, interview, Whakatāne, 1997.

347 Wishie Jaram, interview, Whakatāne, 1992.

348 Sandra Maaka, interview, 1995.

349 Florence Maaka, interview, Whakatāne, 1996.

350 *Data Papers and Conference Agenda, Young Maori Leaders' Conference*, Council of Adult Education, University of Auckland, Auckland, 1959; *Te Ao Hou*, vol. 8, no. 2, Mar 1960, pp. 57–9.

351 In J. G. Wilson and others, *History of Hawke's Bay*, Reed, Dunedin, 1939.

352 Pei Te Hurinui, *King Potatau*.

353 When I was eight, my brother and I sat at the breakfast table eating our porridge while Golan drew a diagram and explained to us the makeup of an atom and the construction of a nuclear bomb.

354 Sandra Maaka, interview.

355 Roger Maaka, interview, Christchurch, 1995.

356 On Golan and cars, see Haami, *Dr Golan Maaka*, pp. 181–3.

357 Sandra Maaka, interview.

358 Haami, *Dr Golan Maaka*, p. 170.

359 Florence Maaka, interview, Whakatāne, 1993.

360 Sandra Maaka, interview, 1995.

361 Roseanne Jones (daughter of Victor Maaka), interview, Waioeka, Nov 1996.

362 K. F. Tyro & K. G. Scarlett (eds), *Te Aute College: 125th Anniversary, 1854–1979*, Te Aute College, Pukehou, 1979, pp. 10, 11, 13.

363 Roger Maaka, interview, Christchurch, 1995.

364 *AJHR*, 1921–22, E-3, p 9.

365 Tyro & Scarlett, *Te Aute College*, p. 25.

366 Florence Maaka, interview, 1993.

367 According to the school register, George Haawea Finau was twenty in 1917.

368 Florence Maaka, interview, Whakatāne, 1994.

369 Sandra Maaka, interview, Whakatāne, 1997.

370 G. Maaka to Annie Maaka, 11 April 1922, Maaka Collection.

371 Walter Lorne Campbell, Journals, 1868–1872, 9 Nov 1870, ATL.

372 Te Aute College Archives, Te Aute College, Pukehou.

373 Sandra Maaka, interview, Whakatāne, 1997.

374 Dormitory no. 2.

375 Reverend F. Bennett.

376 It was common for boys to take apples from the minister's orchard and hide them in their mattresses. On one occasion Golan decided to acquire a few apples. After filling a pillowcase, he heard someone coming, so threw the bag over the hedge – into the middle of the minister's tea party. Roger Maaka, interview, Christchurch, 1995.

377 Mr C. Scully was a staff member.

378 Tom Tibble: first enrolled at Te Aute in 1920.

379 'Chaddo' is Ernest Chadwick, Golan's best friend, who was to marry his sister Nancy.

380 'Vic' is Golan's brother Victor.

381 E. Campbell: first enrolled 1920.

382 Edward, Prince of Wales, was then on a royal visit to New Zealand and was to visit Rotorua.

383 Wiremu W. Mātāmua enrolled at Te Aute in 1918.

384 This was the news that Te Aute boys were to visit Rotorua to attend the welcome for the Prince of Wales.

385 On this day the 40 selected boys left for Rotorua. 'Huks' are girls from Hukarere College.

386 Girls from Rotorua.

387 The Maakas' home at Ōhinemutu, next to Tū-noho-pū marae.

388 Waerenga-a-Hika College boys from Gisborne.

389 Reverend Frederick Bennett.

390 Bill Wakarua.

391 Alex Takarangi from Wanganui, who had represented Hawke's Bay as a wing-threequarter whilst still a pupil at Te Aute in 1896. He captained the New Zealand Māori team which toured Australia in 1910, and played 100 first class games. See A. Carman, *Maori Rugby 1884–1979*, Sporting Publications, Wellington, 1980, pp. 4–5, 249.

392 Reverend Ernest Loten, headmaster of Te Aute from 1920 to 1951.

393 The family's name for their father, Aritaku.

394 Palmerston North.

395 Agriculture was a major subject at the school, and the boys tended the vegetable gardens.

396 Waipukurau.

397 Paraire Tōmoana and Dawson Nikera were old boys of Te Aute and members of the Māori rugby advisory board. Dawson Nikera was a New Zealand Māori representative in 1911; see Carman, *Maori Rugby*, p. 25.

398 Te Angina Bill U. Whakarua from Taranaki: enrolled 1919.

399 The trolley (also known as a jigger) ran on the railway tracks. They possibly went to Lake Poukawa.

400 J. H. Hulton: enrolled 1919. Named Campbell Hulton in the school registers.

401 There were 10,000 spectators. *Te Kopara*, 31 Jul 1920, p. 11.

402 Takapau.

403 Hikurangi Boys' College, at Carterton in Wairarapa. *AJHR*, 1921–22, E-3, p. 10.

404 Golan's father Aritaku.

405 A form of detention.

406 Rīwai Wāwātai: enrolled 1919.

407 Paul Bennett: enrolled 1917.

408 Walker Mōrete: enrolled 1917.

409 Tipi Rōpiha: enrolled 1918.

410 The score published in *Te Kopara*, 31 Jul 1920, p. 11, was 13–3.

411 Pine Tamahōri was an Anglican priest who had been head prefect and captained the 1904 Te Aute College rugby team which toured New South Wales. See R. R. Alexander, *The Story of Te Aute College*, Reed, Wellington, 1979, p. 127.

412 Ratima Timihou: enrolled 1919. Buller has not been identified.

413 A gymnastics bar.

414 George Mackey: enrolled 1917.

415 Sam Ruawai: enrolled 1920.

416 A. Winters: enrolled 1920.

417 Rangi Rūpuha: enrolled 1920.

418 J. M. Henderson, *Ratana: The Man, the Church, the Political Movement*, 2nd edition, Reed, Wellington, 1972, pp. 24–5.

419 Walker, *Ka Whawhai Tonu Matou*, p. 183.

420 G. Maaka, 'Ratana Pa: A General Survey of Conditions at Ratana from a Public Health Perspective', MB ChB thesis, University of Otago, 1931, p. 54.

421 Florence Maaka, interview, Whakatāne, 1997.

422 Sandra Maaka, interview, Whakatāne, 1995.

423 Tiro was another name for Iwikaingata.

424 Te Rangiwhaiata was actually a son of Whangataua and his first wife Reretaupora.

425 Kahungunu's daughter.

426 Golan's mother, Annie Haberfield.

427 Golan's maternal great-grandmother.

428 Golan wrote here: 'Southern hapu = Ngati Huirapa, Ngati Irakehu and Ngati Rakiamoa.'

Chapter 8

429 Kathy Irwin, 'Maori Research Methods and Practices', *Sites*, no. 28, Autumn 1994, pp. 27–8, cited in Linda Tuhiwai Smith, *Decolonizing Methodologies: Research and Indigenous Peoples*, Zed Books/University of Otago Press, Dunedin, 1999, p. 184.

430 Russell Bishop, 'Initiating Empowering Research', *New Zealand Journal of Educational Studies*, vol. 29, no. 1, 1994, p. 176, cited in Smith, *Decolonizing Methodologies*, pp. 184–5.

431 Smith, *Decolonizing Methodologies*, p. 185.

432 Te Aroha McDowell, 'Publishing Maori Material', *Broadsheet*, no. 129, May 1985, pp. 22–3, cited in Dell, 'The Maori Book ', p. 100.

433 McRae, 'From Māori Oral Traditions', pp. 26–7, 39.

434 Michael King, 'Some Maori Attitudes to Documents', in King (ed.), *Tihe Mauri Ora: Aspects of Maoritanga*, Methuen, Wellington, 1978, pp. 14–15.

435 J. E. Traue, 'The Commodification of Information', *New Zealand Studies*, vol. 7, no. 2, Jul 1997, pp. 23–4.

436 Ibid., p. 25.

437 Mita Carter, 'The Preservation of the Maori Oral Tradition', *Oral History in New Zealand*, vol. 3, 1990–91, p. 6.

438 For example, Sir Guy Powles, 'Fundamental Human Rights in 1968', Speech to Wellington Teachers' Training College, 8 Nov 1968, Ombudsman Speeches and Articles, Office of the Ombudsman, ABJY, Acc W4101, box 357, Archives New Zealand, Wellington.

439 Maryanne Cheryl Baker, 'Pharmacy and Rongoa Maori', in Paula Martin (comp.), *He Tiro Arotahi ki te Pūtaiao, te Pāngarau me te Hangarau: Māori into Science, Maths and Technology*, Te Puni Kōkiri, Wellington, 1996, p. 12.

440 O'Regan, 'Old Myths and New Politics', pp. 21–3, 26.

441 *Evening Post*, 4 Jul 1989, cited in Jennifer Garlick, *Māori Language Publishing: Some Issues*, Huia, Wellington, 1998, p. 55.

442 This can be seen, for example, in Ngāi Tahu's aims for its people outlined in the 'Social and Cultural Development' section of the special edition of *Te Karaka, Crown Settlement Offer: Consultation Document from the Ngāi Tahu Negotiating Group*, Christchurch, 1997, p. 52.

443 Hirini Mead, 'Tribal Archival Research: The Ngāti Awa Experience', *Oral History in New Zealand*, vol. 2, 1989, pp. 28, 29.

444 Ibid., p. 28.

445 O'Regan, 'Old Myths and New Politics', p. 26.

446 *Response to the Adult Literacy Report for the Ministry of Eucation, November 1999*, Literacy Aotearoa, Auckland, 1999, p. 10.

447 M. Walker, K. Udy & N. Pole, *Adult Literacy in New Zealand: Results from the International Adult Literacy Survey*, Ministry of Education, Wellington, 1997, p. 1.

448 *Response to the Adult Literacy Report*, p. 11.

449 Jenkins, 'Te Ihi', p. 138.

450 McRae, 'From Māori Oral Traditions to Print', p. 40.

451 Ibid., p. 26.

452 Ray Harlow, *A Word-list of South Island Maori*, Linguistic Society of New Zealand, 1985, pp. vi–ix.

453 J. Spiers, *Moeraki*, Reed, Auckland, 1997, pp. 16–24.

454 Watkin's journal, 8 Sep 1840, cited in Harlow, *Word-list*, p. vii.

455 *Te Matatiki: Contemporary Māori Words*, revised edition, Oxford University Press, Auckland, 1996, p. vii.

456 Bruce Biggs, 'The Maori Language Past and Present', in Erik Schwimmer (ed.), *The Maori People in the Nineteen-Sixties*, Longman Paul, Auckland, 1968, pp. 79–81.

457 *Preserving Family Collections and Care of Archival Materials*, Conservation Services, National Library of New Zealand/Te Puna Matauranga o Aotearoa, Wellington, 1997. See also P. M. Najar, 'Environmental Conditions For National Archives Collections', Con-C83, Archives New Zealand, Wellington, 14 Jan 1992.

458 Hinerangi Himiona, email to author, 20 Jun 2000.

459 Anne Salmond, *Hui: A Study of Maori Ceremonial Gatherings*, Reed, Wellington, 1975, p. 121.

460 Caselberg (ed.), *Maori is My Name*, p. 147. Author's translation.

Te takenga mai o ngā kōrero
Bibliography

Abbreviations:

AJHR — *Appendix to the Journals of the House of Representatives*
ATL — Alexander Turnbull Library, Wellington
AM — Auckland War Memorial Museum Library
GNZMMSS — Sir George Grey Collection, Auckland City Libraries
JPS — *Journal of the Polynesian Society*
MS — manuscript
NZJH — *New Zealand Journal of History*
TPNZI — *Transactions and Proceedings of the New Zealand Institute*
TS — typescript

Unpublished sources:
Archives and Manuscripts
Alexander Turnbull Library, Wellington
Campbell, Walter Lorne, Journals, 1868–1872
Maori Purposes Fund Board papers, MS papers 0189, folder 87
Moore, Thomas, 'Reminiscences of Thomas Moore of Waimarama from 1845', qMS moo, 48040
Polynesian Society Papers, MS Papers 1187, folder 178
Te Atahikoia, Mohi, MS Papers 1354 (copy held by author)
Te Whatahoro Jury, Journals, MS Papers 0189-B054

Archives New Zealand, Wellington
Najar, P. M., 'Environmental Conditions For National Archives Collections', TS, Con-C83, 14 Jan 1992
Powles, Sir Guy, 'Fundamental Human Rights in 1968', Speech to Wellington Teachers' Training College, 8 Nov 1968, Ombudsman Speeches and Articles, Office of the Ombudsman, ABJY, Acc W4101

Auckland City Libraries
Death registers, Māori index: Te Rina Maaka/Maika, folio no. 1001/44; Aritaku Maaka, folio no. 1413/36
Grey New Zealand Māori Autograph Series, GNZMA 215, 467, 626
Okawhare, Wiremu Paratene, to Sir George Grey, 'He Pukapuka no Nga Tupuna', 17 Mar 1853, GNZMMSS 33
Taylor, Richard, 'Manuscript Notes on New Zealand and its Native Inhabitants', Part 2, MSS 297/30

Auckland War Memorial Museum Library
Graham, George, 'The Origin and Meanings of Maori Placenames', TS, MS 120, M 54

Berry Historical Library, Hawke's Bay Museum, Napier
Buchanan, J. D. H., Papers
Colenso, William, Journal (copy)

Maaka Collection (held by author)
Haami, B. J., personal diaries
Waikopiro Minute Book, Native Land Court, 1889

Māori Land Court, Hastings
Napier Minute Books: nos 2, 7, 22a no. 2
Boxes: Okaihau V1 – NA.173, Waimarama V1 – NA.303–305,1886–1905, Waipuka V1 – NA.330

Mitchell Library, State Library of New South Wales, Sydney, Australia
William Colenso, letters written to, c. 1844 – c. 1856, MLMSS.137

Te Aute College, Pukehou
Archives

University of Auckland, Anthropology Department
Mahupuku, Hikawera Wiremu, M29,4cop.4, undated, translation by Pat Hohepa

Waikato University
Brown, Reverend [Alfred], Journal, 1845 (original held at Bernard Sladen Research Library, Tauranga Public Library)

Wellington Public Library
Marsden, M., & T. A. Henare, 'Kaitiakitanga: A Definitive Introduction to the Holistic World View of the Maori', paper prepared for the Ministry for the Environment, Nov 1992

Interviews
Himiona, Hinerangi; Auckland (email), Jun 2000
Jaram, Wishie; Whakatāne, 1992
Jones, Roseanne; Waioeka, Nov 1996
Maaka, Florence; Whakatāne, 1993, 1994, 1996, 1997
Maaka, Matangihau; Whakatāne, 1995; Masterton, Apr 1996
Maaka, Roger; Whakatāne, 1993; Christchurch, 1995, 1996; Wellington, 1997
Maaka, Sandra; Whakatāne, 1995, 1997; Masterton, Apr 1996
Mason, Major; Mangakino, Oct 1996
Metzger, Tiny; Bluff, Feb 1998
Mouatt, Max; Havelock North, Aug 1997
Murdoch, Koa; Whangarei, Dec 1996, Jun 1997
Ngata, Tipene; Waiomatatini, 1989
Royal, Charles; Otaki, Nov 1996
Solomon, Bill; Kaikoura, Jun 1997
Walker, Monty; Auckland, Jan 2000
Wiri, Rapata; Auckland, Nov 1998

Theses
Ballara, Angela, 'The Origins of Ngati Kahungunu', PhD thesis, Victoria University of Wellington, 1991
Broughton, Ruka, 'The Origins of Ngaa Rauru Kiitahi', MA thesis, Victoria University of Wellington, 1979
Jackson, M., 'Literacy, Communications and Social Change: The Maori Case, 1830–1870', MA thesis, University of Auckland, 1967
Jenkins, K., 'Te Ihi, Te Mana, Te Wehi o Te Ao Tuhi: Maori Print Literacy from 1814–1855, Literacy, Power and Colonisation', MA thesis, University of Auckland, 1991
Maaka, G., 'Ratana Pa: A General Survey of Conditions at Ratana from a Public Health Perspective', MB ChB thesis, University of Otago, 1931

Published sources:
Articles and Chapters
Baker, Maryanne Cheryl, 'Pharmacy and Rongoa Maori', in Paula Martin (comp.), *He Tiro Arotahi ki te Pūtaiao, te Pāngarau me te Hangarau: Māori into Science, Maths and Technology*, Te Puni Kōkiri, Wellington, 1996
Ballara, Angela, 'Maika, Purakau', in *Ngā Tāngata Taumata Rau, 1901–1920*, Auckland University Press/Te Tari Taiwhenua, Auckland/Wellington, 1996
Ballara, Angela, 'Te Atahikoia, Mohi', in *The Turbulent Years, 1870–1900: The Maori Biographies from the Dictionary of New Zealand Biography, Volume Two*, Bridget Williams Books/Department of Internal Affairs, Wellington, 1994
Ballara, Angela, 'Wāhine Rangatira: Māori Women of Rank and their Role in the Women's Kotahitanga Movement of the 1890's', in Judith Binney (ed.), *The Shaping of History: Essays from the New Zealand Journal of History*, Bridget Williams Books, Wellington, 2001
Biggs, Bruce, 'Knowledge as Allegory,' in John Morrison, Paul Geraghty & Linda Crowl (eds) *Science of Pacific Island Peoples, Volume Four, Education, Language, Patterns and Policy*, Institute of Pacific Studies, University of the South Pacific, Suva, 1994
Biggs, Bruce, 'The Maori Language Past and Present', in Erik Schwimmer (ed.), *The Maori People in the Nineteen-Sixties*, Longman Paul, Auckland, 1968

Biggs, Bruce, 'The Oral Literature of the Polynesians', *Te Ao Hou*, no. 49, 1964

Binney, J., 'Christianity and the Maoris to 1840: A Comment', *NZJH*, vol. 3, no. 2, 1969

Binney, J., 'Some Observations on the Status of Maori Women', in Barbara Brookes, Charlotte Macdonald & Margaret Tennant (eds), *Women in History 2*, Bridget Williams Books, 1992

Carter, M., 'The Preservation of the Maori Oral Tradition', *Oral History in New Zealand*, vol. 3, 1990–91

Dell, Sharon, 'The Maori Book or the Book in Maori', *New Zealand Libraries*, vol. 45, no. 5, Mar 1987

Downes, T. W., 'History of Ngati-Kahu-ngunu; Chapter I – Continued', *JPS*, vol. 23, 1914

Head L., & B. Mikaere, 'Was 19th Century Maori Society Literate?', *Archifacts*, Jun 1988

Keenan, Danny, 'Aversion to Print? Māori Resistance to the Written Word', in P. Griffith, P. Hughes & A. Loney (eds), *A Book in the Hand: Essays on the History of the Book in New Zealand*, Auckland University Press, Auckland, 2000

King, Michael, 'Some Maori Attitudes to Documents', in M. King (ed.), *Tihe Mauri Ora: Aspects of Maoritanga*, Methuen, Wellington, 1978

Locke, Samuel, 'Historical Traditions of the Taupo and East Coast Tribes', *TPNZI*, vol. 15, 1882

Lowenthal, David, 'History and Memory', *Public Historian*, vol. 19, no. 2, 1997

Maaka, G., 'Health Trends in the Maori Today', in *Data Papers and Conference Agenda, Young Maori Leaders Conference*, Council of Adult Education, University of Auckland, Auckland, 1959; also published in *Te Ao Hou*, vol. 8, no. 2, Mar 1960

McRae, J., 'From Māori Oral Traditions to Print', in P. Griffiths, R. Harvey & K. Maslen (eds), *Book & Print in New Zealand: A Guide to Print Culture in Aotearoa*, Victoria University Press, Wellington, 1997

McRae, J., 'Maori Literature: A Survey', in Terry Sturm (ed.), *The Oxford History of New Zealand Literature*, Oxford University Press, Auckland, 1991

McRae, Jane, 'Transitions', in Penny Griffith, Ross Harvey & Keith Maslen (eds), *Book and Print in New Zealand: A Guide to Print Culture in Aotearoa*, Victoria University Press, Wellington, 1997

Mead, Hirini, 'Tribal Archival Research: The Ngāti Awa Experience', *Oral History in New Zealand*, vol. 2, 1989

Milne, R. S., 'The Inevitability of Administrative Discretion', in R. S. Milne (ed.) *Bureaucracy in New Zealand*, New Zealand Institute of Public Administration/Oxford University Press, Wellington/London, 1957

Murray, Jenny, 'Tenei ano Taku Korero: Here is my Report', *Te Pae Tawhito o te Wā/History Now*, vol. 2, no. 1, May 1996

Ngata, A. T., 'The Maori and Printed Matter', in R. A. Mckay (ed.) *A History of Printing in New Zealand, 1830–1940*, Wellington Club of Printing House Craftsmen, Wellington, 1940

Ngata, Apirana, 'Tribal Organization', in I. L. G. Sutherland (ed.), *The Maori People Today: A General Survey*, Whitcombe & Tombs/Oxford University Press, Christchurch/Auckland, 1940

Orange, Claudia, 'Introduction', *The Turbulent Years, 1870–1900: The Māori Biographies from the Dictionary of New Zealand Biography, Volume Two*, Bridget Williams Books/Department of Internal Affairs, Wellington, 1994

O'Regan, Tipene, 'Old Myths and New Politics; Some Contemporary Uses of Traditional History', *NZJH*, vol. 26, no. 1, 1992

Owens, J. M. R., 'Christianity and the Maoris to 1840', *NZJH*, vol. 2, no. 1, 1968

Parr, C. J., 'A Missionary Library: Printed Attempts to Instruct the Maori, 1815–1845', *JPS*, vol. 70, 1961

Parr, C. J., 'Maori Literacy, 1843–1867', *JPS*, vol. 72, 1963

Pugsley, Chris, 'Walking the Taranaki Wars: Maori Defeat at Mahoetahi, 6 November 1860', *New Zealand Defence Quarterly*, no. 11, 1995

Roberts, Roma Mere, & Peter Wills, 'Understanding Maori Epistemology: A Scientific Perspective', in H. Wautischer (ed.), *Tribal Epistemologies: Essays in the Philosophy of Anthropology*, Ashgate, 1998

Salmond, Anne, 'Maori Epistemologies', in Joanna Overing (ed.), *Reason and Morality*, Tavistock Publications, London

Smith, S. P., 'The Lore of the Whare-wananga: Part 1 – Te Kauwae-runga', *JPS*, vol. 22, 1913

Smith, Takirirangi, 'Doing Research From Home: Tangata Whenua Issues and Māori Research', in Te Pūmanawa Hauora (ed.), *Proceedings of Te Oru Rangahau/Māori Research and Development Conference, 7–9 July, 1998*, 2nd edition, Te Putahi-a-Toi School of Māori Studies, Massey University, Palmerston North, 1999

Tau, Te Maire, 'Mātauranga Māori as an Epistemology', *Te Pouhere Korero*, vol. 1, no. 1, March 1999

Traue, J. E., 'The Commodification of Information', *New Zealand Studies*, vol. 7, no. 2, Jul 1997

Tuhua, Tanguru, 'He Korero Tatai Mo Horehore Pa, I Te Takapau', *JPS*, vol. 15, no. 58, 1906

Van Meijl, Toon, 'Historicising Maoritanga: Colonial Ethnography and the Reification of Maori Traditions', *JPS*, vol. 105, no. 3, 1996

Winitana, C., 'From Words to Wood,' *Mana*, no. 6, Jul–Sep 1994

Books and Pamphlets

Adkin, G. Leslie, *Horowhenua: Its Maori Place-names and their Topographic and Historical Background*, Department of Internal Affairs, Wellington, 1948

Alexander, R. R., *The Story of Te Aute College*, Reed, Wellington, 1979

Bagnall, A. G., *Wairarapa: An Historical Excursion*, Masterton Trust Lands Trust, Masterton, 1976

Bagnall, A. G., & G. C. Peterson, *William Colenso, Printer, Missionary, Botanist, Explorer, Politician: His Life and Journeys*, Reed, Wellington, 1948

Ballara, Angela, *Iwi: The Dynamics of Māori Tribal Organisation from c. 1769 to c. 1945*, Victoria University Press, Wellington, 1998

Bawden, P., *The Years Before Waitangi: A Story of Early Maori/European Contact in New Zealand*, author, 1989

Bayliss, W., *Takapau: The Sovereign Years, 1876–1976*, Hart Printing House, Hastings, 1975

Beattie, H. (ed. Atholl Anderson), *Traditional Lifeways of the Southern Maori: The Otago University Museum Ethnological Project, 1920*, University of Otago Press, Dunedin, 1994

Belich, James, *Making Peoples: A History of the New Zealanders from Polynesian Settlement to the End of the Nineteenth Century*, Penguin, Auckland, 1996

Best, Elsdon, *Fishing Methods and Devices of the Maori*, Dominion Museum Bulletin no. 12, 1929, reprinted by Government Printer, Wellington, 1986

Best, Elsdon, *The Maori School of Learning: Its Objects, Methods, and Ceremonial*, Government Printer, Wellington, 1974

Binney, J., *Redemption Songs: A Life of Te Kooti Arikirangi Te Turuki*, Auckland University Press/Bridget Williams Books, Auckland, 1995

Binney, J., *The Legacy of Guilt: A Life of Thomas Kendall*, Oxford University Press, Auckland, 1968

Bremer, J. E., *The History of Greenhills*, author, Greenhills, 1976

Brown, William, *New Zealand and its Aborigines: Being an Account of the Aborigines, Trade, and Resources of the Colony and the Advantages it now Presents as a Field for Emigration and the Investment of Capital*, Smith, Elder & Co., London, 1845

Buchanan, J. D. H. (ed. D. R. Simmons), *The Maori History and Place Names of Hawke's Bay*, Reed, Wellington, 1973

Butterworth, G. V., & H. R. Young, *Maori Affairs*, GP Books, Wellington, 1990

Care of Archival Materials, Conservation Services, National Library of New Zealand Te Puna Mātauranga o Aotearoa, Wellington, 1997

Carman, A., *Maori Rugby 1884–1979*, Sporting Publications, Wellington, 1980

Caselberg, John (ed.), *Maori is my Name: Historical Maori Writings in Translation*, John McIndoe, Dunedin, 1975

Crown Settlement Offer: Consultation Document from the Ngāi Tahu Negotiating Group, special edition of *Te Karaka*, Christchurch, 1997

Dieffenbach, E., *Travels in New Zealand*, vol. 2, John Murray, London, 1843, Capper Press reprint, Christchurch, 1974

Evison, Harry, C., *The Long Dispute: Maori Land Rights and European Colonisation in Southern New Zealand*, Canterbury University Press, Christchurch, 1997

Fairburn, Miles, *Nearly Out of Heart and Hope: The Puzzle of a Colonial Labourer's Diary*, Auckland University Press, Auckland, 1995

Firth, Raymond, *Economics of the New Zealand Maori*, 2nd edition, Government Printer, Wellington, 1959

Gamow, George, *One, Two Three . . . Infinity: Facts and Speculations of Science*, Viking, New York, 1947

Garlick, Jennifer, *Māori Language Publishing: Some Issues*, Huia, Wellington, 1998

Glen, R. (ed.), *Mission and Moko: The Church Missionary Society in New Zealand, 1814–1882*, Latimer Fellowship of New Zealand, Christchurch, c. 1992

Grant, Sydney, *Waimarama*, Dunmore, Palmerston North, 1977

Haami, Bradford, *Dr Golan Maaka: Māori Doctor*, Tandem, North Shore, 1995

Harlow, Ray, *A Word-list of South Island Maori*, Linguistic Society of New Zealand, 1985

He Kōrero Pūrākau mo Ngā Taunahanahatanga a Ngā Tupuna, New Zealand Geographic Board, Wellington, 1990

Henderson, J. M., *Ratana: The Man, the Church, the Political Movement*, 2nd edition, Reed, Wellington, 1972

Hill, Richard S., *Policing the Colonial Frontier: The Theory and Practice of Coercive Social and Racial Control in New Zealand, 1767–1867, Part 2*, Historical Publications Branch, Department of Internal Affairs, Wellington, 1986

Howard, Basil, *Rakiura: A History of Stewart Island, New Zealand*, Reed, Dunedin, 1940

Illich, I., & B. Sanders, *ABC: The Alphabetization of the Popular Mind*, North Point Press, San Francisco, 1988

Jones, Kevin, *Ngā Tohuwhenua Mai Te Rangi: A New Zealand Archaeology in Aerial Photographs*, Victoria University Press, Wellington, 1994

Kawharu, I. H., *Maori Land Tenure: Studies of a Changing Institution*, Clarendon Press, Oxford/New York, 1977

Keene, Florence, *Tai Tokerau*, author, Whāngārei, c. 1986

Keesing, Felix M., *The Changing Maori, Memoirs of the Board of Maori Ethnological Research*, vol. 4, Thomas Avery & Sons, New Plymouth, 1928

Kendall, Thomas, *A Korao no New Zealand; or, the New Zealander's First Book; Being an Attempt to Compose some Lessons for the Instruction of the Natives*, G. Howe, Sydney, 1815

King, M. (ed.), *Te Ao Hurihuri: Aspects of Maoritanga*, Reed, Auckland, 1992

Lineham, Peter J., *Bible and Society: A Sesquicentennial History of the Bible Society in New Zealand*, Bible Society in New Zealand/Daphne Brasell Associates, Wellington, 1996

McEwen, J., *Rangitāne: A Tribal History*, Reed Methuen, Auckland, 1986

Macgregor, Miriam, *Pioneer Trails of Hawke's Bay*, Reed, Wellington, 1975

McKenzie, D. F., *Oral Culture, Literacy and Print in Early New Zealand: The Treaty of Waitangi*, Victoria University Press, Wellington, 1985

McLean, Mervyn, *Māori Music*, Auckland University Press, Auckland, 1996

Markham, E., *New Zealand or Recollections of it*, Government Printer, Wellington, 1963

Mead, Hirini Moko, *Te Toi Whakairo: The Art of Maori Carving*, Reed, Auckland, 1986

Metge, J., *The Maoris of New Zealand*, Routledge and Kegan Paul, London, 1967

Mitchell, J. H., *Takitimu*, Reed, Wellington, 1944

Ngā Tohu Pūmahara: The Survey Pegs of the Past, New Zealand Geographic Board, Wellington, 1990

Ngata, A. T., *Nga Moteatea*, Part 1, Polynesian Society, Wellington, 1959

O'Malley, Vincent, *Agents of Autonomy: Maori Committees in the Nineteenth Century*, Huia, Wellington, 1998

Ong, Walter, J., *Orality and Literacy: The Technologizing of the Word*, Methuen, London, 1982

Orange, C., *The Treaty of Waitangi*, Allen and Unwin/Port Nicholson Press, Wellington, 1987

Orbell, M., *Maori Poetry: An Introductory Anthology*, Heinemann Educational Books, Auckland, 1983

Pompallier, J. B. F., *Early History of the Catholic Church in Oceania*, H. Brett, Auckland, 1888

Preserving Family Collections, Conservation Services, National Library of New Zealand Te Puna Mātauranga o Aotearoa, Wellington, 1997

Redwood, M. M., *Proud Silk: A New Zealand Racing History*, Reed, Wellington, 1979

Reeves, W. P., *The Long White Cloud: Ao Tea Roa*, Golden Press reprint. Auckland, 1973

Response to the Adult Literacy Report for the Ministry of Education, November 1999, Literacy Aotearoa, Auckland, 1999

Rikihana, H. T., *Te Ao Turoa: Science*, vol. 1, Auckland College of Education, Auckland, 1992

Salmond, A., *Eruera: The Teachings of a Maori Elder*, Oxford University Press, Auckland 1980

Salmond, A., *Hui: A Study of Maori Ceremonial Gatherings*, Reed, Wellington, 1975

Sansom, O., *The Stewart Islanders*, Reed, Wellington, 1970

Shirres, M. P., *Te Tangata/The Human Person*, Accent Publications, Auckland, 1997

Simpson, Miria, *Ngā Tohu o Te Tiriti: Making a Mark*, National Library of New Zealand, Wellington, 1990

Simpson, T., *Te Riri Pakeha/The White Man's Anger*, Hodder and Stoughton, Auckland, 1986

Sinclair, Karen, *Prophetic Histories: The People of the Māramatanga*, Bridget Williams Books, Wellington, 2002

Sinclair, Keith, *Kinds of Peace: Maori People After the Wars, 1870–85*, Auckland University Press, Auckland, 1991

Smith, Linda Tuhiwai, *Decolonizing Methodologies: Research and Indigenous Peoples*, Zed Books/University of Otago Press, Dunedin, 1999

Spiers, J., *Moeraki*, Reed, Auckland, 1997

Tanenuiarangi, University of Auckland, Auckland, 1988

Te Hurinui, Pei, *King Potatau: An Account of the Life of Potatau Te Wherowhero, the First Maori King*, Polynesian Society, Wellington, 1959

Te Taura Whiri i te Reo Māori, Te Matatiki: Contemporary Māori Words, revised edition, Oxford University Press, Auckland, 1996

Tregear, E., *The Maori Race*, A. D. Willis, Wanganui, 1904

Tyro, K. F., & K. G. Scarlett (eds), *Te Aute College: 125th Anniversary, 1854–1979*, Te Aute College, Pukehou, 1979

Vansina, Jan, *Oral Tradition as History*, University of Wisconsin Press, Madison, 1985

Wade, W., *A Journey in the Northern Island of New Zealand*, George Rolwegan, Hobart, 1842, Capper Press reprint, Christchurch, 1977

Walker, M., K. Udy & N. Pole, *Adult Literacy in New Zealand: Results from the International Adult Literacy Survey*, Ministry of Education, Wellington, 1997

Walker, Ranginui, *He Tipua: The Life and Times of Sir Apirana Ngata*, Viking, Auckland, 2001

Walker, Ranginui, *Ka Whawhai Tonu Matou: Struggle Without End*, Penguin, Auckland, 1990

Ward, Alan, *A Show of Justice: Racial 'Amalgamation' in Nineteenth Century New Zealand*, Oxford University Press/Auckland University Press, Auckland, 1974

Wilson, Eva, *Titi Heritage*, Craig Printing Co., Invercargill, 1974

Wright, Harrison M., *New Zealand, 1769–1840, Early Years of Western Contact*, Harvard University Press, Cambridge, Massachusetts, 1959

Zaczek, I., & J. O. Westwood, *The Art of Illuminated Manuscripts: Illustrated Sacred Writings*, Studio Editions, 1996

Electronic Sources

The Bible – The Classic Text: Traditions and Interpretations, 1997, www.uwm.edu/Dept/Library/special/exhibits/calstext/ clspg006.htm, University of Wisconsin, Milwaukee

Newspapers

Hawke's Bay Herald
Huia Tangata Kotahi
Kahiti o Niu Tireni
Te Kopara
Te Wananga

Official Reports

The Maori Land Courts, Report of the Royal Commission of Inquiry, 1980, *AJHR*, 1980, H-3
Report of the Commission Appointed to Inquire into the Subject of the Native Land Laws ('Rees-Carroll Report'), *AJHR*, 1891, Session II, G-1

Television Programmes

Haami, B. (director), 'Tapu', episode of *Waka Huia*, Television New Zealand, 1989
Hiramana-Rua, D. (director), 'A Profile on Bruce Biggs', episode of *Waka Huia*, Television New Zealand, broadcast 7 Jun 1998